Béla Balázs

THEORY OF THE FILM
CHARACTER AND GROWTH OF A NEW ART

Translated from the Hungarian by
Edith Bone

DOVER PUBLICATIONS, INC.
NEW YORK

This Dover edition, first published in 1970, is an unabridged republication, with minor corrections, of the work originally published by Dennis Dobson Ltd., London, in 1952 in their series "International Theatre and Cinema" (general editor, Herbert Marshall). The present edition is published by special arrangement with Dobson Books Ltd.

International Standard Book Number: 0-486-22685-9
Library of Congress Catalog Card Number: 77-130963

Manufactured in the United States of America
Dover Publications, Inc.
180 Varick Street
New York, N.Y. 10014

PUBLISHER'S NOTE, 1970

THEORY OF THE FILM, Béla Balázs' last major work, summarizes, sifts and brings into definitive focus the great film scholar's lifelong thoughts and preoccupations.

Unlike many other theorists, Balázs was a practical man of the theater and film-maker. He was born in Szeged, Hungary, in 1884. As a young man he wrote plays, poems and novels. He supplied the libretti for two works by Bartók: the opera *Kékszakállú herceg vára* (Duke Bluebeard's Castle; composed 1911) and the ballet *A fából faragott királyfi* (The Prince Carved out of Wood; composed 1914–16).

After the unsuccessful Communist revolution in his native country in 1919, Balázs lived in Austria and Germany, and it was the flourishing German film industry that gave him his opportunities as a scenarist and director. His screen credits include the scenarios for *Die Abenteuer eines Zehnmarkscheins* (The Adventures of a Ten-Mark Note; 1926; directed by Viertel) and *Narkose* (Narcosis; 1929; directed by Abel), both discussed in the present book, and (in collaboration) for Pabst's 1931 *Dreigroschenoper* (Threepenny Opera); he was co-director with Leni Riefenstahl of *Das blaue Licht* (The Blue Light; 1932).

When the National Socialists seized power, Balázs left for the Soviet Union, where he remained from 1933 to 1945; he taught at the State Film Institute in Moscow. After the war he returned to Hungary, where he wrote the scenario for Géza Radványi's 1947 film *Valahol Europában* (Somewhere in Europe). After teaching film art in various Iron Curtain countries, he died in Prague in 1949.

Balázs's 1924 volume *Der sichtbare Mensch, oder Die Kultur des Films* (The Visible Man, or Film Culture), a perceptive and prophetic analysis of the potentialities of the silent film, was the first systematic and formal theory of the cinema ever published. It championed the dramaturgical and emotional powers of the close-up, camera angle and set-up, frame composition and cross-cutting; its influence on Pudovkin and others was incalculable. The 1930 volume *Der Geist des Films* (The Spirit of Film) tackled the problems raised by the sound revolution, and pleaded for asynchronous sound.

The author's final book of film theory first appeared in Moscow in

3

1945 as *Iskusstvo Kino* (The Art of Cinema). The Yugoslavian edition appeared in 1947, the Hungarian in 1948 and the German (in Vienna) in 1949 (*Der Film: Werden und Wesen einer neuen Kunst*—The Film: Character and Growth of a New Art). The present volume is a re-publication of the first English edition, translated from the Hungarian.

CONTENTS

Part I

PREFACE

T H E N A M E O F Béla Balázs is probably known in England only
as Béla Bartók's librettist and the author of children's books,
yet among the intelligentsia of Europe he ranks as a classic pioneer
in the sphere of film theory. In particular his two books, published
originally in German, entitled *Der sichtbare Mensch* (1924) and *Der
Geist des Films*, were rated among the most important contributions
to the theory of film art. They were indeed pioneering works, but,
unfortunately, they were not translated and published in English.
The European generalisation about England still seems to hold
good; that we are empiricists in art and despise theory. Certainly
this appears to be so in relation to theatre and cinema, for the
publication of original works in French, German and Russian is
extremely large compared to the number of similar books published
here. It is most important, therefore, that Béla Balázs's last book
should be available in English, for it sums up all the work, thought,
and experience he put into his previous pioneering works, which
have since become classics. It is, alas, his last book. He died as it
was being translated for us.

This work in particular is, I think, one of the most lucid books
on cinema art ever written and the very antithesis of Eisenstein's
intellectual complexity and difficult style. Nevertheless, he and
Eisenstein were both travelling to the same goal, towards an
aesthetic of film art.

The significant thing that Béla Balázs makes clear is the importance of theory and the lack of appreciation of this in relation to
'the only new art'—the film. 'The most important of the arts'
Lenin called it in 1919, pronouncing an axiom which the Americans
have been acting on for a long time! Balázs pointed out in his
earlier books that we have an unprecedented opportunity *to study
the laws governing the evolution of an art in the making*. It is an
art that could only have been born in an industrial civilization and
the universality of the film is primarily due to economic causes. The
making of a film is so expensive that only very few nations have a
home market sufficient for their productions. Added to this factor,
of course, is the ideological one. The American film industry, for
example is not only U.S.A.'s fourth largest industry but also the
Fourth Arm of the State!

11

An important aspect of film art that Belázs brings out is the psychological act of 'identification', which in the film reaches a degree hitherto unattainable in any other medium, and here Eisentein postulated a thesis which is completely in accord with Balázs.

Eisenstein's conception is that cinema is a synthesis of all the arts and that, while Walter Pater said (I quote from memory) 'all art strives to reach the condition of music', Eisenstein said, 'all art strives to reach the form of the sound-colour-stereoscopic cinema', and that though Balázs writes, 'one need not take this . . . to mean that for ages writers had been hatching film themes, film stories and film characters which could not be presented in novels or plays; that these poor authors had to wait decade after decade for the possibility of visual expression, until finally they went to the Lumière brothers and ordered a cinematograph, the new form to fit the new content', yet on the other hand, there is no doubt that great artists from time to time seem to burst the bounds of their art forms, and their content is more powerful than their forms.

Consider what such artists as Michelangelo, Tolstoy, and Balzac could have done with the sound-colour-cinema! They would one and all, I think, have cried to the heavens: Here is the medium I was striving to create, here is the dynamic flow of world and mind, here is both past, present and future, space and time, colour and sound, mind and matter, fused into one unity! Here is the answer to the cry of Chorus in Shakespeare's *Henry V*: 'Oh for a muse of fire that would ascend the brightest heaven of invention!'

As Balázs again points out, monumentality in art is not a question of quantity (as Hollywood often seems to think), 'A film can never be made " monumental " by the number of extras in crowd scenes or the size of the sets, but only by the weight of its theme or the personality of its hero.'

This book then is a pioneer classic in the realm of film theory, brought up-to-date by its author. Many of its one-time original ideas are now commonplace, but others still remain original. These demand the serious attention not only of film critics but of all those who are interested in the theory of art aesthetics and the powerful and all-pervading influence of the cinema.

HERBERT MARSHALL

Bombay, India.
July, 1952.

LIST OF ILLUSTRATIONS

appearing between pp. 128-9

*We are grateful to the British Film Institute for
their co-operation in supplying these photographs.*

NANOOK OF THE NORTH

Rin-Tin-Tin in JAWS OF STEEL
Chaplin and Jackie Coogan in THE KID

Asta Nielsen in DIE EWEGE NATT
Lillian Gish in BROKEN BLOSSOMS

Falconetti in THE PASSION OF JOAN OF ARC
THE BATTLESHIP POTEMKIN

Max Linder
Sessue Hayakawa

IL SOLE SORGE ANCORA
VIVERE IN PACE

ANNA KARENINA

THE GREAT WALTZ
LADY HAMILTON

BERLIN

MOTHER
ARSENAL

DIE LETZTE NACHT
THE FALL OF THE HOUSE OF USHER

LENIN IN OCTOBER
THE THIRTEEN

MONSIEUR VERDOUX
PHILLIPS RADIO

13

PART I

CHAPTER ONE

IN PRAISE OF THEORY

DANGERS OF IGNORANCE

WE ALL KNOW and admit that film art has a greater influence on the minds of the general public than any other art. The official guardians of culture note the fact with a certain amount of regret and uneasiness. But too few of us are sufficiently alive to the dangers that are an inevitable consequence of this fact. Nor do we realize clearly enough that we must be better connoisseurs of the film if we are not to be as much at the mercy of perhaps the greatest intellectual and spiritual influence of our age as to some blind and irresistible elemental force. And unless we study its laws and possibilities very carefully, we shall not be able to control and direct this potentially greatest instrument of mass influence ever devised in the whole course of human cultural history. One might think that the theory of this art would naturally be regarded as the most important field for present-day art theory. No one would deny to-day that the art of the motion picture is *the* popular art of our century—unfortunately not in the sense that it is the product of the popular spirit but the other way round, in the sense that the mentality of the people, and particularly of the urban population, is to a great extent the product of this art, an art that is at the same time a vast industry. Thus the question of educating the public to a better, more critical appreciation of the films is a question of the mental health of the nations. Nevertheless, too few of us have yet realized how dangerously and irresponsibly we have failed to promote such a better understanding of film art.

WHY ARE PEOPLE NOT TAUGHT TO APPRECIATE FILMS?

Nowadays social considerations are taken into account in the cultural sphere no less than in others. Nevertheless, the æsthetics of the film are nowhere included in the official teaching of art appreciation. Our academies have sections for literature and every established art, but none for the new art of our day—the film. It was not until 1947 that the first film-maker was elected to the French *Académie*. At our universities there are chairs for literature and all arts except that of the film. The first Art Academy which included the theory of film art in its curriculum was opened in Prague in 1947. The text-books used in our secondary schools discuss the other arts but say nothing of the film. Millions hear about the æsthetics of literature and painting who will never make use of such knowledge because they read no books and look at no pictures. But the millions who frequent the movies are left without guidance—no one teaches them to appreciate film art.

NEED FOR GENERAL CULTURE

There are numerous film schools in the world and no one denies that there may be need of a theory of the film—for specialists. In Paris, in London, and elsewhere, film institutes and scientific film societies have been formed to study the 'science' of the film. But what is needed is not specialized knowledge: it is a general level of culture. No one who had not the faintest conception of literature or music would be considered well educated. A man who had never heard of Beethoven or Michelangelo would be out of place among people of culture. But if he has not the faintest idea of the rudiments of film art and had never heard of Asta Nielsen or David Wark Griffith, he might still pass for a well-educated, cultured person, even on the highest level. The most important art of our time is that about which one need know nothing whatever. And yet it is an urgent need that we should cultivate enough discrimination to influence the art which shapes the popular taste in the highest degree. Until there is a chapter on film art in every text-book on the history of art and on æsthetics; until the art of the film has a chair in our universities and a place in the curriculum of our secondary schools, we shall not have firmly established in the consciousness of our generation this most important artistic development of our century.

CREATIVE CULTURE

This is all the more important as what is at stake is not merely the proper valuation of the film, but the fate of the film itself, for this depends on our appreciation, and we are responsible for it. It has always been the rule in the history of art and culture that the two were functions of each other in dialectic interaction. Art educated the taste of the public, and the better taste of the public demanded and rendered possible the development of art to higher levels.

In the case of the film this is a hundred times more so than in the case of any other art. It is conceivable for a writer to be in advance of his time and write in the solitude of his study a great book not appreciated in his own time; a painter may paint a picture, a composer compose music which only posterity with its higher culture and understanding can value. Such poets, painters or composers may perish, but their work lives.

But in the case of the film a lack of proper appreciation kills, not the artist in the first place, but the work of art itself, smothering it even before it is born. The film as a product of a large-scale industry costs too much and is too complicated a collective creative process for any individual genius to create a masterpiece in defiance of the tastes or prejudices of his own day. And this applies not only to the capitalist film industry which envisages immediate cash returns. Even a socialized film production cannot make films for the public of some coming century. A certain degree of success—in other words, appreciation—is an inexorable material postulate for the birth of any film. The situation is paradox: in the sphere of film art the public must be available before the film, the making of which is rendered possible only by an appreciation ensured in advance, on which the producers of the film can count. What is required is not a passive appreciation which enjoys what is already available, but an inspiring, encouraging, *creative* appreciation; we need theoretical understanding and a sort of æsthetics which does not draw conclusion from already existing works of art but demands and expects such works of art on the basis of theoretical forecasts. What is wanted is a responsible public and canny æstheticists.

That is the justification for the film societies which have now sprung up in most civilized countries. There have, of course, long been societies of music-lovers and the like, whose object was to afford opportunities for the enjoyment of the less popular and more valuable works of art and to give support to good art and good artists, but only such art and artists as already existed. The theoretically expert members of film societies have a different task : they offer a ready-made public to the producer thereby encouraging him to dare try something new and good. After all there are few capitalists who make bad films on principle and would not willingly make good films if good box-office returns were assured in advance —and if they knew a good film from a bad one. The public bears part of the responsibility for the development of the art of the film and a sense of this responsibility is slowly beginning to spread at last. From a Swiss audience I first heard the word 'film-conscious' in the sense in which others use the word 'class-conscious' and it is to be hoped that other picture-goers will increasingly become film-conscious in this sense.

There are few among present-day æstheticists who deny in principle the artistic possibilities of the film. But many of them regard this new art as embryonic. Such critics would like to wait for some Shakespeare of the film and draw conclusions from the deathless works of the film classics. It remains to be asked : how will they recognize such works without a theoretical, æsthetic understanding of the film? Where will they find the standards, the evaluating principles with which to demonstrate and explain the qualities of a film?

Here is a great opportunity for æstheticists not merely to register and expound æsthetic values produced without their aid, but to participate in the production of such values and in the creation of the spiritual conditions which make them possible.

THEORY AS A NEW COLUMBUS

A theory which demonstrates the direction and purpose of the intrinsic laws of development will not be merely an owl of Minerva which, as Schlegel puts it, does not begin its flight until dusk. It will be not only an *a posteriori* theory summing up foregone conclusions, but an initiating theory pointing into the future and drawing charts of unknown oceans for some future Columbus. It will be an inspiring theory that will fire the imagination of future seekers for new worlds and creators of new arts. We need not console ourselves with the argument that a 'general' good taste nurtured on other arts can be a sufficient directive influence for the development of a completely new art. One of the aims of this book is precisely to prove that the deeply rooted old conceptions and valuations of an artistic culture nurtured on the old arts was the greatest obstacle to the development of film art in Europe. It was the old principles, inapplicable to a new art, which smothered the new principles at birth. Yet an aeroplane is not a bad motor-car because you can't drive it on a road. The traditional arts which have proved themselves by the momentum of a millennium of practice have less need of theoretical support than have those which have barely appeared above the horizon of the present.

A GREAT OPPORTUNITY MISSED

The fact that the art of the film is not yet fully developed offers an unprecedented opportunity for æstheticists to study the laws governing the evolution of an art in the making. Twenty-five years ago, in my *Der sichtbare Mensch,* I already sounded the alarm, but then and since then, it was in vain. Aestheticists, historians of art, psychologists were offered the opportunity of watching a new art being born before their eyes. For the film is the only art whose birthday is known to us—the beginnings of all the others are lost in the fog of antiquity. The symbolic myths which tell of their birth throw no light on the mystery of why and how these arts and not others came into being, why and how they took the forms they took and why and how they came to be the most important manifestations of the human race. No digging in the ground and no archæology can answer these whys and hows nor explain the part played by incipient art in primitive societies. We do not know the social and economic conditions in which those arts came into being, nor the state of human consciousness which gave them birth. So our scholars have only hypotheses or more or less daring surmises to fall back upon. But about fifty—or rather thirty—years ago a completely new art was born. Did the academies set up research groups? Did they observe, hour by hour and keeping precise records, how this embryo developed and in its development revealed the laws governing its vital processes?

The scholars and academies let this opportunity pass, although for many centuries it was the first chance to observe, with the naked eye so to speak, one of the rarest phenomena of the history of culture: the emergence of a new form of artistic expression, the only one born in our time, and in our society and therefore the only one with the material, intellectual and spiritual determinants of which we are entirely familiar. It would have been worth while to seize this opportunity because—if for no other reason—knowledge of the evolutionary process of this new form of artistic expression would *per analogiam* have provided a key to many secrets of the older arts.

CHAPTER TWO

ANCIENT HISTORY

MOVIES AND LARGE-SCALE INDUSTRY

I CALL THIS chapter ancient history, because it deals with the period when moving pictures were a fairground sideshow, not an art.

It was in March 1895 that the Lumière brothers in France completed their film camera. But the new means of expression and the new form-language of film art were not born until ten or twelve years later, in the United States. Thus the technical facilities for film-making were already in the hands of a wealthy capitalist group at the end of the last century, but French cinematography nevertheless failed to produce a single manifestation of the new art. So the art of the film did not automatically grow out of the French cinematographic camera, nor was it a mechanical result of the general laws of vision. Other forces were required to bring into existence the new art and it is not by chance that it was born, not in Europe, but in the United States.

The technique of cinematography took shape in the very beginning of the twentieth century, and it was not by accident that it emerged at the time when other intellectual products were also beginning to be produced on a large industrial scale. It was in this same period that the giant publishing houses, the great theatrical concerns and concert agencies, the newspaper trusts and wholesale picture-dealing were born. The wholesale industrialization of art and literature did not start with the film, but the film arrived when this trend was just gathering momentum.

PHOTOGRAPHIC THEATRE

The new invention was immediately used for the large-scale exploitation of dramatic art. The cinematographic camera made it possible to substitute a machine-made—one might say 'industrial'—production for the actual flesh-and-blood 'hand-made' performance of the stage. It was turned into a commodity capable of being reproduced in unlimited quantities, and distributed at low cost. The first great general contract in this industry was the agreement between the firm of Pathé Frères and the Société des Auteurs Dramatiques which provided for the photography of stage performance and the distribution of the films thus obtained.

In those years cinematography was merely a fairground sideshow, a moving picture of some sensational event or a means to the mass reproduction of stage performances. It was not an autonomous art ruled by its own laws. Nevertheless, even though the film was still only photographed theatre, the wider technical possibilities soon led film producers to photograph scenes which would have been impossible on a closed stage and even on an open-air stage of the usual kind—the stage of the film play was soon all the earth. Thus even the photographed theatre, from the very start, widened and enriched the dramatic art of the closed stage not only by spectacular effects but by such subjects and actions which were made possible only by the fact that natural phenomena could now be shown and therefore dramatized.

NEW SUBJECTS

Urban Gad, the famous Danish film producer, wrote a book on the film as far back as 1918. This wise and sound book makes no mention as yet of the new form-language proper to the new art—at that time Urban Gad knew nothing of this. Hence he dealt chiefly with the specific new subjects suitable for film presentation. According to him every film should be placed in some specific natural environment which must affect the human beings living in it and play a part in directing their lives and destinies. Thus a new personage is added to the *dramatis personæ* of the photographed play: nature itself, a personage who could not have appeared on the ordinary stage. But the new *dramatis personæ* followed the same rules as the old familiar stage personalities and settings. The stage was widened but its basic principles remained the same, even though the play may have been enriched by certain dramatic features through the present action of the immediate effect of nature on the moods and feelings of human beings which sometimes exercise a decisive influence on their fate.

This novelty, this enrichment of subject matter, became the specific characteristic of the photographed theatre. It is natural that under the pressure of competition it developed in a direction in which the old theatre could not follow it. In the first years of the movies the emphasis was mainly on movement. This was the time of Westerns, in which galloping horses, jumping, rapid travel, running, climbing, swimming, became the most important elements of a film story. Very often that was all there was to it. The film showed what one could not see anywhere else.

NEW CHARACTERS

Soon, however, new characters appeared in the films, characters which could only rarely and under great difficulties appear on the real stage. Children and animals took the stage —new characters in the old art of photographed theatre. Some of the first film stars were the famous panther of Pathé, the no less famous Alsatian Rin-Tin-Tin and the gifted and enchanting infant prodigy Jackie Coogan, Charlie Chaplin's pal, the Kid, an unforgettable little artist of the very highest order. These were characters of a new kind who had been introduced into the old art of the theatre by the new technical possibilities. Thus it was that even in its infancy the film brought new subjects, new stories and even new characters into the world, long before it could develop its own specific means of expression, its own peculiar form-language.

SLAPSTICK COMEDY

At this time a new specific art form was born: the slapstick comedy. Its hero was not so new and original a character as children and animals were; he was only a reincarnation of our old friend the clown, complete with stooge. These two, borrowed from the circus ring, are the most ancient figures in all the history of the theatre. But the specific art of the clown and comedian had no possibility of further development in the ring and on the music-hall stage. The wider space required for a development of their style was provided by the open-air play, of which the film was a photographic image.

The first such films had a stereotyped ending, no less standardized than the final kiss of the later film-with-the-happy-ending. The stereotyped finale of the old slapstick comedy was a general rush. The hero gets into hot water and runs away; he is pursued by one man, by two men, by thirty men and finally by every single character in the film, irrespective of whether they had anything to do with the fugitive or not. A human avalanche was let loose, carrying everything before it in a senseless and purposeless rush. This movement, quite divorced as it was from the story, amused people; they saw in it the essence of the motion picture and in fact the substratum of human life.

In the course of the subsequent development of film art the slapstick comedy still remained a hardy perennial, just as children and animals never ceased to be popular film characters. Thus a definite variety of film art with a distinctive style of its own was born *before* the specific new method of film art and the new form-language of the film was developed. What is the explanation for this?

The photographed play had a peculiarity distinguishing it from the live stage: it was silent. With the subsequent development of the silent film the place of the dialogue was taken by a detailed, expressive play of features and gestures, shown in close-up. In the beginning the motion picture was mute even as to facial expression, for the scenes were seen as a whole, in long shot, as in the theatre. Hence it was necessary to act in dumb-show, with exaggerated grotesque gestures which could be seen from a distance and which, if seen now, make an irresistibly amusing impression on the spectators. Thus one of the deficiencies of the primitive motion picture, its muteness, served as a style-creating element through the comic

quality of the dumb-show. A new dramaturgy of strictly pantomimic comic situations was born; a comedy of situations
which needed neither the elucidating word, nor the individual-
izing play of facial expression.

EXAMPLES

Let me tell the story of a fine example of this immemorial
art form: Max Linder, one of the first film comedians, goes
out to buy a bathtub. Having bought it, he wants to carry it
home himself. But the tub is large and there are many laughs
in the way he tries to lift it and carry it. After a series of
grotesque acrobatic contortions he finally puts the tub on his
head, like a gigantic hat. The tub is heavy and gradually
weighs its bearer down. Finally Linder crawls along on all
fours, completely hidden by the tub. The tub thus appears to
walk along on its own on the crowded pavement, frightening
passers-by and annoying the dogs who crowd around it and
bark their heads off. Tub reaches Linder's house at last, climbs
up the stairs and wants to enter Linder's flat. But it is wider
than the door. Linder now crawls out from beneath the
tub and because he cannot get it into the flat, puts it on the
landing in front of the door and badly wanting a bath, proceeds to fill the tub with water brought in jugfuls from the flat.
He then calmly strips and gets into the tub. At this moment
two ladies come up the stairs. The modest Linder dives under
the water. But the ladies have seen him and indignantly call
the caretaker. The caretaker tries to remove Linder by force,
but he resists by using the most effective weapon—he splashes
water at the caretaker. Here is that grain of psychological
reality which in a farce, among all the absurdities, has the
greatest comic effect. For one real and convincing feature
lends a spurious reality to all the others. The huge caretaker
is more afraid of the water than of a bludgeon. This appears
credible to everyone. He sends for the police. Linder splashes
away fiercely, heroically and the police are daunted. This, too,
is convincing by now. Finally firemen arrive who overcome
the water weapon with a water weapon of their own.

This bit of fun is most filmic, not only because a number

of things are made visible in it which cannot be shown on the real stage, but also because these new *motifs* represent a type of grotesque psychological reaction which could not have been shown in the past.

The first brilliant shorts made by Charlie Chaplin were in a similar style. His struggle with a demoniac rocking-chair from which, once seated, he cannot escape. Or his duel with the malicious revolving door that always turns him out into the street again. Or the first lesson in roller-skating, when the skates strapped to his feet rebel and declare their independence. The deeper meaning of Chaplin's 'clumsiness' lies in the fact that his struggle with objects not only reveals their demoniac personality but turns them into equal, even superior, opponents. They defeat Chaplin because he, in his unobjectivized humanity, cannot adapt himself to their mechanical nature. This art grew out of the very essence of the silent film, out of the essence of the silent, but distant, undifferentiated and hence theatre-like picture. At that time movement had not yet acquired that intimate emotional significance which could be observed only in close-up. On the contrary, the whole of the movement, the amusing struggle of the hero, provided the comic effect.

It is characteristic that the birth of the sound film and the talkie marked the end of this type of slapstick comedy which had given us the first world-famous film stars such as Max Linder, Prince, Cretinetti and Charlie Chaplin. The great comedians of the second generation, Harold Lloyd and Buster Keaton, appeared when the silent film was already fully developed, when the new art was already using camera angles and close-ups. For this reason these new protagonists had more of the individual, psychologizing character-actor, even in their performances as comedians. Nevertheless they were unable to adapt their art to the needs of the sound film, because their humour was born of the spirit of the silent photographed stage. Even for the great Charlie Chaplin the change-over to the sound film brought a profound crisis, the significance of which is to be discussed later.

From its earliest years the film also had yet another special feature. The film could conjure better than any platform magician. George Méliès, himself originally a professional illusionist and conjurer, soon discovered what miracles could be performed with the aid of film technique: men and objects could be made to disappear, to fly through the air, to change into each other. There is scarcely a technical trick of which the camera is capable, which Méliès did not use in the very first years of cinematography. But what he did was nevertheless only photographed theatre. For if some cunning stage trick were to make it possible to make characters vanish, fly through the air or change into something else on the real stage, this would still not change the eternal forms and basic principles of the theatre.

CHAPTER THREE

A NEW FORM-LANGUAGE

IF THE FILM had from its infancy produced specific new subjects, new characters, a new style, even a new art form, why then do I say that it was not yet a new art, but merely a photographic copy of a stage performance? When and how did cinematography turn into a specific independent art employing methods sharply differing from those of the theatre and using a totally different form-language? What is the difference between photographed theatre and film art? Both being equally motion pictures projected on to a screen, why do I say that the one is only a technical reproduction and the other an independently creative art?

The basic formal principle of the theatre is that the spectator sees the enacted scene as a whole in space, always seeing the whole of the space. Sometimes the stage presents only one corner of a larger hall, but that corner is always totally visible all through the scene in question, and everything that happens in it is seen within one and the same frame.

The second basic formal principle of the theatre is that the spectator always sees the stage from a fixed unchanging distance. True, the photographed theatre already began to photograph different scenes from different distances, but within one and the same scene the distance was never changed.

The third basic formal principle of the theatre is that the spectator's angle of vision does not change. The photographed theatre did change the perspective sometimes from scene to scene, but within one and the same scene the perspective never changed, any more than the distance.

These three basic formal principles of the stage are of course interconnected, they form the groundwork of dramatic style and means of expression. In this connection it makes no difference whether we see the scenes on the living stage or in photographic reproduction; nor does it matter whether the scenes presented are such as could not be shown on the stage at all, but only in the open air and by means of photographic technique.

It was these three basic principles of theatrical art that were discarded by the art of the film—it begins where the three principles no longer apply and are supplanted by new methods. These are:

1. Varying distance between spectator and scene within one and the same scene; hence varying dimensions of scenes that can be accommodated within the frame and composition of a picture.

2. Division of the integral picture of the scene into sections, or 'shots'.

3. Changing angle, perspective and focus of 'shots' within one and the same scene.

4. Montage, that is the assembly of 'shots' in a certain order in which not only whole scene follows whole scene (however short) but pictures of smallest details are given, so that the whole scene is composed of a mosaic of frames aligned as it were in chronological sequence.

This revolutionary innovation in visual artistic expression came about in the United States of America, in Hollywood, during the first world war. David Griffith was the name of the genius to whom we owe it. He not only created masterpieces of art, but an art that was totally new.

One of the specific characteristics of the art of the film is that not only can we see, in the isolated 'shots' of a scene, the very atoms of life and their innermost secrets revealed at close quarters, but we can do so without any of the intimate secrecy being lost, as always happens in the exposure of a stage performance or of a painting. The new theme which the new means of expression of film art revealed was not a hurricane at sea or the eruption of a volcano: it was perhaps a solitary tear slowly welling up in the corner of a human eye.

A good film director does not permit the spectator to look at a scene at random. He leads our eye inexorably from detail to detail along the line of his montage. By means of such a sequence the director is enabled to place emphasis where he sees fit, and thus not only show but at the same time interpret the picture. It is in this that the individual creativeness of a film-maker chiefly manifests itself. Two films in which story and acting are exactly the same, but which are differently cut, may be the expression of two totally different personalities and present two totally different images of the world.

CHAPTER FOUR

VISUAL CULTURE

THE BIRTH OF film art led not only to the creation of new works of art but to the emergence of new human faculties with which to perceive and understand this new art.

It is a great pity that the scholars dealing with the arts have up to now concerned themselves chiefly with already existing works of art and not at all with the subjective faculties which, created through a dialectical interaction, enable us to see and appreciate the newly-emerging beautiful things. Although objective reality is independent of the subject and his subjective consciousness, beauty is not merely objective reality, not an attribute of the object entirely independent of the spectator, not something that would be there objectively even without a corresponding subject, even if there were no human beings on earth. For beauty is what we like—we know of no other beauty —and this human experience is not something independent, but a function changing with races, epochs and cultures. Beauty is a subjective experience of human consciousness brought about by objective reality; it has its own laws, but those laws are the universal laws of consciousness and to that extent of course not purely subjective.

The philosophy of art has in the past devoted little attention to the subject, the carrier of an artistic culture, whose sensibility and receptivity not only develop under the influence of the arts, but may actually be created by them. What is required is not merely a history of art but a history of art running to and linked with a history of mankind.

It is the purpose of this book to investigate and outline that sphere of the development of human sensibility which developed in mutual interaction with the evolution of the art of the film.

33

FILM CULTURE

The evolution of the human capacity for understanding which was brought about by the art of the film, opened a new chapter in the history of human culture. Just as musical hearing and musical understanding develop under the influence of music, so the development of the material richness of film art leads to a parallel development of film vision and film appreciation. The forms of expression of the silent film developed gradually, but the rate of development was fast enough and together with it the public developed the ability to understand the new form-language. We were witnesses not only of the development of a new art but of the development of a new sensibility, a new understanding, a new culture in its public.

THE COLONIAL ENGLISHMAN

There is a story about an English colonial administrator, who, during the first world war and for some time after it, lived in a backward community. He regularly received newspapers and periodicals from home, thus knew of films, and had seen pictures of the stars and had read film reviews and film stories; but he had never seen a motion picture. As soon as he reached a place where there was a cinema, he went to see a film. A number of children around him seemed to enjoy it very much, but he was completely baffled by what he saw and was quite exhausted when at last the film came to an end.

'Well, how did you like it?' asked a friend.

'It was very interesting,' he said, 'but what was it all about?'

He had not understood what was going on, because he did not understand the form-language in which the story of the film was told, a form-language every town-dweller already knew at that time.

THE SIBERIAN GIRL

This story was told to me by a friend in Moscow. A cousin had arrived on a visit from a Siberian collective farm—an intelligent girl, with a good education, but who had never seen a motion picture (this of course was many years ago). The Moscow cousins took her to the cinema and having other plans, left her there by herself. The film was a burlesque. The Siberian cousin came home pale and grim. 'Well, how did you like the film?' the cousins asked her. She could scarcely be induced to answer, so overwhelmed was she by the sights she had seen. At last she said: 'Oh, it was horrible, horrible! I can't understand why they allow such dreadful things to be shown here in Moscow!'

'Why, what was so horrible then?'

'Human beings were torn to pieces and the heads thrown one way and the bodies the other and the hands somewhere else again.'

We know that when Griffith first showed a big close-up in a Hollywood cinema and a huge 'severed' head smiled at the public for the first time, there was a panic in the cinema. We ourselves no longer know by what intricate evolution of our consciousness we have learnt our visual association of ideas. What we have learnt is to integrate single disjointed pictures into a coherent scene, without even becoming conscious of the complicated psychological process involved. It is amazing to what extent we have, in a couple of decades, learnt to see picture perspectives, picture metaphors and picture symbols, how greatly we have developed our visual culture and sensibility.

WE HAVE LEARNED TO SEE

Thus the new technique of the film camera produced a new way of presentation and a new way of telling a story. The new picture language was developed, polished and differentiated to an incredible degree in the course of some twenty years. We can almost measure this process by harking back twenty years, when we ourselves would probably not have understood films which are quite obvious to spectators to-day. Here is an instance. A man hurries to a railway station to take leave of his beloved. We see him on the platform. We cannot see the train, but the questing eyes of the man show us that his beloved is already seated in the train. We see only a close-up

of the man's face, we see it twitch as if startled and then strips
of light and shadow, light and shadow flit across it in quicken-
ing rhythm. Then tears gather in the eyes and that ends the
scene. We are expected to know what happened and to-day we
do know, but when I first saw this film in Berlin, I did not
at once understand the end of this scene. Soon, however,
everyone knew what had happened: the train had started
and it was the lamps in its compartment which had thrown
their light on the man's face as they glided past ever faster
and faster.

Another example. A man is sitting in a dark room in gloomy
meditation. The spectator knows from the previous scene that
a woman is in the next room. We see a close-up of the man's
face. Suddenly a light falls on it from one side. The man raises
his head and looks towards the light with an expression of
hopeful expectation. Then the light fades from his face and
with it the expression of hope. He lowers his head in disappointment. Complete darkness falls slowly. It is the last shot
of a tragic scene. No more is needed. What happened here?
Every picture-goer knows and understands this language now.
What happened was that the door of the next room opened
for a moment, the woman came to the threshold of the lighted
room, hesitated, but turned back and closed the door for ever.
Even this 'for ever' could be felt in the slow and complete
darkening of the picture. Precisely the fact that no more was
shown stimulated our imagination and induced the right mood
in us. Therein lay its subtlety.

WHY ARE OLD FILMS FUNNY?

To-day we understand not only the situation presented in
a picture but every shade of its significance and symbolic
implications. The rapidity of our evolution towards this new
understanding can be measured by looking at old films. We
laugh aloud, especially at the grimmest tragedies, and can
scarcely believe that such antics could be taken seriously a
mere twenty years ago. What is the reason for this? Other
old works of art do not appear funny to us and we rarely feel
like laughing even at the most naïve and primitive art.

The reason is that old art usually expresses the mentality of a bygone age in adequate form. But what we see in a film we relate to our own selves, it is not yet 'history' and we laugh at our own recent selves. It is not yet a historical costume that can be beautiful and dignified, however strange it may be—it is merely the fashion of the last year but one which strikes us as comic.

Primitive art is the adequate expression of primitive taste and skill. The primitiveness of old films gives the impression of grotesque impotence. A spear in the hand of a naked savage is not as comic as a pike in the hands of a Home Guard. While a fifteenth-century Portuguese sailing-ship is a lovely sight, the early steam-engines and motor-cars are ridiculous because we see in them not something quite different, something no longer existent, but recognize a ridiculous, imperfect form of what is still in use to-day. We laugh at it as we laugh at the antics in the monkey-house—because the monkeys are like ourselves.

For the culture of the film has developed so rapidly that we still recognize our own selves in its clumsy primitiveness. It is for this reason that this culture is of so great an importance for us, this art which is accessible to millions of ordinary people.

ART DOES NOT DEVELOP

We should realize that, while art has a history, it has no development in the sense of growth or increase in æsthetic values. We do not consider the paintings of Renoir or Monet more precious or perfect than those of Cimabue or Giotto. There is no development in the objective side of art but there is development on the part of those who enjoy art or are connoisseurs of art. Artistic *culture* has not only a history, it also has an evolution in a certain direction. Subjective human sensibility, the faculty of understanding and interpreting art, has demonstrably developed in continuous cultures, and when we speak of a development of subjective human faculties, we do not mean the development of æsthetic values. For instance the discovery and application of perspective in art did not in itself imply an increase in artistic values. The rules of perspective are learned in school to-day by every ungifted dauber, but that does not make him a greater artist than Giotto,who knew nothing of these rules. The former will not be a greater artist, but his visual sensibility, his culture will be on a higher level. The discovery of the rules of perspective drawing played a much greater part in the evolution of general human culture than in the evolution of art. It enriched the culture of the eye far more than that of painting. It did of course pervade the routine of painting, but it is much more important that it has come to be an indispensable element in the everyday life of civilized man.

CHAPTER FIVE

DER SICHTBARE MENSCH

THIS CHAPTER WHICH deals with the visual culture developed through the silent film is taken from my book *Der sichtbare Mensch*. In it I hailed the silent film as a turning-point in our cultural history, not suspecting that the sound film would soon come to oust it. The truth which stated a then existing reality has remained true, but the reality it dealt with has bolted like a runaway horse and has made new observations and interpretations necessary. Nevertheless, this chapter may be of interest not merely as a chapter in the history of film theory. Nor does it perhaps retain its interest only because the picture still remains the essence of the film and its visual content. Lines of development are never rigidly set. They often proceed in a roundabout way, throwing the light of old knowledge on to new paths through dialectical interaction. Because I believe that we have now come to such a doubling back in the development of the film, when the already once accomplished and then again lost achievements of the silent film are about to be revalued and restored, I want to quote here what I wrote in 1923 about the silent film:

The discovery of printing gradually rendered illegible the faces of men. So much could be read from paper that the method of conveying meaning by facial expression fell into desuetude.

Victor Hugo wrote once that the printed book took over the part played by the cathedral in the Middle Ages and became the carrier of the spirit of the people. But the thousands of books tore the *one* spirit, embodied in the cathedral, into thousands of opinions. The word broke the stone into a thousand fragments, tore the church into a thousand books.

The visual spirit was thus turned into a legible spirit and visual culture into a culture of concepts. This of course had its social and economic causes, which changed the general face of life. But we paid little attention to the fact that, in conformity with this, the face of individual men, their foreheads, their eyes, their mouths, had also of necessity and quite concretely to suffer a change.

At present a new discovery, a new machine, is at work to turn the attention of men back to a visual culture and give them new faces. This machine is the cinematographic camera. Like the printing press, it is a technical device for the multiplication and distribution of products of the human spirit; its effect on human culture will not be less than that of the printing press.

For not to speak does not mean that one has nothing to say. Those who do not speak may be brimming over with emotions which can be expressed only in forms and pictures, in gesture and play of feature. The man of visual culture uses these not as substitutes for words, as a deaf-mute uses his fingers. He does not think in words, the syllables of which he sketches in the air like the dots and dashes of the Morse code. The gestures of visual man are not intended to convey concepts which can be expressed in words, but such inner experiences, such non-rational emotions which would still remain unexpressed when everything that can be told has been told. Such emotions lie in the deepest levels of the soul and cannot be approached by words that are mere reflexions of concepts; just as our musical experiences cannot be expressed in rationalized concepts. What appears on the face and in facial expression is a spiritual experience which is rendered immediately visible without the intermediary of words.

In the golden age of the old visual arts, the painter and sculptor did not merely fill empty space with abstract shapes and forms, and man was not merely a formal problem for the artist. Painters could paint the spirit and the soul without becoming 'literary', for the soul and the spirit had not yet been confined in concepts capable of expression only by means of words; they could be incarnated without residue. That was the happy time when paintings could still have a 'theme' and an 'idea', for the idea had not yet been tied to the concept and to the word that named the concept. The artist could present in its primary form of manifestation the soul's bodily incarnation in gesture or feature. But since then the printing press has grown to be the main bridge over which the more remote interhuman spiritual exchanges take place and the soul has been concentrated and crystallized chiefly in the word. There was no longer any need for the subtler means of expression provided by the body. For this reason our bodies grew soulless and empty—what is not in use, deteriorates.

The expressive surface of our body was thus reduced to the face alone and this not merely because the rest of the body was hidden by clothes. For the poor remnants of bodily expression that remained to us the little surface of the face sufficed, sticking up like a clumsy semaphore of the soul and signalling as best it could. Sometimes a gesture of the hand was added, recalling the melancholy of a mutilated torso. In the epoch of word culture the soul learnt to speak but had grown almost invisible. Such was the effect of the printing press.

Now the film is about to inaugurate a new direction in our culture. Many million people sit in the picture houses every evening and purely through vision, experience happenings, characters, emotions, moods, even thoughts, without the need for many words. For words do not touch the spiritual content of the pictures and are merely passing instruments of as yet undeveloped forms of art. Humanity is already learning the rich and colourful language of gesture, movement and facial expression. This is not a language of signs as a substitute for words, like the sign-language of the deaf-and-dumb— it is the visual means of communication, without intermediary of souls clothed in flesh. Man has again become visible.

Linguistic research has found that the origins of language lie in expressive movement, that is, that man when he began to speak moved his tongue and lips to no greater extent than the other muscles of his face and body—just as an infant does to-day. Originally the purpose was not the making of sounds. The movement of tongue and lips was at first the same spontaneous gesturing as every other expressive movement of the body. That the former produced sounds was a secondary,

adventitious phenomenon, which was only later used for practical purposes. The immediately visible message was thus
turned into an immediately audible message. In the course
of this process, as in every translation, a great deal was lost.
It is the expressive movement, the gesture, that is the aborigi-
nal mother-tongue of the human race.

Now we are beginning to remember and re-learn this tongue.
It is still clumsy and primitive and very far removed as yet
from the refinements of word art. But already it is beginning
to be able sometimes to express things which escape the artists
of the word. How much of human thought would remain unexpressed if we had no music! The now developing art of
facial expression and gesture will bring just as many submerged
contents to the surface. Although these human experiences are
not rational, conceptual contents, they are nevertheless neither
vague nor blurred, but as clear and unequivocal as is music.
Thus the inner man, too, will become visible.

But the old visible man no longer exists to-day and the new
visible man is not yet in existence. As I have said before, it
is the law of nature that unused organs degenerate and disappear, leaving only rudiments behind. The animals that do
not chew lose their teeth. In the epoch of word culture we
made little use of the expressive powers of our body and have
therefore partly lost that power. The gesturing of primitive
peoples is frequently more varied and expressive than that of
the educated European whose vocabulary is infinitely richer.
A few more years of film art and our scholars will discover
that cinematography enables them to compile encyclopædias
of facial expression, movement and gesture, such as have long
existed for words in the shape of dictionaries. The public,
however, need not wait for the gesture encyclopædia and gram-
mars of future academies: it can go to the pictures and learn
it there.

We had, however, when we neglected the body as a means
of expression, lost more than mere corporal power of expression. That which was to have been expressed was also
narrowed down by this neglect. For it is not the same spirit,
not the same soul that is expressed once in words and once in
gestures. Music does not express the same thing as poetry in

a different way—it expresses something quite different. When we dip the bucket of words in the depths, we bring up other things than when we do the same with gestures. But let no one think that I want to bring back the culture of movement and gesture in place of the culture of words, for neither can be a substitute for the other. Without a rational, conceptual culture and the scientific development that goes with it there can be no social and hence no human progress. The connecting tissue of modern society is the word spoken and written, without which all organization and planning would be impossible. On the other hand fascism has shown us where the tendency to reduce human culture to subconscious emotions in place of clear concepts would lead humanity.

What I am talking about is only art and even here there is no question of displacing the more rational art of the word. There is no reason why we should renounce one sort of human achievement in favour of another. Even the most highly developed musical culture need not crowd out some more rational aspect of culture.

But to return to the simile of the bucket: we know that the wells that dry up are the wells from which no water is dipped. Psychology and philology have shown that our thoughts and feelings are determined *a priori* by the possibility of expressing them. Philology is also aware that it is not only concepts and feelings that create words, but that it is also the other way round: words give rise to concepts and feelings. This is a form of economy practised by our mental constitution which desires to produce unusable things just as little as does our physical organism. Psychological and logical analysis has shown that words are not merely images expressing our thoughts and feelings but in most cases their *a priori* limiting forms. This is at the root of the danger of stereotyped banality which so often threatens the educated. Here again the evolution of the human spirit is a dialectical process. Its development increases its means of expression and the increase of means of expression in its turn facilitates and accelerates its development. Thus if then the film increases the possibilities of expression, it will also widen the spirit it can express.

Will this newly developing language of facial expression and expressive gesture bring human beings closer to each other or the contrary? Despite the tower of Babel there were concepts common to all behind the different words and one could also learn the languages of others. Concepts on the other hands, have, in civilized communities, a content determined by convention. A universally valid grammar was an even more potent unifying principle holding together the individuals who in bourgeois society were prone to become estranged and isolated from each other. Even the literature of extreme subjectivism used the common vocabulary and was thus preserved from the loneliness of final misunderstanding.

But the language of the gestures is far more individual and personal than the language of words, although facial expression, too, has its habitual forms and conventionally accepted interpretations, to such an extent that one might—and should —write a comparative 'gesturology' on the model of comparative linguistics. Nevertheless this language of facial expression and gesture, although it has a certain generally accepted tradition, lacks the severe rules that govern grammar and by the grace of our academies are compulsory for us all. No school prescribes that you must express your cheerfulness by this sort of smile and your bad humour with that sort of wrinkled brow. There are no punishable errors in this or that facial expression, although children doubtless do observe and imitate such conventional grimaces and gestures. On the other hand, these are more immediately induced by inner impulses than are words. Yet it will probably be the art of the film after all which may bring together the peoples and nations, make them accustomed to each other, and lead them to mutual understanding. The silent film is free of the isolating walls of language differences. If we look at and understand each other's faces and gestures, we not only understand, we also learn to feel each other's emotions. The gesture is not only the outward projection of emotion, it is also its initiator.

The universality of the film is primarily due to economic causes—which are always the most compelling causes. The making of a film is so expensive that only very few nations have a home market sufficient to make film production pay. But one of the preconditions of the international popularity of any film is the universal comprehensibility of facial expression and gesture. Specific national characteristics will in time be permissible only as exotic curiosities and a certain levelling of 'gesturology' will be inevitable. The laws of the film market permit only universally comprehensible facial expressions and gestures, every nuance of which is understood by princess and working girl alike from San Francisco to Smyrna. We now already have a situation in which the film speaks the only universal, common world language understood by all. Ethnic peculiarities, national specialities sometimes can lend style and colour to a film, but can never become factors in causing the story to move on, because the gestures which convey the meaning and decide the course of the action must be uniformly comprehensible to every audience everywhere, otherwise the producer will lose money on the film.

The silent film helped people to become physically accustomed to each other and was about to create an international human type. When once a common cause will have united men within the limits of their own race and nation, then the film which makes visible man equally visible to everyone, will greatly aid in levelling physical differences between the various races and nations and will thus be one of the most useful pioneers in the development towards an international universal humanity.

CHAPTER SIX

THE CREATIVE CAMERA

W H A T   W E   S E E on the screen is a photograph; that is, it was not created on the screen as a painting is created on the canvas but was already previously existent and visible in reality. It had to be enacted in front of the camera, otherwise it could not have been photographed. Thus the actual artistic creation, the original creative act is performed in the studio or on location; at all events before the camera in space and before the shooting in time. Then and there the actors acted and the technicians did their jobs. Everything had first to be reality before it could become a picture. Hence the film we see on the screen is merely a photographic reproduction, or to be exact, the reproduction of a histrionic performance.

Or do we see things in the film, on the screen, which we could not have seen in the studio even if we had been present when the film was made? What are the effects which are born only on the celluloid, are born only in the act of projecting the film on to the screen? What is it that the film does not re-produce but produce, and through which it becomes an independent, basically new art after all?

We have already said it: the changing distance, the detail taken out of the whole, the close-up, the changing angle, the cutting, and what is the most important: a new psychological effect achieved by the film through the devices just mentioned. This new psychological effect is identification.

Even if I am present at every shot, if I look on as every scene is enacted in the studio, I can never see or feel the pictorial effects which are the results of camera distances and angles, nor can I become aware of the rhythm which is their outcome. For in the studio I see each scene and each figure as a whole and am unable to single out details with my eye.

In reality we can never see the face of things in the microscopic detail of a close-up, even if we stand beside the camera when the shot is made. The cut-out of the close-up is a function akin to the composition in a painting. What is left out and what is included have a significance of their own and this significance is provided only by the camera and transmitted to us only by the picture projected on the screen.

The angle is what gives all things their shape and the same thing taken from different angles often gives a completely dissimilar picture. This is the strongest means of characterization the film possesses; and it is not reproduction but genuine production. The cameraman's vision, his artistic creative work, the expression of his personality, can be seen only in the screen projection.

Finally there is the cutting, the ultimate integrating work on the film, which is quite apart from the shooting of the picture and which creates the rhythm and that process of association of ideas which again cannot be reproduction, if for no other reason, because there is no original to reproduce in this phase of film creation, not even as much as the painter has in his model. Montage, the mobile architecture of the film's picture-material, is a specific, new creative art.

Such are the basically novel elements of film art. These are the things which the invention in France of the cinematographic camera did not automatically produce, but which were evolved in Hollywood decades later.

WE ARE IN THE PICTURE

Some people think that the new means of expression provided by the camera are due only to its mobility, which not only shows us new things all the time but does so from incessantly changing angles and distances and that this constitutes the historical novelty of the film.

True, the film camera has revealed new worlds until then concealed from us: such as the soul of objects, the rhythm of crowds, the secret language of dumb things.

But all this provided only new knowledge, new themes, new subjects, new material. A more important, more decisive, more historical novelty was that the film showed not other things, but the same things shown in a different way—that in the film the permanent distance from the work fades out of the consciousness of the spectator and with it that inner distance as well, which hitherto was a part of the experience of art.

IDENTIFICATION

In the cinema the camera carries the spectator into the film picture itself. We are seeing everything from the inside as it were and are surrounded by the characters of the film. They need not tell us what they feel, for we see what they see and see it as they see it.

Although we sit in our seats for which we have paid, we do not see Romeo and Juliet from there. We look up to Juliet's balcony with Romeo's eyes and look down on Romeo with Juliet's. Our eye and with it our consciousness is identified with the characters in the film, we look at the world out of their eyes and have no angle of vision of our own. We walk amid crowds, ride, fly or fall with the hero and if one character looks into the other's eyes, he looks into our eyes from the screen, for, our eyes are in the camera and become identical with the gaze of the characters. They see with our eyes. Herein lies the psychological act of 'identification'.

Nothing like this 'identification' has ever occurred as the effect of any other system of art and it is here that the film manifests its absolute artistic novelty.

A NEW PHILOSOPHY OF ART

The film camera went to America from Europe. Why did film art nevertheless come from America to Europe? Why did Hollywood rather than Paris first hit on the new and specific forms of expression of the new art? This was the first time in history that Europe learnt an art from America.

The reason is that the film is the only art born in the epoch of capitalism. The roots of all the others reach far back into the past and they all to a greater or lesser degree bear the stamp of older ideologies. To this must be added the traditions of bourgeois æsthetics and a philosophy of art which preached the absolute authority of pre-capitalist, chiefly ancient art and of its 'eternal laws'. The bourgeoisie made antique art, born of other societies and ideologies, the absolute standard and the sole norm of all art. Every academy, every official body concerned with art, accepted this attitude. Such an attitude to art made civilized Europe unfavourable ground for the sudden leap into the completely new twentieth-century art which the traditionless and unbiassed Americans could lightly accept.

In the shadow of the conservative French *Académie*, in the neighbourhood of the treasures piled up in the Louvre, near the ancient Comédie Française where the Alexandrines of Corneille and Racine were still spoken as they had been two hundred years ago, such an innovation would have been immeasurably more difficult than in the brand-new cultural vacuum of Hollywood. The ideology of the American people was not fettered by old æsthetic and cultural traditions. But let us see how the traditional European attitude to art differs from the American.

PRINCIPLE OF THE MICROCOSM

A basic principle of European æsthetics and art philosophy from the ancient Greeks to our own time has been that there is an external and internal distance and dualism between spectator and work of art. This principle implies that every work of art by force of its self-contained composition, is a microcosm with laws of its own. It may *depict* reality but has no immediate connection and contact with it. The work of art is separated from the surrounding empiric world not only by the frame of the picture, the pedestal of the statue, the footlights of the stage. The work of art, by force of its intrinsic nature, as a result of its self-contained composition and own specific laws, is separated from natural reality and precisely because it depicts the latter, cannot be its continuation. Even if I hold a painting in my hand, I cannot penetrate into the painted space of the picture. I am not only physically incapable of this, but my consciousness cannot do it either. It should be said here, however, that this feeling of insuperable distance was not always and everywhere present in all nations. For instance the Chinese of old regarded their art with a different eye and their attitude found expression in tales such as this:

There was once a painter who one day painted a landscape. It was a beautiful valley with wonderful trees and with a winding path leading away towards the mountains. The artist was so delighted with his picture that he felt an irresistible urge to walk along that path winding away towards the distant mountains. He entered the picture and followed the path towards the mountains and was never seen again by any man.

Another story tells of a young man who saw a beautiful picture of lovely maidens disporting themselves in a meadow full of flowers. One of the maidens caught his eye and he fell in love with her. He entered the picture and took the maiden for his wife. A year later a little child appeared in the picture.

Such tales could never have been born in the minds of men brought up in European ideas of art. The European spectator feels the internal space of a picture as inaccessible, guarded by its own self-sufficient composition.

But such strange stories as those Chinese tales could easily have been born in the brain of a Hollywood American. For the new forms of film art born in Hollywood show that in that part of the world, as in old China, the spectator does not regard the inner world of a picture as distant and inaccessible. Hollywood invented an art which disregards the principle of self-contained composition and not only does away with the distance between the spectator and the work of art but deliberately creates the illusion in the spectator that he is in the middle of the action reproduced in the fictional space of the film.

IDEOLOGY OF THE PIONEERS

It would be contrary to all experience and probability and would require a special explanation, if such a tradition-breaking new art had not been born out of progressive ideologies. It is by no means an accident that the initiator of the revolution in cinematography, the genius David Griffith, made films which were not only new in their form but radically democratic and progressive in their content. His great four-part serial

Intolerance, made at the time of the first world war, was the most courageous pacifist manifestation of the time and turning against imperialist chauvinism he depicted the methods of big business in this way:

An American manufacturer's business is doing badly. He needs some sort of publicity to build it up. So the manufacturer gives money to his sister to build orphanages. There is no particular need for orphanages but charity always provides good publicity. The orphanages cost a great deal of money and as there are no orphans about, stand empty. The money for the orphanages has to come from the manufacturer's factories, so he reduces wages. The workers go on strike against the wage-cut. The manufacturer brings in blacklegs. The strikers stop the blacklegs from entering the factory. The manufacturer's factory police fire on the strikers. A number of them are killed. The factory is working again and the orphanages now have plenty of orphans. Everything is fine. Happy ending.

This film was made in 1916, an epic of bourgeois cinematography.

Charlie Chaplin, who himself belongs to the first great generation that created the art of the film, always depicted poor and persecuted human beings. Of course Charlie's immortal figure is not the revolutionary image of the exploited factory worker or agricultural labourer, but that of a 'Lumpenproletarian' who defends himself with charming cunning against the heartlessness of the rich and revenges himself by petty means. Nevertheless, taken as a whole, the first great Hollywood generation which created the new form-language of the film was progressive and democratic in its ideology and in the spirit and content of its films. It is out of this spirit that the first and only bourgeois art was born.

CHAPTER SEVEN

THE CLOSE-UP

A S W E H A V E already said, the basis of the new form-
language is the moving cinematographic camera with its constantly changing viewpoint. The distance from the object and
with it the size and number of objects in the frame, the angle
and the perspective all change incessantly. This movement
breaks up the object before the camera into *sectional pictures*,
or 'shots', irrespective of whether that object is moving or
motionless. Sectional pictures are not details of a whole film.
For what is being done is not to break up into its constituent
parts a picture already taken or already envisaged. The result
of this would be detail; in this case one would have to show
every group and every individual in a crowd scene from the
same angle as the one from which they are seen in the total
picture; none of the people or things could move—if they did,
they would no longer be details of the same total. What is
done is not to break up into detail an already existent, already
formed total picture, but to show a living, moving scene or
landscape as a synthesis of sectional pictures, which merge
in our consciousness into a total *scene* although they are not
the parts of an existent immutable mosaic and could never
be made into a total single *picture*.

WHAT HOLDS THE SECTIONAL PICTURES TOGETHER?

The answer to this question is: the montage or cutting, the
mobile composition of the film, an architecture in time, not
space, of which much more is to be said later. For the time
being we are interested in the psychological question of why
a scene broken up into sectional pictures does not fall apart
but remains a coherent whole, remains in the consciousness

of the spectator a consistent unity in both space and time. How do we know that things are happening simultaneously and in the same place, even though the pictures pass before our eyes in temporal sequence and show a real passing of time?

This unity and the simultaneity of pictures proceeding in time is not produced automatically. The spectator must contribute an association of ideas, a synthesis of consciousness and imagination to which the film-going public had first to be educated. This is that visual culture of which we have spoken in previous chapters.

But the sectional picture (or 'shot') must be correctly ordered and composed. There may be shots which slip out of the whole and in respect of which we no longer feel that we are in the same place and see the same scene as in the preceding shots. This is a matter for the director who can, if he chooses, make the spectator feel the continuity of the scene, its unity in time and space even if he has never once shown him a total picture of the whole scene for his orientation.

This is done by including in every shot a movement, a gesture, a form, a something which refers the eye to the preceding and following shots, something that protrudes into the next shot like the branch of a tree or a fence, like a ball that rolls from one frame to the other, a bird that flies across, cigar smoke that curls in both, a look or gesture to which there is an answer in the next shot. But the director must be on his guard not to change the angle together with the direction of movement— if he does, the change in the picture is so great as to break its unity. The sound film has simplified this job of remaining in step. For sound can always be heard in the whole space, in each shot. If a scene is enacted, say, in a night club, and we hear the same music we will know that we are in the same night club even if in the shot itself we see nothing but a hand holding a flower or something of the sort. But if we suddenly hear different sounds in this same shot of a hand we will assume, even if we don't see it, that the hand holding the flower is now in a quite different place. For instance, to continue the picture of the hand holding the rose—if instead of dance music we now hear the twittering of birds, we will not be surprised if, when the picture widens into a long shot, we see a garden and the owner of the hand picking roses. This sort of change-over offers opportunities for good effects.

SOUND IS INDIVISIBLE

This totally different nature of sound has a considerable influence on the composition, montage and dramaturgy of the sound film. The sound camera cannot break up sound into sections or shots as the cinematographic camera can break up objects. In space, sound is always heard indivisibly and homogeneously; that is, it has the same character in one part of space as in any other; it can only be louder or softer, closer or more distant and mixed with other sounds in differing ways. In the night club, for instance, we may first hear only dance music and then the loud talking and laughter of a noisy company at one of the tables may almost drown it.

SOUND IN SPACE

All sound has an identifiable place in space. By its pitch we can tell whether it is in a room, or a cellar, in a large hall or in the open air. This possibility of placing sound also helps to hold together shots the action of which takes place in the same space. The sound film has educated our ear—or might and should have educated it—to recognize the pitch (timbre) of sound. But we have made less progress in our aural than in our visual education. In any case, the sound film which could use sound as its artistic material in a similar way as the silent film had used the visual impression, was soon superseded by the talkie, which was in a sense a step backwards towards the photographed theatre.

THE FACE OF THINGS

The first new world discovered by the film camera in the days of the silent film was the world of very small things visible only from very short distances, the hidden life of little things. By this the camera showed us not only hitherto unknown objects and events: the adventures of beetles in a wilderness of blades of grass, the tragedies of day-old chicks in a corner of the poultry-run, the erotic battles of flowers and the poetry of miniature landscapes. It brought us not only new themes. By means of the close-up the camera in the days of the silent film revealed also the hidden mainsprings of a life which we had thought we already knew so well. Blurred outlines are mostly the result of our insensitive short-sightedness and superficiality. We skim over the teeming substance of life. The camera has uncovered that cell-life of the vital issues in which all great events are ultimately conceived; for the greatest landslide is only the aggregate of the movements of single particles. A multitude of close-ups can show us the very instant in which the general is transformed into the particular. The close-up has not only widened our vision of life, it has also deepened it. In the days of the silent film it not only revealed new things, but showed us the meaning of the old.

VISUAL LIFE

The close-up can show us a quality in a gesture of the hand we never noticed before when we saw that hand stroke or strike something, a quality which is often more expressive than any play of the features. The close-up shows your shadow on the wall with which you have lived all your life and which you scarcely knew; it shows the speechless face and fate of the dumb objects that live with you in your room and whose fate is bound up with your own. Before this you looked at your life as a concert-goer ignorant of music listens to an orchestra playing a symphony. All he hears is the leading melody, all the rest is blurred into a general murmur. Only those can really understand and enjoy the music who can hear the contrapuntal architecture of each part in the score. This is how we see life: only its leading melody meets the eye. But a good film with its close-ups reveals the most hidden parts in our polyphonous life, and teaches us to see the intricate visual details of life as one reads an orchestral score.

LYRICAL CHARM OF THE CLOSE-UP

The close-up may sometimes give the impression of a mere naturalist preoccupation with detail. But good close-ups radiate a tender human attitude in the contemplation of hidden things, a delicate solicitude, a gentle bending over the intimacies of life-in-the-miniature, a warm sensibility. Good close-ups are lyrical; it is the heart, not the eye, that has perceived them.

Close-ups are often dramatic revelations of what is really happening under the surface of appearances. You may see a medium shot of someone sitting and conducting a conversation with icy calm. The close-up will show trembling fingers nervously fumbling a small object—sign of an internal storm. Among pictures of a comfortable house breathing a sunny security, we suddenly see the evil grin of a vicious head on the carved mantelpiece or the menacing grimace of a door opening into darkness. Like the *leitmotif* of impending fate in an opera, the shadow of some impending disaster falls across the cheerful scene.

Close-ups are the pictures expressing the poetic sensibility of the director. They show the faces of things and those expressions on them which are significant because they are reflected expressions of our own subconscious feeling. Herein lies the art of the true cameraman.

In a very old American film I saw this dramatic scene: the bride at the altar suddenly runs away from the bridegroom whom she detests, who is rich and who has been forced on her. As she rushes away she must pass through a large room full of wedding presents. Beautiful things, good things, useful things, things radiating plenty and security smile at her and lean towards her with expressive faces. And there are the presents given by the bridegroom: faces of things radiating touching attention, consideration, tenderness, love—and they all seem to be looking at the fleeing bride, because she looks at them; all seem to stretch out hands towards her, because she feels they do so. There are ever more of them—they crowd the room and block her path—her flight slows down more and more, then she stops and finally turns back.

The Thirteen

This is the title of a film by Romm. The significant dramatic life the close-up gives to things is not an artistic monopoly to the silent film. Michael Romm used it in his film *The Thirteen* when the sound film was already fully developed. Desert marauders have surrounded a little group of soldiers. One man on horseback is sent out to bring help. We alternately see the life-and-death struggle of the twelve left behind—a struggle that cannot last long—and the long and dangerous ride of the solitary horseman across the sands of the desert. On him depends the life of the other twelve and therefore his struggle and his fate interest us more than the others, whose battle from behind a parapet of sand offers little variety to the eye. The enemy against whom the solitary rider matches his strength is the *length* of the road. How is the director to show this? By showing the rider riding and riding again? The spectator would tire of this even sooner than the rider himself. And so Romm doesn't show us the rider at all, only his trail in the sand. It tells us more than any riding, or even the rider's face, ever could. For this trail shows what is the most terrible—the awful length of the road. We see a great panorama of the boundless desert and on its smooth surface a single solitary forlorn line of footprints lost in the immensity of space stretching endlessly to a distant horizon. How much time and footage would the director have required to produce by means of riding scenes the effect he achieved by a single panoramic picture?

Then the close-ups of the trail mark the beginning of an exciting drama. For the trail changes its shape, it takes on a physiognomy—it shows us the fatigue and then exhaustion of the increasingly uncertain feet and our imagination is stimulated by the fact that we cannot see, but merely deduce or guess the condition of the man by the state of the trail. Then far away on the horizon we see something lying prostrate on the ground and we do not know at first whether it is man or horse. The suspense is exciting. But presently we see human footprints in the desert sand. That we have not seen a close-up of the dead horse brings home the significance of the close-up more than anything else. For at bottom the spectator is afraid; he does not really want to see what is lying there and thereby conjures up more intensely than ever the close-up lurking in his own imagination!

Afterwards we see only the trail of the man on foot, sinking into the sand up to the knees. One can see that he is staggering —his footprints are a zig-zag—then the erratic trail sinks below the remote horizon—and the goal is still far away.

Then we see a rifle lying in the sand. A close-up shows the precious weapon—no man would throw such a thing away while he could still muster the strength to carry it. Then a sabre is lying on the ground . . . Close-ups show how the man gradually jettisons his equipment, show his efforts, his suffering, his unbending will, his stubborn struggle forward. He himself has not been shown us even once, but the picture our imagination paints of him is all the more harrowing. We see the tragic ballad of that endless road and every new sign, every new object is a new verse in it.

If the director had shown us the man himself, how often would he have had to show us practically the same picture over and over again? The human face, if it registers nothing but effort and exhaustion all the time, could not contain so much variety as that trail. Only at the end of the road do we see the man himself at the climax of his dramatic struggle. We see him still crawling forward on all fours, then we see him sink down and swoon. Now the man's facial expression also finds its mark, in our hearts, because the director did not use up this effect too soon. Here is a classical example of how the close-up should be used.

On the stage the living, speaking human being has a far greater significance than dumb objects. They are not on the same plane and their intensity is different. In the silent film both man and object were equally pictures, photographs, their homogeneous material was projected on to the same screen, in the same way as in a painting, where they are equally patches of colour and equally parts in the same composition. In significance, intensity and value men and things were thus brought on to the same plane.

Even in the talkie the speaking human being is still only a

picture, a photograph. The word does not lift him out of the community of the common material. For this reason even the sound film still offers the possibility of a consistent style; for instance a scurrilously grotesque evil-faced personage may, like some hidden family trait, take on a resemblance to the scurrilously grotesque malevolence of the character. Or else objects surrounding a charming, smiling girl can all be smiling and graceful.

Having discovered the soul of things in the close-up, the silent film undeniably overrated their importance and sometimes succumbed to the temptation of showing 'the hidden little life' as an end in itself, divorced from human destinies; it strayed away from the dramatic plot and presented the 'poetry of things' instead of human beings. But what Lessing said in his *Laokoon* about Homer—that he never depicted anything but human actions and always described objects only inasmuch as they took part in that action—should to this day serve as a model for all epic and dramatic art as long as it centres around the presentation of man.

CHAPTER EIGHT

THE FACE OF MAN

*The basis and possibility of an art of the film is that everyone
and everything looks what it is*

EVERY ART ALWAYS deals with human beings, it is a
human manifestation and presents human beings. To para-
phrase Marx: 'The root of all art is man'. When the film close-
up strips the veil of our imperceptiveness and insensitivity from
the hidden little things and shows us the face of objects, it still
shows us man, for what makes objects expressive are the
human expressions projected on to them. The objects only reflect our own selves, and this is what distinguished art from
scientific knowledge (although even the latter is to a great
extent subjectively determined). When we see the face of
things, we do what the ancients did in creating *gods* in man's
image and breathing a human soul into them. The close-ups
of the film are the creative instruments of this mighty visual
anthropomorphism.

What was more important, however, than the discovery of
the physiognomy of things, was the discovery of the human
face. Facial expression is the most subjective manifestation of
man, more subjective even than speech, for vocabulary and
grammar are subject to more or less universally valid rules
and conventions, while the play of features, as has already been
said, is a manifestation not governed by objective canons, even
though it is largely a matter of imitation. This most subjective
and individual of human manifestations is rendered objective
in the close-up.

A NEW DIMENSION

If the close-up lifts some object or some part of an object
out of its surroundings, we nevertheless perceive it as existing
in space; we do not for an instant forget that the hand, say,

which is shown by the close-up, belongs to some human being. It is precisely this connection which lends meaning to its every movement. But when Griffith's genius and daring first projected gigantic 'severed heads' on to the cinema screen, he not only brought the human face closer to us in space, he also transposed it from space into another dimension. We do not mean, of course, the cinema screen and the patches of light and shadow moving across it, which being visible things, can be conceived only in space; we mean the expression on the face as revealed by the close-up. We have said that the isolated hand would lose its meaning, its expression, if we did not know and imagine its connection with some human being. The facial expression on a face is complete and comprehensible in itself and therefore we need not think of it as existing in space and time. Even if we had just seen the same face in the middle of a crowd and the close-up merely separated it from the others, we would still feel that we have suddenly been left alone with this one face to the exclusion of the rest of the world. Even if we have just seen the owner of the face in a long shot, when we look into the eyes in a close-up, we no longer think of that wide space, because the expression and significance of the face has no relation to space and no connection with it. Facing an isolated face takes us out of space, our consciousness of space is cut out and we find ourselves in another dimension: that of physiognomy. The fact that the features of the face can be seen side by side, i.e. in space—that the eyes are at the top, the ears at the sides and the mouth lower down—loses all reference to space when we see, not a figure of flesh and bone, but an expression, or in other words when we see emotions, moods, intentions and thoughts, things which although our eyes can see them, are not in space. For feelings, emotions, moods, intentions, thoughts are not themselves things pertaining to space, even if they are rendered visible by means which are.

MELODY AND PHYSIOGNOMY

We will be helped in understanding this peculiar dimension by Henri Bergson's analysis of time and duration. A melody, said Bergson, is composed of single notes which follow each other in sequence, i.e. in time. Nevertheless a melody has no dimension in time, because the first note is made an element of the melody only because it refers to the next note and because it stands in a definite relation to all other notes down to the last. Hence the last note, which may not be played for some time, is yet already present in the first note as a melody-creating element. And the last note completes the melody only because we hear the first note along with it. The notes sound one after the other in a time-sequence, hence they have a real duration, but the coherent line of melody has no dimension in time; the relation of the notes to each other is not a phenomenon occurring in time. The melody is not born gradually in the course of time but is already in existence as a complete entity as soon as the first note is played. How else would we know that a melody is begun? The single notes have duration in time, but their relation to each other, which gives meaning to the individual sounds, is outside time. A logical deduction also has its sequence, but premise and conclusion do not follow one another in time. The process of thinking as a psychological process may have duration; but the logical forms, like melodies, do not belong to the dimension of time.

Now facial expression, physiognomy, has a relation to space similar to the relation of melody to time. The single features, of course, appear in space; but the significance of their relation to one another is not a phenomenon pertaining to space, no more than are the emotions, thoughts and ideas which are manifested in the facial expressions we see. They are picture-like and yet they seem outside space; such is the psychological effect of facial expression.

SILENT SOLILOQUY

The modern stage no longer uses the spoken soliloquy, although without it the characters are silenced just when they are the most sincere, the least hampered by convention: when they are alone. The public of to-day will not tolerate the spoken soliloquy, allegedly because it is 'unnatural'. Now the film has brought us the silent soliloquy, in which a face can speak with the subtlest shades of meaning without appearing unnatural and arousing the distaste of the spectators. In this silent monologue the solitary human soul can find a tongue more candid and uninhibited than in any spoken soliloquy, for it speaks instinctively, subconsciously. The language of the face cannot be suppressed or controlled. However disciplined and practisedly hypocritical a face may be, in the enlarging close-up we see even that it is concealing something, that it is looking a lie. For such things have their own specific expressions superposed on the feigned one. It is much easier to lie in words than with the face and the film has proved it beyond doubt.

In the film the mute soliloquy of the face speaks even when the hero is not alone, and herein lies a new great opportunity for depicting man. The poetic significance of the soliloquy is that it is a manifestation of mental, not physical, loneliness. Nevertheless, on the stage a character can speak a monologue only when there is no one else there, even though a character might feel a thousand times more lonely if alone among a large crowd. The monologue of loneliness may raise its voice within him a hundred times even while he is audibly talking to someone. Hence the most deep-felt human soliloquies could not find expression on the stage. Only the film can offer the possibility of such expression, for the close-up can lift a character out of the heart of the greatest crowd and show how solitary it is in reality and what it feels in this crowded solitude.

The film, especially the sound film, can separate the words of a character talking to others from the mute play of features by means of which, in the middle of such a conversation, we are made to overhear a mute soliloquy and realize the difference between this soliloquy and the audible conversation. What a flesh-and-blood actor can show on the real stage is at most that his words are insincere and it is a mere convention that the partner in such a conversation is blind to what every spectator can see. But in the isolated close-up of the film we can see to the bottom of a soul by means of such tiny movements of facial muscles which even the most observant partner would never perceive.

A novelist can, of course, write a dialogue so as to weave into it what the speakers think to themselves while they are talking. But by so doing he splits up the sometimes comic, sometimes tragic, but always awe-inspiring, unity between spoken word and hidden thought with which this contradiction is rendered manifest in the human face and which the film was the first to show us in all its dazzling variety.

'POLYPHONIC' PLAY OF FEATURES

The film first made possible what, for lack of a better description, I call the 'polyphonic' play of features. By it I mean the appearance on the same face of contradictory expressions. In a sort of physiognomic chord a variety of feelings, passions and thoughts are synthesized in the play of the features as an adequate expression of the multiplicity of the human soul.

Asta Nielsen once played a woman hired to seduce a rich young man. The man who hired her is watching the results from behind a curtain. Knowing that she is under observation, Asta Nielsen feigns love. She does it convincingly: the whole gamut of appropriate emotion is displayed in her face. Nevertheless we are aware that it is only play-acting, that it is a sham, a mask. But in the course of the scene Asta Nielsen really falls in love with the young man. Her facial expression shows little change; she had been 'registering' love all the time and done it well. How else could she now show that this time she was really in love? Her expression changes only by a scarcely perceptible and yet immediately obvious nuance— and what a few minutes before was a sham is now the sincere expression of a deep emotion. Then Asta Nielsen suddenly remembers that she is under observation. The man behind the curtain must not be allowed to read her face and learn that she is now no longer feigning, but really feeling love. So Asta now pretends to be pretending. Her face shows a new, by this time threefold, change. First she feigns love, then she genuinely shows love, and as she is not permitted to be in love in good earnest, her face again registers a sham, a pretence of love. But now it is this pretence that is a lie. Now she is lying that she is lying. And we can see all this clearly in her face, over which she has drawn two different masks. At such times an invisible face appears in front of the real one, just as spoken words can by association of ideas conjure up things unspoken and unseen, perceived only by those to whom they are addressed.

In the early days of the silent film Griffith showed a scene of this character. The hero of the film is a Chinese merchant. Lillian Gish, playing a beggar-girl who is being pursued by enemies, collapses at his door. The Chinese merchant finds her, carries her into his house and looks after the sick girl. The girl slowly recovers, but her face remains stone-like in its sorrow. 'Can't you smile?' the Chinese asks the frightened child who is only just beginning to trust him. 'I'll try,' says Lillian Gish, picks up a mirror and goes through the motions of a smile, aiding her face muscles with her fingers. The result is a painful, even horrible mask which the girl now turns to-wards the Chinese merchant. But his kindly friendly eyes bring a real smile to her face. The face itself does not change; but a warm emotion lights it up from inside and an intangible nuance turns the grimace into a real expression.

In the days of the silent film such a close-up provided an entire scene. A good idea of the director and a fine perform-ance on the part of the actor gave as a result an interesting, moving, new experience for the audience.

MICROPHYSIOGNOMY

In the silent film facial expression, isolated from its sur-roundings, seemed to penetrate to a strange new dimension of the soul. It revealed to us a new world—the world of micro-physiognomy which could not otherwise be seen with the naked eye or in everyday life. In the sound film the part played by this 'microphysiognomy' has greatly diminished because it is now apparently possible to express in words much of what facial expression apparently showed. But it is never the same —many profound emotional experiences can never be ex-pressed in words at all.

Not even the greatest writer, the most consummate artist of the pen, could tell in words what Asta Nielsen tells with her face in close-up as she sits down to her mirror and tries to make up for the last time her aged, wrinkled face, raddled with poverty, misery, disease and prostitution, when she is expecting her lover, released after ten years in jail; a lover who has retained his youth in captivity because life could not touch him there.

ASTA AT THE MIRROR

She looks into the mirror, her face pale and deadly earnest. It expresses anxiety and unspeakable horror. She is like a general who, hopelessly encircled with his whole army, bends once more, for the last time, over his maps to search for a way out and finds there is no escape. Then she begins to work feverishly, attacking that disgustingly raddled face with a trembling hand. She holds her lipstick as Michelangelo might have held his chisel on the last night of his life. It is a life-and-death struggle. The spectator watches with bated breath as this woman paints her face in front of her mirror. The mirror is cracked and dull, and from it the last convulsions of a tortured soul look out on you. She tries to save her life with a little rouge! No good! She wipes it off with a dirty rag. She tries again. And again. Then she shrugs her shoulders and wipes it all off with a movement which clearly shows that she has now wiped off her life. She throws the rag away. A close-up shows the dirty rag falling on the floor and after it has fallen, sinking down a little more. This movement of the rag is also quite easy to understand—it is the last convulsion of a death agony.

In this close-up 'microphysiognomy' showed a deeply moving human tragedy with the greatest economy of expression. It was a great new form of art. The sound film offers much fewer opportunities for this kind of thing, but by no means excludes it and it would be a pity if such opportunities were to be neglected, unnecessarily making us all the poorer.

Baltic Deputy

In this film there is a fine long monologue without words, in a close-up of the old professor's face. Professor Polezhayev has joined the Bolsheviks and therefore none of the guests invited to his birthday party has come. He is left alone at an empty table laid for many guests. The table is a depressing sight and the professor's wife weeps. Suddenly the old man turns away and goes to his laboratory. There he looks, not at the empty festive table, but at a bench laden with retorts, test-tubes and other apparatus, cheerfully glittering tools of his life's work, his ever-faithful loyal friends. This alone would make a fine close-up. But the expression coming to the professor's face is an even finer one. Here is sorrowful defiance, a proud faith in spite of everything, a great mute vow of fidelity to the revolution, all in an unspoken soliloquy. Russian audiences broke into spontaneous applause when they saw this scene.

Not only psychological subtleties or moving emotions can be shown in such close-ups, but greater things too, all the pathos of human greatness. The simple, immediately convincing expression on a human face avoids the danger of over-ornate phrases, or rhetoric. (Of course only if the expression is convincing. The play of features can also have an insincere rhetoric of its own.) I remember Shchukin playing Lenin in the film *Lenin in October*, notably in the scene where he is talking to a little child. The warmth of a paternal tenderness is still on his face when the news is brought of the assassination of his close friend and comrade Uritski. He does not utter a word, only turns his face away. He remains silent for a long time, but his face is all the more eloquent in a microphysiognomic close-up. The expression of love and tenderness does not fade off his face, but is slowly overlaid by another emotion: pain. Then comes the third layer: we see anger hardening into inexorable, fear-inspiring hatred. These four emotions are all seen together and simultaneously on Shchukin's face like a chord of four notes.

The director let this scene follow immediately on the scene with the child, because he wanted to show in this synthesis of emotions the true soul of the great revolutionary. He wanted to show what was most important: that hardness was only the reverse side of tenderness, that the revolutionary could hate so fiercely only because he could love so tenderly.

SPEECH AND FACIAL EXPRESSION

In the silent film the actor spoke, just as he does in the talkie. But in the close-ups of the silent film we *saw* the actor talking and this, too, was expressive play of features. Those who can see a speaker as they listen to what he says, see and hear something different from those who only hear.

In the silent film the way in which an actor moved his mouth in speaking was also a means of facial expression. That is why we all understood the actors of all nationalities so well. We understood what was meant when a man hissed his words from between clenched teeth, or spat them out like the darting tongue of a poisonous snake. This was acting, in the true sense of the word. We knew what it meant when a drunk pushed out his words with a heavy tongue through slack lips. We understood when the hero let the words drop contemptuously from the corner of his mouth. This was one of the most interesting features of the close-up, for there were a thousand different ways of speaking when the words were only seen, but not heard, by the audience.

SPEECH IN THE SOUND FILM

The actor in the silent film spoke in a way intelligible to the eyes, not the ears. He could do this precisely because he had no need to speak in a manner intelligible to the ear, he had no need to shape his mouth for the proper pronunciation of sounds, to open his mouth for a broad 'a' or purse it for a 'u'. The reason for any movement of the mouth was only to express some emotion—it was not a rational gesture conforming to the requirements of articulate intelligible speech. This art of expression was virtually killed by the talkie, because a mouth that speaks intelligibly to the ear, can no longer remain intelligible to the eye. It is no longer a spontaneous vehicle of expression, like the other features of the face—it has become a sound-producing instrument.

It is for this reason that the sound film avoids as much as possible the showing in close-up of human faces in the act of speaking, for at such times a part of the face, to wit the mouth, is devoid of expression and because it nevertheless is in active movement, it often appears grotesque. This disadvantage meant that we had to abandon those close-ups which threw a light into the microphysiognomic depths of the human heart, at least while a character on the screen was speaking.

But even so every speaking face on the screen retained an expressiveness just sufficient to render unpalatable the synchronized substitution of another language for the original. Not only because every word of the dubbed text had to be adapted to the movement of the speaking mouth, often resulting in a ridiculous and unnatural phraseology—there is also an inevitable inartistic, sham quality in all synchronization, because every language has inseparably pertaining to it a play of features characteristic of the people speaking the given language. To speak English and accompany the speech with Italian gestures is a monstrosity and the audience felt this. It is for this reason that dubbing has been abandoned more and more in favour of translated titles.

ASTA SPEAKS

In one of her old silent films *(Vanina or The Wedding under the Gallows)* Asta Nielsen attempts to deliver her lover from prison under sentence of death. She has obtained the keys, she is in his cell, the road to freedom is open. But only for a few minutes. The lover is lying in numb despair on the straw and refuses to budge. Now Asta begins to talk to the prisoner, putting all her own energy and determination into her words. She speaks rapidly, desperately, with furious ardour. We cannot hear what she is saying. No title tells us. There is no need for it. The situation speaks for itself. It is obvious that she is trying to put heart into him and repeating again and again: 'Come, there is no time to lose, come or we must both perish!' This is not the real text of Asta's tremendous, visible exhortation—the real text is the fierce struggle between love and fear which no words could express. Seeing her as she speaks makes a deeper impression than if we saw her tear her hair or claw her face in despair. She speaks like this for a long time; and so much audible speech would have been quite unbearable.

Most instructive is the case of Michael Romm and his film of Maupassant's *Boule de Suif*. Romm made this film as a silent film although the sound film was already fully developed at the time. The silence of this film and everything resulting from it was thus no technical necessity, but intentional and deliberately accepted style—rather like the etcher's renunciation of colour. In this silent film Romm did in fact achieve many pictorial and dramatic effects which would have been impossible in a sound film.

The story is well-known, but will bear repetition: a little Parisian tart, escaping in a bus from the Prussians with a number of other passengers, is demonstratively treated with contempt by her fellow-travellers, who, while quite willing to eat generously proffered food, keep her at arm's length in all other respects. The bus is held up by a Prussian patrol and the officer commanding it refuses to allow the fugitives to proceed unless the little cocotte spends the night with him. Two nuns who form part of the strictly virtuous company are the most zealous in trying to persuade the reluctant prostitute to comply with the Prussian officer's demands. Under the pelting rain of their words the little street-walker bows her head. We see the nuns' mouths move with hysterical rapidity. A few minutes before, when they were praying in the immobile poses of statues, no one would have believed that they were capable of such violent passions. The arguments the nuns use to persuade the girl are presented to the audience in two short titles and their essence is that as she is a whore anyway one man more or less would make no difference to her; on the other hand she would be acting in a way to please God if she slept with the German. Much more convincing and effective than their words, however, is their manner of speaking and this can be shown only visually. The incessant, irresistible cataract of words, their cruel, determined, unbearably violent insistence is much more convincingly shown by the *visible,* rapid ceaseless motion of the lips than could ever be conveyed by making *audible* the same, or slightly varied, arguments repeated over and over again. The latter would show only hypocrisy. The former show a fierce passion as well. The loquacity itself is characteristic, but it would have been both tiring and boring to listen to it all. In a sound film the stream of words could never have rushed on with such rapidity— the words would have been unintelligible at such a pace. The motions of speech were here far more expressive and convincing than any spoken words could have been; hence they could be shown only in a silent film.

DUMB SHOW

The characters in the silent film spoke, but their speech was only visible, not audible. Only the pantomime has genuinely mute characters and hence this is a basically different form of art. Pantomime is mute not only to the ear but to the eye. For the pantomime is not only a silent art, it is the art of being silent, expressing what rises from the depths of silence. The gestures and mimicry of pantomime are not an accompaniment to words which have been spoken and which we cannot hear, but the expression, by means of gestures, of the profound experience of music, the music that lives in the depths of silence. It is interesting to observe that in a film in which we see onlookers watching dancers dancing, the motionless public appears more realistic to us than the dancers who are in rapid movement. The reason for this is that the immobility of the audience is the familiar everyday behaviour of all onlookers, while the movements of the dancers express a distant, exotic experience outside our workaday usage.

KEEPING SILENT NO SOLUTION

I must anticipate a little here, as the problem of silence will arise again later. The unsolved inner contradictions of the sound film are manifested among other things in the fact that nearly every director prefers to avoid much speaking and wants scripts in which there is as little dialogue as possible. This in itself discredits the talkie and shows that it is an un-

natural form of art—rather as though a painter were to prefer
painting pictures without colours.

This problem cannot on any account be solved by making
the characters speak little or not at all. The silence of pantomime characters is an inherent quality of this *art form*. But
in the film it is a quality, a characteristic of the *personages,* not
of the art form. If a human being is silent, although he or
she might speak (either audibly as in the talkie or only visibly,
as in the silent film) then we attribute this silence to his or her
character or to the dramatic situation. We cannot use this
powerful means of characterization just for the purpose of
avoiding dialogue; the result would be that all the characters
in our films would be grotesquely surly and taciturn for no
apparent reason.

TEMPO OF MIMICRY

The mute soliloquies of physiognomy, the wordless lyrics of
facial expression can convey many things for the registering of
which other arts possess no instruments. Not only can facial
expression itself tell us things for which we have no words—
the rhythm and tempo of changes in facial expression can also
indicate the oscillation of moods which cannot be put into
words. A single twitch of a facial muscle may express a
passion for the expression of which a long sentence would be
needed. By the time the character would get to the end of
such a sentence, his mood may have changed more than once
and the words would perhaps no longer be true when he spoke
them. The most rapid tempo of speech lags behind the flow
and throb of emotions; but facial expression can always keep
up with them, providing a faithful and intelligible expression
for them all.

There is another Griffith film in which the heroine (Lillian
Gish) is a naïve, trustful girl who is seduced by an unscrupu-
lous cynic. The seducer tells her with a sneer that he has
deceived her. Lillian Gish, the loving, trusting girl, cannot
believe her ears, or rather she is incapable of realizing all at
once that her life is in ruins. She knows that what the man
says is true, but would nevertheless like to believe that he is

joking. For it is impossible that he should be so evil. In this helpless, breathless struggle, this alternating between faith and despair, Lillian Gish laughs and weeps by turns perhaps a dozen times, while she stares at her seducer without saying a word. This two-minute dumb-show, which one could see in close-up, was one of the great artistic achievements of 'microphysiognomics'. It would in itself suffice to immortalize the art of the silent film—the silent film which has since died.

It is impossible to express such an oscillation of emotions in their original rhythm by means of the spoken word. Described in a novel it would take pages, the reading of which would require much more time than the described scene itself. Here again we find an emotional reality which can be shown adequately by the film alone. But not only by the silent film. There is no technical obstacle to such scenes in a sound film. But the sound films of to-day seem to have torn the strings from their own instruments. In their primitive banality they do not know and do not wish to know the possibilities of their own medium and squander the rich heritage of the silent film.

MUTE DIALOGUES

In the last years of the silent film the human face had grown more and more visible, that is, more and more expressive. Not only had 'microphysiognomy' developed but together with it the faculty of understanding its meaning. In the last years of the silent film we saw not only masterpieces of silent monologue but of mute dialogue as well. We saw conversations between the facial expressions of two human beings who understood the movements of each others' faces better than each others' words and could perceive shades of meaning too subtle to be conveyed in words.

A necessary result of this was—as I will show in detailed analysis later in connection with the dramaturgy of the film— that the more space and time in the film was taken up by the inner drama revealed in the 'microphysiognomic' close-up, the less was left of the predetermined 8,000 feet of film for all the external happenings. The silent film could thus dive into the depths—it was given the possibility of presenting a passionate life-and-death struggle almost exclusively by close-ups of faces.

Dreyer's film *Jeanne d'Arc* provided a convincing example of this in the powerful, lengthy, moving scene of the Maid's examination. Fifty men are sitting in the same place all the time in this scene. Several hundred feet of film show nothing but big close-ups of heads, of faces. We move in the spiritual dimension of facial expression alone. We neither see nor feel the space in which the scene is in reality enacted. Here no riders gallop, no boxers exchange blows. Fierce passions, thoughts, emotions, convictions battle here, but their struggle is not in space. Nevertheless this series of duels between looks and frowns, duels in which eyes clash instead of swords, can hold the attention of an audience for ninety minutes without flagging. We can follow every attack and riposte of these duels on the faces of the combatants; the play of their features indicates every stratagem, every sudden onslaught. The silent film has here brought an attempt to present a drama of the spirit closer to realization than any stage play has ever been able to do.

DETAILS OF FACES IN CLOSE-UP

Everything I have said until now about facial expression and play of features referred to the *whole* face. This sort of facial expression is more or less under control—a man may, if he wishes, prevent his feelings from showing in his face—he may even feign other emotions, dissemble, tell a lie with his facial expression.

But the camera can get so close to the face that it can show 'microphysiognomic' details even of this detail of the body and then we find that there are certain regions of the face which are scarcely or not at all under voluntary control and the expression of which is neither deliberate nor conscious and may often betray emotions that contradict the general expression appearing on the rest of the face.

This has a great artistic value and significance because speech, that is the speech of an adult and sober human being, has no involuntary and unconscious elements. If someone wants to tell a lie and is a capable liar, his words will serve him almost to perfection. But his face has areas over which he has no control. He may knit his brows and wrinkle his forehead as much as he likes, the camera creeps up quite close and shows that his chin, which has no dirigible mimicry, is weak and frightened for all the bravado of the rest of the face. In vain does his mouth smile ever so sweetly—the lobe of his ear, the side of a nostril shown in isolated magnification reveal the hidden coarseness and cruelty.

In one of Eisenstein's films there is a priest, a handsome, fine figure of a man. His noble features, his inspired eyes are made even more radiant by a glorious voice. He is like the sublime image of a saint. But then the camera gives an isolated big close-up of one eye; and a cunningly watchful furtive glance slinks out from under his beautiful silky eyelashes like an ugly caterpillar out of a delicate flower. Then the handsome priest turns his head and a close-up shows the back of his head and the lobe of his ear from behind. And we see the ruthless, vicious selfishness of a coarse peasant expressed in them. This expression of the nape of the neck and ear-lobe is so incisive, so irresistibly convincing and so disgusting that when the noble face reappears, it is like a deceptive screen concealing a dangerous enemy. The expression of the whole face cannot cover up the expression of its details, if these details betray a different, more profound truth. Graphology claims to read the writer's true character from the handwriting even if what is written down is an untruth, but the ability to read handwriting in this way is a very rare gift. The art of reading faces was about to become the very useful property of the masses, thanks to the silent film.

I CAN SEE THAT I CANNOT SEE

In the early days of the silent film 'microphysiognomics' had already shown that one can read more in a close-up of a face than what is visibly written on it. On a face, too, one can read 'between the lines'.

The Japanese actor Sessue Hayakawa was a film star of

the early silent film. His speciality was an iron immobility of feature and his feelings and passions did not show in his face. His acting was notable for his restraint, his failure to act. How then did he nevertheless express his emotions so intelligibly that we understood what was going on in the film and were interested in the fate of the character he played?

Once he acted this scene: he is captured by robbers and bound, then unexpectedly confronted with his wife whom he had believed in safety and who is now also a captive. He must not betray the fact that he knows this woman—his life and hers depend on concealing this. The bandits have him covered with their guns and watch his face intently. A movement of a muscle, the slightest hint of any love, tenderness, anxiety, surprise or fear, any indication of what is going on inside him, would betray them both and be their death. But Hayakawa's hard Japanese face is a mask of stone. Nothing shows in his indifferent face of what we know is ravaging his heart. He looks into his wife's frightened eyes with a hard look and we are convinced that the bandits believe him when he says that he does not know this woman.

Nevertheless we can see something in his eye. Not really something, for we could not say what it is. But we can see that there is something there that we cannot see. We can read between the lines of the petrified features—not only excitement and a deep affection, but a consoling encouragement that tells the wife's frightened, fixed stare: 'Speak not, move not, know me not. Fear not, all will be well!' It is the 'microphysiognomics' of the close-up that have given us this subtlest play of features, almost imperceptible and yet so convincing. The invisible face behind the visible had made its appearance, the invisible face visible only to the one person to whom it addresses itself—and to the audience.

SIMPLIFIED ACTING

In films in which a slight movement can express a deep passion and the tragedy of a soul can manifest itself in the twitching of an eyebrow, broad gesturing and grimacing become unbearable. The technique and style of 'microphysiognomics' greatly simplified the acting of film actors. Both gestures and play of features had to be toned down in comparison with the technique of the live stage. This is one of the reasons why the acting style of very old films now appears exaggerated and ridiculous. The microscopic close-up is an inexorable censor of 'naturalness' of expression; it immediately shows up the difference between spontaneous reaction and deliberate, unnatural, forced gesture. Only nature moves naturally, even in human beings, and only the unconscious reflex-like reactions of the soul impress the onlooker as natural gestures.

Even the best film actors are told by the director when a close-up is about to be made: 'Do what you like as long as you don't "act". Don't do anything at all, just feel and imagine the situation you are in and what then appears in the face of its own accord as it were and flexes the muscles in gesture is enough.' The close-up puts emphasis on the most delicate nuances.

We cannot use glycerine tears in a close-up. What makes a deep impression is not a fat, oily tear rolling down a face—what moves us is to see the glance growing misty, and moisture gathering in the corner of the eye—moisture that as yet is scarcely a tear. This is moving, because this cannot be faked.

CHANGES IN TASTE

The simplification of acting brought about by the close-up changed more than the style of acting. There was also a change in taste accompanying the change of trend which substituted a neo-naturalistic tendency for the neo-romanticism of Rostand and Maeterlinck on the western European stage. After the first world war and the hysterical emotional fantasies of expressionism, a 'documentary', dry, anti-romantic and anti-emotional style was the fashion in the film as in the other arts.

The simplified acting demanded by the close-up conformed to the new taste for the objective and unromantic and this circumstance did much to popularize the American style of acting in Europe.

SIMPLE FACES

Not only romantic acting went out of fashion but romantic faces as well. Especially among the male stars, popularity was diverted to those who had commonplace faces. Conrad Veidt's romantic, exalted, almost expressionist head, which brought him world success in the years immediately following the first world war, no longer appealed to the public. Not only was he crowded out by ordinary commonplace faces—he himself did his best to tone down his eccentric appearance and look as commonplace as possible, in order to be able to compete with rival stars. The decorative, out-of-the-ordinary face now seemed a mask and no longer seemed attractive. Beauty, too, grew less important, for in the intimacy of the close-up the intimate details of the face gained in significance and such details could be discovered by the camera—and the spectator —in ugly faces no less than in handsome ones.

SIMPLE VOICES

A related phenomenon is the aversion of the modern director to his characters having too fine and too well-trained voices—except when they play a professional singer or something of the sort, of course. A too fine voice is not 'natural' and gives the impression of an artistic performance and not of a presentation of real life. A song sung by an untrained voice is more intimate and human in its effect.

NATURE SEEMS UNNATURAL

The value placed on being natural increased to such an extent that directors often attempted to do away with professional actors altogether and take their characters 'from the street'. So far as extras were concerned it was certainly easier to find the right types among the crowds in the street if it was only a matter of episodic parts which involved no acting, and required merely being present and showing some sort of a face. But if the perfectly suitable type had to act and particularly if he had to speak, the bad, amateurish acting often nullified the effect produced by the suitable physiognomy.

NATURE TURNED TO ART

To try to cut raw nature into a film is a dangerous business. The fanatics of 'naturalness' (such as Eisenstein and Pudovkin were at one time), simply brought in extras from the street and expected them to move naturally in the set, because they were not actors. But such strangers could not be natural, precisely because they were not actors and hence the studio was something unnatural to them, making them unnatural themselves. But such adherents of the natural did even more than this: they attempted to cut real, natural facial expressions and gestures caught by the camera in the street, into the artistic sequences of their films. They tried to produce art by means of montage, by piecing together natural snapshots. If they wanted a woman looking in terror into the barrel of a gun directed at her and the acting of an actress was not natural enough for their requirements, they went out and searched for a truer one in the street. A woman screamed in terror because the pram with her baby in it overturned by accident. She was photographed without her knowledge and then this really unselfconscious, naturally terrified face was cut into the picture to face the gun.

I am quoting this instance only as an illustration of the method. This method is always a deception; it is rendered possible only by the fact that our physiognomic culture is not as yet sufficiently sensitive to be able to differentiate between terrors induced by different causes—or different laughters for that matter. The close-up which has made us so sensitive to the naturalness of a facial expression will sooner or later develop our sensitivity further, so that we shall be able to discern in a facial expression its cause as well as its nature. Even now we often meet with the paradoxical situation that in the good acting of a good actor things appear perfectly natural, while the photographed reproduction of actual reality does not seem natural at all, as for instance in snapshots of a running man or horse.

Sometimes directors are compelled to produce facial expressions by means outside the story, as for instance in the case of children or primitive exotic characters. The more exotic and foreign the play of features, the more convincing it will be—we are insufficiently acquainted with Zulus or Chens to know when the expression is faked.

EDUCATION IN PHYSIOGNOMICS

In his book on film production, Pudovkin describes in detail the method by means of which he could harness the natural unconscious reactions he evoked and create a conscious artistic effect. But it is precisely this same book that shows how great and conscious an artist is required if unconscious nature is to be thus used and formed into a work of art. A vast physiognomical sensitivity is required if unconscious facial expressions are to be correctly assessed and used; if the expressions on faces, taken from a variety of situations and scenes, are to be so collated as to bring them into relation with each other and respond to each other like the phrases of a dialogue. This great director of silent films had the sure and sensitive eye which could discern in a chance face picked up in the street the very shade of expression required in a given scene. But in the sound film this method could be applied only to detail close-ups of silent crowd scenes.

CHILDREN AND SAVAGES

The acting of children is always natural, for make-believe is a natural thing to them. They do not want to 'register' this or that, like an actor; they just pretend that they are not what they are but something else and that they are not in the situation in which they are but in some other. This is not acting—it is a natural manifestation of youthful consciousness and it can be observed not only in the human young but in the young of other species as well. It is a transposition such as occurs in dreams, or in a trance. All those who have worked with children on the stage or in films will know that children should not be 'directed', they must be played with. It is not their acting which is natural—their nature is play-acting. The same can be observed in savages or primitives. The close-up often reveals unusual gestures and mimicry—unusual, that is, from the white man's viewpoint. If we understand them, they have a particularly fresh and immediately strong effect. But it often happens that we fail to understand them.

Among the red Indians and Chinese for instance the expression of pain or deep sorrow often looks like a smile to our eyes. Not always and not immediately do we know what it is intended to convey. But if we recognize it for what it is, an expression of pain, it moves us deeply, precisely because it is unusual.

GROUP PHYSIOGNOMIES

There was no need of close-ups to show us the typical *common traits* of the great coloured races, the group physiognomies recognizable as Negro, Chinese, Eskimo, etc. On the contrary these exotic faces seemed all alike to us only because we knew them so superficially. Here the close-up was needed to show us the individual differences between one Chinese and the other, one Negro and the other.

Nor was it a discovery to see characteristic English or French, Italian or German types in the films. We had known them well enough before. The film could at most improve our knowledge of the type by showing us new varieties.

In any case, it is difficult to say which type of face is really representative of any nation or race. Is there an undisputed, generally accepted English face? If so, what is it like? And why should that particular face be the truly typical and not some other face? As there is a science of comparative linguistics, so there should be a comparative science of gesture and mimicry, with research into these in order to find the common fundamental forms of expressive movement. The film offers the means to establish such a science.

CLASS FACES

An important innovation introduced by the film was the

'typing' of class faces and facial expressions. Not stereotyped figures such as the 'over-refined degenerate aristocrat' contrasted with the 'coarse, powerful labourer'. We know that these were rough generalizations and the close-up tore off these primitive masks. Behind the external, conventional characteristics, the close-up revealed the hidden, impersonal class traits in individual faces. These class characteristics are often more obvious than national or racial characteristics and the face of a French miner, for instance, is more like the face of a German or English miner, than like the face of a French aristocrat. The mixtures of national, racial and class characteristics show many interesting combinations and variations, but they all show human beings, human types.

It is not by accident that the discovery and presentation of a rich gallery of class physiognomies fell to the lot of Soviet cinematography. Eyes sharpened by the revolutionary class struggle saw more than just the difference between 'rich' and 'poor'. No theoretical type-analysis could show social stratifications more completely than the 'typing' of certain Soviet films. Who does not remember Eisenstein's *October*? In it not only the faces of workers and of aristocrats are juxtaposed in open conflict with each other. The bourgeois liberals and the moderate Socialist intellectuals also wear their distinctive mark on their foreheads, and when the sailor bars their way on the bridge, face faces face, and two different conceptions of the world clash in two different, unmistakable physiognomies.

A classic example of this is the magnificent scene in Dovzhenko's civil war film *Arsenal*. The scene shows the lull before the storm, the storm being the rising in Kiev. The title says 'Waiting for the First Shot'. The city is waiting in the night, motionless, with bated breath. No one is asleep. Everyone is waiting. For the first shot.

Who is waiting? How are they waiting? Now in a series of brief scenes the film shows a cross-section of the social body of a whole city. The workman harks out. The soldier watches. The artisan listens. The merchant strains his ears. The factory-owner is on the alert. The teacher, the clerk, the landowner, the artist, the declassed down-and-out, the Bohemian—they are all looking expectantly into the darkness. How do we know who they are? The title does not tell us. It is written in their faces, unmistakably showing their class and showing it immanently in individual physiognomies; showing not man in his social class, but social class in men. When, after this scene, fighting breaks out in the streets, it is not only machine-guns and bayonets that are engaged in battle, but live human faces as well.

OUR UNKNOWN FACES

The human face is not yet completely discovered—there are still many white patches on its map. One of the tasks of the film is to show us, by means of 'microphysiognomics', how much of what is in our faces is our own and how much of it is the common property of our family, nation or class. It can show how the individual trait merges with the general, until they are inseparably united and form as it were nuances of one another. Written psychology has often attempted to find by analysis the dividing line between the individual and the general. The 'microphysiognomics' of the film can differentiate more subtly and accurately than the most exact of words and hence it acquires, beside the artistic significance, an important scientific function, supplying invaluable material to anthropology and psychology.

THE SECOND FACE

In the mingling of the individual and racial character two expressions are superimposed on each other like translucent masks. For instance, we often see a degenerate specimen of an ancient, long-civilized, refined race. The anatomy of an English aristocrat's face may bear a noble, handsome expression, the physiognomy of an ancient racial culture. But the close-up may show concealed beneath it the coarse and depraved expression of a base individual. Or the film may show the inverse variant: the soulful, beautiful physiognomy hiding between the typically coarse and ugly features of an uncultured race.

'Microphysiognomics' can show, behind the faces we can

control, those other faces which we cannot influence because they have already hardened into anatomy.

MICRODRAMA

This is another necessary consequence of micromimicry. The detailed psychology of the close-up picture occupied so much space (and so many feet) in the film, that less and less room was left for the story. The richer the episodes were in inner content, the fewer episodes had room in the film, the length of which is as unalterably predetermined as that of a sonata.

But there was no longer any need for a multitude of adventurous episodes, for a piling of event on event. The extensivity of the early *colportage* style gave way to intensity; the story turned inward, deepened, penetrated the soul. The development of the close-up changed the whole style of the film story and scenario. The stories now dealt with the hidden subtle adventures of the soul.

Great novels rich in incident were no longer found suitable for filmic treatment. What was wanted were not intricate and adventurous, but plain and simple stories. The specific imagination and inventiveness of the film-makers manifested itself in the pictorial forming of details and not in the visual activity of bustling scenes. What the film-makers now liked to show were scenes which could scarcely be described in words, which could be understood only when seen. In this way the silent film grew less and less 'literary', following in this respect the trend at that time prevalent in the art of painting.

DRAMATIC STATE

The technique of the close-up which thus simplified the story of the film and deepened and brought to dramatic life its smallest details, succeeded in lending dramatic tension to a mere state or condition, without any external event at all. It was able to make us feel nerve-rackingly the sultry tension underneath the superficial calm; the fierce storms raging under the surface were made tangible by mere microscopic movements, by the displacement of a hair. Such films were unsurpassed in showing the Strindbergian moods in the savagely antagonistic silences of human beings confined together in narrow spaces. The micro-tragedies in the peace and quiet of ordinary families were shown as deadly battles, just as the microscope shows the fierce struggles of micro-organisms in a drop of water.

CAMERA RHYTHM

By the movement of the camera or the flickering of the montage even the physical immobility of such static conditions could be mobilized and dramatized. This is a means of expression completely specific to the film. If for some reason or another movement is arrested in a scene on the stage or in the studio, then nothing moves there any more and there can be no question of tempo or rhythm. The film, however, possesses this specific possibility that the scene that is being shot may be completely frozen and motionless and yet the scenes projected on to the screen can nevertheless be in violent and varied motion. The characters may not move, but our glance may leap from the one to the other as it is carried by the camera. Men and things do not move but the camera shifts rapidly and excitedly from the one to the other and the movement of motionless pictures collated by the cutting may have a swift, wild rhythm, making us feel the inner movement of the scene in despite of its outer immobility. The scene in its entirety may be motionless in deadly numbness, like a stationary great machine. But the rushing close-ups show the throbbing of some tiny wheel of the clockwork. We see an eyelid twitch, a lip curl in the motionless figures, their immobility replete with utmost tension.

Lupu Pick, who was one of the greatest German directors of the silent film, once made a crime film. In it safe-breakers burgling a bank vault inadvertently lock themselves into the underground vault. There is no way out of the trap and the mined vault would be blown up in ten minutes. A clock on the wall shows the passing of the minutes. Nine men dash to and fro in mad frenzy, searching for a way out. All in vain. There are three minutes left. They all stand still and stare numbly at the hands of the clock. They are waiting. Nothing moves in the vault save the hands of the clock. This utmost tension could not be increased any further by even the most frenzied movement of the characters. They even hold their breath, so complete is their numb immobility.

On the stage such immobility is possible only for very brief periods. After a few moments the scene would become empty and dead, because nothing happens in it. But in the film a lot of things can happen even when the characters are motionless. For the camera can move even while they do not. The quick cross-cutting of close-ups can move. In the bank vault just mentioned the camera rushes to and fro and the pictures move faster and more fiercely than the actors could. The actors are motionless and silent. But the flickering close-ups, the 'microphysiognomies', speak. They show not a general picture of fear, but the horrible symphony of every phase in nine distinct mortal agonies of terror. The crescendo of fear is shown by the increasingly rapid rhythm of ever shorter close-ups in an ever-quickening montage.

An ant-heap is lifeless if seen from a distance, but at close quarters it is teeming with busy life. The grey, dull texture of everyday life shows in its microdramatics many profoundly moving happenings, if we look at it carefully enough in close-up.

COMMONPLACE   DRAMATIZED

In the heyday of the silent film there was a vogue for realistic films featuring the commonplace and dramatizing the things we usually leave unheeded. It was at this time that King Vidor made his great film showing the workaday life of the average American man-in-the-street. It is a monotonous affair and yet, how many moving, terrifying, and happy little events occur in it, hidden melodies contained in a monotone.

Of course this technique achieves its greatest effects when it spreads out the crucial moment of an action film in the ritardando of detail close-ups, showing that crucial moment in instantaneous sections of time when everything still hangs in the balance, the pointer of the scales is still oscillating and it is not yet certain in which direction it will finally point.

CRUCIAL MOMENT

Let us look at the final scene of Reisman's masterpiece: *The Last Night*. A military train steams into a railway station in Petrograd, which has been occupied by the revolutionaries. It is a mysterious, closed train. Has it brought friends or enemies? We don't know. Bayonets bristle at every window and door of the train, but not a face do we see. Rifle barrels point at the train from every door and window of the station buildings. Who is in there? Friend or foe? No man wants to be the first to step out on to the deserted platform. Expectation and silence. Only the hissing of steam is heard. All action has stopped. But the fate of the station, of the town, perhaps of the whole revolution turns on what will happen in the next few minutes. This frozen state of tension, of doubt and expectation, is not really motionless however. Its elements are agog with nervous impatience. In the restless cross-cutting of close-ups, tiny gestures of boiling excitement sizzle and bubble. Finally an old peasant woman steps on to the platform alone and unarmed, goes to the military train and speaks, asks questions . . .

Of course this scene could not have achieved such powerful tension if the whole film had shown such immobility; the effect is similar to a pause suddenly occurring in a dynamic burst of music.

REALITY INSTEAD OF TRUTH

The development of the microdramatics of the close-up to a stage when experiments were made to produce, not only films without dramatic action, but even films without a central dramatic hero, will be dealt with in later chapters, together with other developments. But one thing should be noted here: if stories without plot and incident, single-situation stories escaped the reproach of being 'literature', this had disadvantages as well as advantages, for there was an increasing tendency to make films of which only the details were interesting, while the whole story was over-simple and trivial.

There was of course an ideological reason for this, as for every other fashion in art. The escapism which, almost from the start, was the dominant tendency in the bourgeois film was here given a new direction. Having first escaped to the fairy-tale romanticism of exotic adventure, the film now escaped to the small detail of the new naturalist style. In its fear of the whole truth, it hid its head like an ostrich in the sand of tiny particles of reality.

CHAPTER NINE

CHANGING SET-UP

CHANGING SET-UP IS the second great creative method of film art. In this again it differs from the principles and methods of every other art. In the theatre we see everything from the same viewpoint, from the same angle, that is in the same perspective. The photographed theatre could not change this very much. It sometimes changed the angle or perspective from scene to scene but never within the same scene. Different paintings have different perspectives and this is their essential artistic creative element, their artistic characteristic. But the perspective of every single painting is one and immutable; hence the outline of every object shown in the picture is finite, a single definite shape. It may have an expressive physiognomy, but never a changing expression, such as the movement of changing outlines, which changing set-ups can give to things in a film.

Only the changing set-up enabled cinematography to develop into an art. No lighting effects could have done it if the camera could not have been moved in relation to the object. Cinematography would have remained mechanical reproduction.

SYNTHESIS OF THE PHOTOGRAPHED IMAGE

The free, individual possibilities of the set-up bring about in the image the synthesis of subject and object which is the basic condition of all art. Every work of art must present not only objective reality but the subjective personality of the artist, and this personality includes his way of looking at things, his ideology and the limitations of the period. All this is projected into the picture, even unintentionally. Every picture shows not only a piece of reality, but a point of view as well. The set-up of the camera betrays the inner attitude of the man behind the camera.

Even the most faithful portraits, the best likenesses, if they are works of art, reproduce not only the sitter but the artist as well. A painter has many ways of painting his own self into his pictures. Composition, colour, brushwork all show at least as much of him as of the objective reality he depicts. But the personality of the film-maker can manifest itself in one thing only: the set-up, which also determines the composition of the shot.

SUBJECTIVITY OF THE OBJECT

Every object, be it man or beast, natural phenomenon or artefact, has a thousand shapes, according to the angle from which we regard and pin down its outlines. In each of the shapes defined by a thousand different outlines we may recognize one and the same object, for they all resemble their common model even if they do not resemble each other. But each of them expresses a different point of view, a different interpretation, a different mood. Each visual angle signifies an inner attitude. There is nothing more subjective than the objective.

The technique of the set-up renders possible the identification which we have already met as the most specific effect of film art. The camera looks at the other characters and their surroundings out of the eyes of one of the characters. It can look about it out of the eyes of a different character every instant. By means of such set-ups we see the scene of action from the inside, with the eyes of the *dramatis personæ,* and know how they feel in it. The abyss into which the hero is falling opens at *our* feet and the heights which he must climb rear themselves into the sky before *our* faces. If the landscape in the film changes, we feel as if *we* had moved away. Thus the constantly changing set-ups give the spectator the feeling that he himself is moving, just as one has the illusion of moving when a train on the next platform starts to leave the station. The true task of film art is to deepen into artistic effects the new psychological effects made possible by the technique of cinematography.

'DÉJÀ VU'

This identification of the picture and the spectator (for the picture incorporates the point of view of those with whose eyes it is seen) makes it possible for the film to recall to mind, by the repetition of certain set-ups, the persons who at one time or another had seen that certain picture in the film. A face or a landscape must reappear in the memory as it was seen in reality, else it would not again conjure up the same mood. On the other hand a repetition of the set-up can stimulate the memory of some past experience and produce the well-known psychological effect of 'having seen it before'.

In the film *Narcosis* which Alfred Abel and I made in Berlin a long time ago, the hero, after many years, meets again a girl he had forgotten and who has changed so much that he does not recognize her. The girl does not tell him who she is but arranges a scene identical with the one in which her fate was decided. She sits in the same chair, in front of the same fire, her face lit up by the flames in the same way. She makes the man take the same chair out of which he looked at her in the old days. She reconstructs the same set-up in which the man got his first impression of her. The film repeats the old picture and the spectator has no doubt that the scene will recall the old experience to the hero.

MORE ABOUT IDENTIFICATION

The physiognomy of every object in a film picture is a composite of two physiognomies—one is that of the object, its very own, which is quite independent of the spectator—and another physiognomy, determined by the viewpoint of the spectator and the perspective of the picture. In the shot the two merge into so close a unity that only a very practised eye is capable of distinguishing these two components in the picture itself. The cameraman may pursue several aims in choosing his angle. He may wish to stress the real objective face of the object shown; in that case he will search for the outlines which express this character of the object most adequately—or he may be more concerned with showing the state of mind of the spectator, in which case he will, if he wants to convey the impressions of a frightened man, present the object at a distorting angle, lending the object a terrifying aspect; or if he wants to show us the world as seen by a happy man, give us a picture of the object from the most favourable, flattering angle. By such means is achieved the emotional identification of the spectator with the characters in the film, and not only with their position in space but with their state of mind as well. Set-up and angle can make things hateful, lovable, terrifying, or ridiculous at will.

Angle and set-up lend the pictures in a film pathos or charm, cold objectivity or fantastic romantic qualities. The art of angle and set-up are to the director and cameraman what style is to the narrator and it is here that the personality of the creative artist is the most immediately reflected.

ANTHROPOMORPHOUS WORLDS

Everything that men see has a familiar visage—this is an inevitable form of our perception. As we cannot sense things outside space and time, so we cannot see them without physiognomy. Every shape makes a—mostly unconscious—emotional impression on us, which may be pleasant or unpleasant, alarming or reassuring, because it reminds us, however distantly, of some human face, which we ourselves project into it. Our anthropomorphous world-vision makes us see a human physiognomy in every phenomenon. This is why, as children, we were frightened of the grinning furniture in a dark room or the nodding trees in a dark garden and this is why, as adults, we rejoice in the landscape which looks back at us with friendly and intelligent recognition, as if calling us by name. This anthropomorphous world is the only possible subject of all art and the poet's word or the painter's brush can bring life into none but a humanized reality.

In the film it is the art of angle and set-up that reveals this anthropomorphous physiognomy in every object and it is one of the postulates of film art that not an inch of any frame should be neutral—it must be expressive, it must be gesture and physiognomy.

GOETHE ON THE FILM

The omniscient Goethe seems already to have been speaking of this great mission of the film when he wrote in his *Contributions to Lavater's Physiognomic Fragments*:

The things surrounding men do not merely act upon them —men react on their surroundings too and while they allow things to change them, they in return change things. The clothes and household goods of a man permit a sure conclusion to be drawn as to his character. Nature forms man and man forms nature and this, too, is a natural process. Man set down in the middle of an immense world, cuts himself a little world out of it and hangs it full of his own images.

Hangs it full of his own images. This vision of the magnificently rational thinker, Goethe, can be realized in no art more completely than in the film, which can, by means of angle and set-up, choose and stress those outlines of every object which lend it a living characteristic physiognomy.

Such surprisingly live outlines are often unusual. In everyday life it is not thus we see things. But the truth is that in everyday life we usually don't see them at all. Custom spreads a veil over our eyes. Baudelaire wrote in his diary: 'What is not deformed is not perceptible'. Only by means of unaccustomed and unexpected outlines produced by striking set-ups, can old, familiar and therefore never seen things hit our eye with new impressions.

Things may, of course, be deformed to a degree which makes them unrecognizable. In such cases the work of art, consisting of a synthesis of the subject and object, is so heavily weighted in favour of the subjective element that it ceases to be a reproduction of some reality and hence loses its value. The dangers of such arbitrary subjectivity will be discussed later in connection with the *avant-garde* and 'absolute' film styles.

OBJECTIVE SUBJECTIVISM

Frequently, however, the film aims at demonstrating precisely the excessive subjectivity of a character by showing the world, from his viewpoint and out of his mood, as completely deformed. The film can show not only a drunk reeling along the street, but those distorted reeling houses as well, which the drunk sees with his drunken eye. His subjective vision is reproduced by the film as objective reality.

A film once showed the same street in four entirely different aspects, when four different people walked along it, each seeing it in his own fashion. We saw the same houses, shopwindows, street lamps, poster hoardings, once with the eyes of a fat and contented shopkeeper, once with the eyes of an empty-bellied unemployed workman, of a happy lover, of an unhappy lover—the objects were the same but their pictures were very different, although all that was different was the set-up and angle.

THEME WITH VARIATIONS

This sort of thing can be compared with a theme with variations, a mighty example of which can be seen in Dovzhenko's film *Ivan*. The film shows the building of the great Dnieprostroi dam four times. First it is seen by Ivan, the peasant lad who has just come from his village to find work on the great project. It is a night picture and shows a terrifying, infernolike chaos. Smoking, flame-belching furnaces, incomprehensible, mythical monsters. A confused, impenetrable, titanic jungle of enormous iron beams and wheels within wheels. It is the peasant boy's vision of an industrial building site and the cameraman with his set-up has drawn its terrifying outlines.

The next time we see the site, it is with the eyes of Ivan who is now a full-fledged industrial worker. Now it is a picture of order and purpose. A steel structure of reason moving precisely on pinion-wheels of logic. Clear, exact, transparent, it is as if the inner mechanism of a creative brain had been laid bare. Ivan is working there and he knows what he is doing and why.

Then we see the giant hydro-electric station in the making a third time, but not with the eyes of Ivan. This time the eyes belong to a woman whose son has been crushed to death by the giant machines. She rushes across the site in despair, surrounded by the murderous devices that killed her boy. The set-up is different and how different are their faces! They are no longer sensible mechanisms serving a reasonable purpose, but fierce and incalculable antediluvian monsters which lash out with their heavy arms at the puny men who stray within their reach. The terrifying wild beasts of a primeval jungle, they are now the deadly enemies of man. Nevertheless Dovzhenko still shows us the same building site—only the different set-up makes it reflect the terrors of an unhappy bereaved mother.

There is a fourth variation to the theme. The mother has rushed into the building office with her complaint and her accusations. She bursts into the room of the chief engineer, who is just reporting the accident to the authorities. The woman waits and hears what is being said. Her son, a member of the Komsomol, volunteered for a dangerous bit of rescue work in the interests of the project and of the country. The woman does not wait to hear the end of the telephone conversation. She has heard enough. Her son was a hero. She walks out of the office and goes back to her work along the same road she came. She sees the same giant dredgers and derricks as before. But she sees them with a different eye. She holds her head erect and there is pride in every feature. The same machines now seem sublime steel columns of some gigantic temple. She walks amid grandeur and beauty and we hear the strains of a great psalm, a swelling hymn of fruitful labour and it is as though the pictures themselves were singing.

These variations of the same picture were not projections of the author's subjective moods, but objective presentations of the subjective emotions of the characters. After all, we show dream pictures in the films. Dream pictures are so subjective that they are not images of some outside reality; they are born from the inner images of the memory. Nevertheless dreaming is a natural, existing objective phenomenon, the specific material of film art.

PHYSIOGNOMY OF SURROUNDINGS AND BACKGROUND

Even the stage, if it is good, will not tolerate neutral scenery, i.e. backgrounds which are not drenched as it were with the blood of the scene which is being enacted in front of it. Even the painter of stage scenery wants to project the mood of the scene on to the set, as a sort of visual echo of what is happening on the stage. But unlike the film-maker, he cannot show any changes of mood that occur during the scene.

The eternal and insoluble contradiction between the living actor and the dead scenery, the flesh-and-blood figure and the painted perspective of the background anyway places the background outside the play; it relegates the background to the background as it were. Not so in the film. There man and background are of the same stuff, both are mere pictures and hence there is no difference in the reality of man and object. The film, like the painting, thus offers the possibility of giving the background, the surroundings, a physiognomy no less intense than the faces of the characters—or, as in Van Gogh's late pictures, an even more intense physiognomy, so that the violent expressive power of the objects makes that of the human characters pale into insignificance.

Usually, of course, there is no contradiction between the facial expression of the characters and the physiognomy of the surrounding objects. The expression of the human face radiates beyond the outlines of the face and is repeated in the images of furniture, trees or clouds. The mood of a landscape, or of a room, prepares us for the scene to be enacted in it. All this the film-maker achieves by means of his set-up.

LANDSCAPES

How is the countryside turned into landscape? Not every bit of nature is a landscape in itself. The countryside has only a topography, which is a thing that can be exactly reproduced on a military map. But the landscape expresses a mood, which is not merely objectively given; it needs the co-operation of subjective factors before it can come into existence. The phrase is 'the mood of the landscape' but there is no mood save that of some human being and those who look at the countryside with the greatest objectivity—a farmer, for instance—would be least likely to see any sort of 'mood' in it. 'Mood' is the feeling of the painter, the artist, not of the ploughman, the shepherd, or the wood-cutter, whose business with nature is not of the soul but of the body, a practical, not artistic activity.

The landscape is the physiognomy of some countryside, as seen by the painter who can put it on his canvas, but also by the cameraman who can shoot it with an appropriate set-up. It is as though the countryside were suddenly lifting its veil and showing its face, and on the face an expression which we recognize though we could not give it a name. There have already been several landscape artists of genius in the film, artists of that moving landscape which has not only a physiognomy, but mimicry and gesture too. On these landscapes the clouds gather, the mist drives, the reeds tremble and shiver in the wind, the branches of the trees nod and toss and the shadows play hide-and-seek—these are film landscapes which wake at daybreak and darken to tragedy at the setting of the sun. There is no painter born whose motionless pictures could match this experience.

HOW DOES REALITY BECOME A THEME ?

The 'soul of nature' is our own soul which the cameraman picks out of the objective shapes of the countryside. Nature was not always naturally a subject and material for art. Man first had to permeate nature with his own humanity, turn nature into something human. The great art of the Christian Middle Ages knew nothing of this 'soul of nature' and the self-sufficient and meaningful beauty of the landscape. Nature was merely a background, the space in which human events and scenes were played out. In Europe it was the art of the Renaissance which first transformed lifeless nature into living landscape. It is well known that Petrarch was the first to whom it occurred to climb a mountain peak solely for the pleasure of looking down from there on the beauty of the countryside below. Tourist travel is an entirely modern phenomenon. The history of art shows us how and when new spheres of reality are opened up to art, become presentable as it were. For instance, not every kind of human labour is as old a theme of art as is agricultural work. In the tilling of the soil men have felt from time immemorial the unobjectivized relationship of man to his occupation! It has ever been natural and reasonable, like the suckling of a child—it is what men live by. But factory work was for a long time outside the sphere of poetry and art and its transition to the dignity of artistic theme is still difficult, because for a long time it had no human physiognomy, was not imbued with a human soul. It appeared inhuman, mechanical, forced, unnatural labour; to use Marx's classic expression, it seemed objectivized action, because man was only a part of the machine and his human individuality had no opportunity to find expression. For this reason man's humanity did not radiate into the machine and therefore it was no thing of beauty, no subject for art.

THE WORKER AND THE PHYSIOGNOMY OF THE MACHINE

By this attitude to the machine, art again expressed a real situation, even though only a negative one. With the growth of the revolutionary consciousness of the working-class the great human significance and dignity of industrial labour also became recognized. In Meunier's miners, in Frank Brangwyn's etchings, and many other works of great artists the industrial worker and his labour appear as artistic themes.

What had happened? Had industrial labour, which had been ugly, now suddenly become beautiful? No. But in the light of the increasingly revolutionary consciousness of the workers, the workers themselves acquired a defiant dignity and a changed physiognomy. And it was their rebellious anger which lent the tormenting, exploiting, inhuman machine a hateful, diabolically animated physiognomy. Thus it was that the factory came to be a subject for artistic presentation, especially of film presentation. It provided no idyllic features, like the life of the ploughman and shepherd. A modern, revolutionary, realistic art showed in the film with increasing frequency the face of man-devouring mechanical monsters that were the instruments of man's exploitation. The set-ups devised by revolutionary directors and cameramen unmasked the true face of the machine. Such is for instance the unforgettable documentary Joris Ivens made of the Phillips wireless factory. The conveyor belt and the women working at it are shown so expressively that the spectator holds his breath in fear that the girls may not be able to deal quickly enough with the avalanche of parts sweeping towards them.

It is not by accident that the physiognomy of industrial plant and machines so often shown in Soviet films are in contrast so friendly and encouraging. The set-up is different. And the cameraman's set-up is different because the attitude of the workers to those machines is different—they are no longer considered exploiters and tormentors of the workers but aids, instruments, co-operators in the building of the workers' own lives. This is all a matter of set-up and therefore peculiar to the film.

Karl Grune once made a very interesting film about miners. The story had a revolutionary slant, but much more revolutionary was the spirit of the actual shots and set-ups. The subject was the pit itself and the main characters were the shafts and galleries, the machines and the work. What it showed was not the facts of coal-getting, in the manner of a documentary —it presented by means of special set-ups, the physiognomy of those same facts, seen not objectively but emotionally. The cage which carried the colliers down to the coalface had a grim face stonily set in an inexorable expression. It seemed a dreadful prison cell when its door closed and the miners looked out from behind bars as it began to descend to the depths. Grune saw this descent to the dangers of the pit with the eyes of the colliers and photographed it from their inner angle of vision.

PHYSIOGNOMY AND SYMBOL

One scene of this film showed the dressing-room in which the miners changed. They took off their civilian clothes, put on their working clothes and hung their civilian clothes on hooks provided for this. There was a close-up of these clothes hanging on their hooks and they looked like a row of men hanging on a gibbet. It was a tormenting sight. Everyone could understand the symbolic meaning of this physiognomy. The picture said: 'Look, here hangs the man the collier has had to discard. He has to leave this man behind. What goes down in the cage to the pit is only a machine—nothing more'.

The heavy black smoke pouring out of chimneys and cascading down to the ground symbolized who knows how much hopeless, frustrating longing. A silent film, it did not give the alarm by sounding sirens—it showed it by the thick streams of steam shooting out of the steam whistles, but in them one could see the despairing shriek of thousands.

One picture showed the hero with the door of the cage just closing on him and in that instant he sees a rival accost his wife. Like a caged wild beast the husband glares from behind the grating of the door, a helpless prisoner in the iron-barred prison-cell of toil which begins to sink irresistibly down with him. The set-up showed a clear and deep symbolism no one could fail to understand.

SET-UP ACCELERATING RHYTHM

A classic example of this occurs in Eisenstein's *Battleship Potemkin*. A mutiny has broken out and there is fighting between officers and ratings. It is not an organized, disciplined, tactically led battle of coherent groups, but a wild fierce struggle on deck among ropes and woodwork, on stairs and ladders, in cabins and gun-turrets, rushings and tumblings, blows, wrestling, the wallowing of bodies locked in struggle, the flailing of legs and arms, a chaotic clash of irreconcilable enemies. This magnificent stormy rhythm cannot be speeded up. And yet it must be. Because the monotonous gloom of a desert landscape is increased by its remaining uniformly the same. But the rhythm of a hurricane, if it remains the same for two minutes, tires the spectator. What is by its nature motionless can remain motionless for ever. But movement in art requires either a *crescendo* or a *diminuendo*, else it grows tedious.

Eisenstein was faced with the task of increasing the speed and movement of a scene in which direction and acting no longer offered possibilities of a higher speed. What he did was to increase, not the violence of the scene, but the violence of the pictures of the scene. The struggle itself was no fiercer than before. But the set-ups in which it appeared on the screen grew fiercer and fiercer. At first we saw the savage fight from the plain full-front angle. But when we began to tire of this, the combatants were shown from below, from above, from the strangest angles, so that not only did the men stand on their heads or take flying leaps, but the pictures too, and their physiognomies were ever more haggard and distorted than the faces of the struggling men. But the fight goes on and the violence of the shots must be increased still more. Now the tussle is shown not only from steep and oblique angles—the camera takes shots between taut ropes, from behind gratings, across the rungs of ladders and the iron treads of companionways. The gestures of the combatants cannot be made any fiercer, but the ropes, the gratings, the rungs chop up the shots. Men are merely at each other's throats, but the shots do more; they dismember them, by means of set-ups and angles.

DISTORTION

The bounds of realist art may be defined thus: the artist may see any however unusual and strange physiognomy in his object, but as long as he sees it *in* the object and cuts it *out* of it, as Michelangelo cut the figures he saw in his mind out of the block of marble, so long as he derives the physiognomy of his work of art *from* his object and does not project it *into* the object, so long is his art realistic. The artist is a realist as long as he does not change the structure and meaning of his object by subjectively drawn outlines. A caricature may distort as much as it pleases, as long as the distorted face remains recognizable. But if we no longer recognize the face, the caricature is no longer funny, for the comic quality lies in the resemblance and the recognition. If there is no longer any recognition of the object, then there is no longer any distortion of something we know, but just a grimace without relation to anything else. Distortion, whether its purpose is satire or serious psychological analysis, must always be the distortion of something. If that something is no longer present in the picture then the meaning and significance of the distortion is also gone. For if we exaggerate something, but no one knows what we are exaggerating, then no one can discern that it *is* exaggeration.

UNFAMILIAR OUTLINES

What I said obtains in painting and sculpture, where it is entirely in the hands of the artist to decide how and where he draws his outlines. But however surprising the outlines produced by a camera angle may be, the basic shape of the object cannot be changed by this means. Then can it overstep the boundaries of realism?

Yes, it can. The picture of an object can be unreal even if it is an exact photographic reproduction of the object. This happens when the object is unrecognizable. There are certain perspectives and angles the strangeness, characteristic quality and unusual originality of which are cancelled out because they are overdone, so that one can no longer recognize the object to be represented. A reproduction of an object can be unusual and surprising only if we are familiar with the object from a different angle, have been accustomed to seeing it in a different way, that is if we know what the object is. There was a vogue at one time for riddle photographs in illustrated papers. The reader had to guess what the photograph was supposed to show. The unusual angle of the shot made the object unrecognizable. The film must avoid such riddles.

IMPOSSIBLE OUTLINES

There is yet another method of photography which is also unreal artistically. This is to show objects from angles or in set-ups in which the human eye cannot see them in normal circumstances. The automatic camera can be brought into positions in which a live human being could never be. One can swallow a camera and make a photograph of the human stomach from the inside. It is of incalculable value to science that we can thus extend our visual observation beyond the limits of immediate natural human vision. But to art such pictures are without value. If the theme *catexochen* of art is the inner experience (that is, not the scientific perception of the object in itself but the reflection of the objective world in our sensual perception); if the relationship of object and subject coupled in art expresses the emotional relationship of healthy man to the outer world, then no picture can be a realistic work of art if it can be seen by human beings only through the intermediary of some mechanical contrivance and never as a typical, natural, immediate experience.

UNUSUAL ANGLES DENOTE UNUSUAL CONDITIONS

Very unusual angles must be motivated by the condition of the character through whose eyes we look at the thing presented. A picture will be unusual if it is seen by a fever-sick person, or if we look at it and show it as seen by a very short-sighted eye. But it is not enough to give a mere logical explanation of the strangeness, the unusual character of a shot, we must also give an artistic motivation of such unusual set-ups. For unusual angles produce unusual physiognomies and those in their turn produce unusual moods. But such moods must always be the result of deliberate purpose on the part of the film-maker, they must always emanate from the content of the scene, the state of mind of the characters—otherwise they will remain mere empty tricks of form.

It would not be realistic to show things seen by a feverish or drunken man realistically. But the face of things is changed by other things beside a high temperature or too much alcohol; passion, hatred, love or fear can have the same result. On the other hand a director often intends only to emphasize the exotic nature of a scene or of the place where a scene is enacted and may use an unusual angle for this purpose. For instance an opium den may be a quite ordinary room, but the fantastic quality of the things happening there can be conveyed visually by showing the room from an unusual angle.

FILM CARICATURES

The photo-caricature is more effective, because it can be more convincing, than the drawn caricature. For the photograph cannot suppress facts completely, not even the facts of shape. The camera can take only what is really visible if we look at the object from a certain angle in a certain way. The photographic caricature is more murderous because it is more authentic.

Eisenstein and his brilliant cameraman, Tisse, gave us a magnificent caricature of an office. The angles of the close-ups of typewriter and inkstand, pen and rubber-stamp, pencil and pencil-sharpener lend these objects a grotesque monumentality, give them important, even majestic physiognomies and breathe a demoniac life of their own into them. The technical requisites of the office, which appear more important than the human beings in it, provide a biting satire on bureaucracy.

Such improbable magnifications are achieved not merely by camera set-ups but by certain photo-technical 'effects', hence they are not, properly speaking, 'natural' impressions. In such cases the spectator must be advised in advance that the pictures are deliberately intended to be satirical caricatures. For if the spectator expects to find objective reality in such pictures, they will appear unreal to him; only if he looks at them as pictorial fantasies will he discover a deep reality in them.

EXPRESSIONISM IN THE FILM

Every emotion which shows in the face shows inasmuch and because it changes the normal features of the face, or rather moves them in some way from their quiescent position. The stronger the emotion, the greater the distortion of the face. A perfectly 'normal' face, if such a thing existed at all, would be expressionless, empty, would not be a physiognomy at all.

The expressionists hold that only the expression (which is the bodily manifestation of the spirit) matters at all—the physical material of the face is merely an obstacle and the soul-revealing physiognomy should be freed from the raw, unilluminated material of the flesh. The true expressionists proclaimed that the artist who sees and reproduces a physiognomy should not allow himself to be limited by the natural outlines of the face. Why should not the expressive lines of the face be drawn beyond the boundaries set by anatomy? Why should not the smile be broader than the natural mouth? Why not, if doing so would increase its expressive significance? The emotions of men are always greater than can be expressed by gesture within the miserably narrow limits of their bodily being. The swing of our arm always lags behind the inner *élan* of our spirit. Our 'natural' expressive movements are always rudimentary and incomplete, because our boundless emotions are hemmed in by our bodily limitations.

The film guarantees the authenticity of the expressionist distortion, because the spectator knows that the picture is a photograph and cannot therefore arbitrarily change the shape of its object. For this reason the expressionist style could nowhere be as convincing and effective as in the film where there is no way of checking up whether the angle and set-up bring *out* of the object only such expressions as they found *in* it.

The Cabinet of Dr Caligari

Expressionism in the film has many degrees, from the expressivity of the theme, where the style is determined merely by the collating of curious motives, surroundings and backgrounds, to the complete and pure expressionism embodied in the famous *Cabinet of Dr Caligari,* which deserves a chapter to itself in the history of film art and in which the physiognomy and mimicry of things achieved the same democratic animation as the faces and gestures of the human characters. At the peak of the development of the silent film there was scarcely a director of any talent who would have tolerated neutral, lifeless backgrounds and would not have striven to suggest, in the shapes of the set, a vague parallel to the expressive line in the faces and gestures of the characters, thus expanding human emotions by visual means into an atmosphere pervading the whole picture. This expressionism of physiognomic resonance had at that time already come to be an obligatory element of film technique. But in the *Caligari* film there was more than this; in it all the objects surrounding the human characters had become their active and equal partners. Houses, furniture and other things all grimaced like the living personages and looked at the human actors as though with eyes. The director, Robert Wiene, felt the need of some apology for presenting this filmic vision of the delusions of persecution mania and added this sub-title to the title of his film: 'How a madman sees the world'.

We do actually see madmen and a lunatic asylum in the film, but they too are shown in such apparition-like visions. Who is it who sees *them* with such strange eyes? Obviously the beholder must be outside the story and it is obvious that it is the author, the film-maker himself, who is the madman seeing the world in this strange fashion.

The problematic character of this very interesting and inspiring film lies in the fact that in it the film to a great extent ceased to be creative art, for its interesting physiognomic effects were *not* brought about by camera angles and set-ups which lend the real objects of a real world characteristic, passion-twisted outlines. In this film the camera showed photographic reproductions of finished expressionist paintings—it was *not* the camera that gave the slants and distorted the outlines. The houses were built crookedly in the studio, the lampstandards were set up at crazy angles and the trees were the work of the scenery-painters. The camera did nothing but photograph and did not demonstrate how individual moods can deform the normal aspect of things. *The Cabinet of Dr Caligari* was a film-painting, the picture of a picture, not primary but second-hand.

DECORATIVE SCENERY

It is for this reason that all stylized scenery is unsatisfactory in a film. One may reproduce anything in nature in a film studio, but it must be a faithful copy of nature and look just like the natural thing, transplanted into the studio for reasons of technical convenience, lighting, etc. Even in the studio, it still remains merely an object for the creative artistry of the camera. The creative work of stylization should be left to the lighting, the set-up, in other words to the shooting. Only thus will the result be first-hand film art.

FILM-IMPRESSIONISM

In comparing the film with the live stage, it is usually regarded as an advantage of the former that it can show crowd scenes. Even the largest stage can accommodate comparatively few people, while the film can use tens of thousands of extras if need be. However, the film director who can produce the effect of large crowds only by actually showing a multitude of people is not much of a director. To mention only one instance: far larger crowds can be suggested by putting them behind a smoke-screen than the film could actually show in an open space. What gives the impression of large crowds is not the actual numerical multitude. In the perspective of an endless desert even a hundred thousand men can appear a mere handful. It is the business of perspective and set-up to produce the illusion required, and the use of such impressionist methods affords great scope for this sort of filmic effect. A hundred raised fists crowded into the narrow space of a single shot can make us sense the violence of mass passion far more intensely than say a disciplined march of ten thousand demonstrators.

The cameraman can also suggest things which cannot for one reason or another be actually shown. The set-up and angle must stimulate the imagination and direct it into certain channels. Often the most accurate and careful photographic views of a town convey nothing of its real physiognomy. The dark silhouette of a bridge, a gondola rocking under it in the water-reflected light of a lantern, marble stairs dipping into dirty water can reproduce far more of the atmosphere of Venice than the most authentic and accurate photographs of the great row of palaces along the Canal Grande.

IMPRESSIONS OF EVENTS

Happenings, events, also have an emotional colouring of their own which can often be shown more intensively in a well-angled detail shot than in an objective photograph of a whole scene. Steam rushing out of sirens, fingers knocking on a window, the slanted picture of a tocsin bell suddenly cut in, frightened eyes and screaming mouths in distorted perspective will show panic far more alarmingly than a long shot of a frightened mob.

This complementary, imagination-prodding impressionism is best suited to the spirit of the film because the moving and rapidly changing close-ups keep the spectator on the alert and seem to bring him progressively closer from the periphery to the centre of the action. He will wait with increasing tension for a glimpse of the whole and when at last he sees it—although this is not even always necessary—the picture will no longer be merely what it is. The spectator will see more in it than it actually shows; he will see into it all the preceding pictures.

SUBJECTIVE IMPRESSIONISM

The position is quite different when the shots intend to convey certain impressions but not to present some objective reality. In such cases what matters is the subjective experience, for the picture is not meant to present reality, merely a passing mood. This is a similar degenerative phenomenon of bourgeois art as the merely journalist expressionism which has peeled facial expression off the face and physiognomy off the object, creating abstract, floating 'expressions' that no longer express anything.

Just as expressionism had its *Caligari* film, so subjectivist impressionism had its own classic (because the most completely realized) paradigm. It is no accident that this, too, was a German film, like *The Cabinet of Dr Caligari*. The Germans are more dogmatic in their art than others; they tried to put their theories consistently into practice and were not guided by the sensibility of instinctive good taste.

The title of this German film was *Phantom* and it was a film version of a novel by Gerhart Hauptmann. It proposed to show the world as seen by an excited over-imaginative person who refuses to accept objective reality. Fantasies, fixed ideas, the delusions of persecution mania were projected on to the same plane as the ordinary pictures of everyday life and the fantastic seemed more real than reality, the boundaries between the two were wiped away and finally reality, too, appeared as a shadowy vision.

The impressionist style of *Phantom* was so sustained and consistent that in long stretches of the film no logical structure of events could be discerned at all. Moods, snapshots, passed before the spectators' eyes in incoherent flashes just as they had floated past the inner eye of the drunken hero. The title of one section was actually 'The staggering sun'. It is impossible to relate its contents in rational terms. Streets of swaying houses swim past the eyes of the motionless hero. Flights of stairs rear themselves in front of him and then sink into the depths without his moving a muscle. For what is important is not what happens—only impressions matter. A diamond necklace glitters in a shop window ... A face emerges from behind a bunch of flowers ... A hand reaches out and grips another hand ... The columns of a vast hall teeter drunkenly ... Car lamps flare up and are extinguished ... A revolver is lying on the ground ... The 'meaningless' alignment of such details by editing is possible because angle and set-up show that they are not intended to be pictures of real things, hence we do not expect them to reproduce objective reality—we accept them as figments of the memory and imagination and there is nothing to prevent them from thus lining up into a row of pictures.

This film shows *only* the things which made an impression on the hero. Nothing else is shown at all, only close-ups of disjointed moments, and we feel no real time-lapse in it and cannot tell whether we are seeing the history of years or of days.

INDIRECT SET-UP

It often happens that the camera shows not the person or scene itself but only its image in a mirror, or a shadow of it on the wall. This may be a means of preparation, destined to increase the effect of what is coming; this applies especially in the case of shadows cast before, which by making us imagine the figure belonging to them, create in advance an appropriate atmosphere. Such indirect indications of something to come always contain some threatening, promising or curiosity-arousing mystery. No horror can be so horrible, no beauty so enchanting, if really seen, as the horror or enchantment suggested by its shadow.

Often such indirect shots are used by directors to avoid effects which would be too crude. If the story requires a murder or some other act of revolting violence, some dreadful disaster or some nauseating spectacle, the vehicle is frequently an indirect set-up. Nor do film-makers like to show figures of great pathos in the always illusion-dispelling reality of the direct picture. If for instance the figure of Jesus appeared in a biblical film, directors of good taste usually avoided making him appear in the flesh and preferred to present him by means of reflections of his influence and activities. But if he did make a personal appearance, it was usually as a shadow thrown on to a wall.

There are certain tragic scenes which would appear trivial in direct pictures and lose their tragic character. If a director shows these in indirect shots, he does not do so in order to avoid crude effects; on the contrary his object is to heighten the effect of some scene in danger of becoming banal. For in a direct shot we see only the scene itself; for instance a man about to shoot himself, a revolver in his hand, the hand raised to fire the shot. Even if something else is actually visible on the screen, the glaring nature of the scene blots it out. But if we see only a shadow of the scene on a wall, then we see the wall, the room of which it is a part and the physiognomy of the things which witness the deed. If we see something in a mirror, we see the mirror and its character together with the reflected image. Man and the scene he plays do not stand before us so nakedly, so without atmosphere. The real animation of the background increases the real animation of the scene itself.

In a film I once saw there was a sheet of water reflecting the shore, the moon, clouds and other shadows of the night. Then another mirrored image appeared below. A woman leaned over the water and the mirrored image down there in the water *fell upwards*, towards the surface, towards the spectator. Then one heard a splash and saw the water in movement. We didn't see the woman herself, yet we knew what had happened. Such indirect shots often have a subtle poetic effect, like an unspoken word, because they conjure up associations and avoid the often clumsy and imperfect rationality of calling a spade a spade.

SYMBOLIC ANGLES

In *The End of St Petersburg,* one of Pudovkin's great silent films, he shows us a picture of the city twice. Both show the Neva embankment; the first is a reflection in the waters of the river, of the row of palaces along the bank. Houses, palaces, gardens standing on their heads, dreamlike, in an improbably tremulous restless picture. It is a dream of Venice, an illusion, a mirage. At the end of the film the city is no longer St Petersburg. Its name is Leningrad. The shot shows the same row of houses, but from a different angle. It is a frontal shot. Everything is standing squarely planted on the earth. The heavy stones throw heavy shadows and there is nothing tremulous about them. This is solid reality, no dream, no fleeting illusion, no mirage. These houses will stand for ever unshaken. This is what the picture shows, this is what the set-up says, quite unmistakably.

THE HUMAN FACE AS A MIRROR

A much-used device of microdramatics is to show a thing only in its effects, to show not the spectacle but the beholder. By this means we come to know not only what happened but also how someone reacted to it. A well-tried method in dialogue is always to show the listener, never the speaker. In the sound film the speaker is always present anyway, or rather his voice is and the shot shows the double melody of the word and with it the facial expression it evokes.

METAPHORS OF THE SET-UP

In one of the Soviet films there is a peasant revolt. We see the far bank of the Volga taken against the light at sunset.

Pointed, thorny outlines of reed and bush pierce the air in the distance of the other bank. Suddenly the reeds and bushes seem to grow denser. New pointed, thorny silhouettes emerge from the ground in terrifying numbers. They cluster together and move away and we realize that what we saw were the straightened scythes of the insurgent peasant army. We see that they have 'grown out of the earth' like the reeds and the bushes. It is the set-up which made us see them in this way. Such a metaphor, written, would have been trivial—seen, it is of elemental power.

In an American film two policemen drag a poor girl before the judge. The angle shows the policemen as two mighty terrifying, gigantic colossi who fill up the whole frame. Between the two is a narrow slit, in which we see the thin, fragile little figure of the girl. This one picture alone foreshadowed the sentence and the whole fate of the girl.

The hidden pattern of angles, the physiognomy of set-ups, touch off the association of our ideas and conjure up thoughts, moods and emotions, as metaphors do in poetry.

In the immortal scene in Eisenstein's *Battleship Potemkin* where dead and wounded are lying on the great flight of steps, the set-up shows bloodstained and tearstained human faces. Then it shows the Cossacks who fire on the crowd. But it shows only their boots. Not men, mere boots trample down those human faces. The boots have such oafish, stupid, base physiognomies that the spectator clenches his fists in anger. Such is the effect of picture-metaphors.

Such picture-metaphors often have a satirical edge, as for instance in one of Pudovkin's films, where the council of war held by the bourgeois generals was shot at an angle which put the heads of the generals out of the picture and all one could see was a row of headless, much-bemedalled chests in military tunics.

Another fine metaphor of this kind occurs in Eisenstein's *October,* which shows St Petersburg in the first days of the revolution. The Winter Palace is being besieged. But we see few battle scenes. We see the first shot fired by the battleship *Aurora* and immediately afterwards we see the magnificent chandelier of the throne-room quiver. The set-up shows the chandelier in all its imperial brilliance, with thousands of glittering, sparkling, pendant crystals, irresistibly recalling a crown, an obvious symbol of the shining majesty of the Tsar. But it has quivered! At first almost imperceptibly. But there is now no longer any need to show the cause of that quivering, the gunfire from the *Aurora*. The majestic chandelier begins to shiver slightly. When a thousand crystals swing and tremble and sparkle, they show such a superhuman, gigantic quaking that it seems to contain the panic of the whole Russian aristocracy and bourgeoisie. This single brilliant set-up of Tisse, the cameraman, is so expressive that there is no need for detailed battle scenes. The chandelier begins to swing. Nothing could increase the breath-taking tension. It swings out further and further—a crack shows in the ceiling, one hook holding the chandelier is loosened, the crack widens and then the whole magnificent, glittering contraption falls crashing to the ground. There is no need for any explanation of the symbolism here.

In *Battleship Potemkin* small sailing-boats bring food from the shore to the ship. The matter itself is nothing particular and the scene is simple enough. But the angle, looking down from the deck of the battle-cruiser, is so contrived that the whole frame is crammed with the bustling little boats and the bulging sails all seem to repeat the same encouraging gesture, the same call to action.

Then the little boats reach the great ship and lower their sails, as is natural. Only they do it all at the same time and this simultaneity of the movement turns it into a gesture, the gesture of a ceremonial salute. As though the little boats had taken off their hats to the great ship.

In such metaphoric sequences the objects photographed are real: the Cossack boots, the chandelier in the Winter Palace, the little sailing-boats are all real—the set-up merely gives them a deeper meaning, a second, symbolical significance, without depriving them of their own, real, normal meaning. The shot would be comprehensible, as the detail of an ordinary film scene, even to those who failed to grasp this second meaning.

Herein lies the artistic value of such set-ups. They are not allegories which have only a symbolic meaning and the immed-

iately perceived pictures of which are in themselves meaningless. What would a cross in itself mean to us, if we were
ignorant of its traditional significance, its connection with reli-
gion, with Christianity? A question mark would mean nothing
to us if we had not learned about it in school. No less meaningless are the allegories constructed for the purpose of signify-
ing something different from what they actually say; they have
no reality in themselves.

EMPTY PHRASES AND 'KITSCH' IN PICTURES

Set-up and angle should only reveal or stress the mood
already present in the object or the scene, but never put in
what is not inherent in it—that would be a lie. If the physiognomic atmosphere of the picture diverges from or exaggerates
what is appropriate to the scene, the result is filmic bombast,
Kitsch, rather like a trite bit of verse recited with great bathos
or some banality accompanied by music dripping with sentimentality. The camera may stress hidden meanings present in
the object but cannot supply anything that is lacking in it,
otherwise the picture will be like a dry factual report sobbed
out in tones of utmost emotion.

Even less genuine and sincere will the picture be if the
director attunes the set in advance to reflect an emotional
atmosphere. The camera ceases to be an artistic medium when
the 'beauty' it should create is laid on in advance and put in
front of its lens. The same often applies to lighting effects.
Angle and set-up are authentic film instruments because in
one way or another they show reality, and their product is
after all a photograph. But a director who modifies his objects
and tidies up reality before it is shot, robs the film of its claim
to authenticity.

DANGEROUS BEAUTY

Over-beautiful, picturesque shots are sometimes dangerous
even if they are the result of good camera work alone. Their
over-perfect composition, their self-sufficient closed harmony
may lend them a static, painting-like character and thereby

lift them out of the dynamic stream of the action. Such beauty has its own centre of gravity, its own frame and does not reach beyond itself to the preceding and the subsequent. *'Je hais le mouvement qui déplace les lignes'*, wrote Baudelaire in his sonnet on beauty. But the film is art in motion.

THE WORK OF ART AS OBJECT

The film is faced with a peculiar problem if it has to reproduce not nature but an already existing work of art, a painting, a sculpture, a puppet play, i.e. when the camera merely copies what a painter or sculptor or carver has already created as a work of art. But if such works of art are presented as a visual experience of a character in the film, from the angle, both external and internal, from which the character views them, then the cameraman is confronted with a very intricate and interesting task.

The terrifying Asiatic Gothic of the medieval icons photographed in Eisenstein's *Ivan the Terrible* shows not only already existing works of art but the savage superstitions and visions of a tormented people. When in Alexander Korda's *Lady Hamilton* the prospective husband leads the poor ignorant girl past all the accumulated works of art in his mansion, the camera shows not only works of art but the good taste and culture of a superior social environment, which are destined to have a decisive influence on the heroine and thus have an important dramaturgic function.

Works of art may thus play a part in front of the camera, reverting, as it were, to the state of raw material, imposing on the camera the difficult task of adding to the given expression of the object a further, secondary expression by means of angles and set-ups. This secondary expression is that of the effect made on the spectator. In fact a gifted cameraman can show a picture or sculpture in the same way as an orchestra conductor can give voice to a musical score. In such productions two artistic personalities are merged in one another.

STYLE AND SET-UP

This duality, resulting from the artistic re-creation of an already existing work of art, is strikingly manifested in the transition of one style into the other. If the object is the furniture of a room, for instance, all the austere simplicity of the directoire style will be of no avail if the camera work is baroque. What is decisive is not the style of the object but of the shot. The theme may be an ancient Greek temple but the angle may give it a Gothic character if the cameraman pleases.

Similar things may be observed in other arts. In the Musée Guimet in Paris there is a china tea-service made in a Chinese pottery for the Versailles court of the king of France. The simon-pure rococo designs of the decorations were sent out to China where pastoral scenes between French *marquis* and *marquises* were conscientiously copied on the Chinese tea-cups. Nevertheless the whole is so Chinese in character that looking at the Versailles lords and ladies from the distance of a few yards, one might easily take them for Chinese mandarins or Chinese empresses. The Chinese brushwork and manner restyled the French rococo designs.

The inverse example of Dresden china is well known. The traditional ancient Chinese designs acquired a comfortable corpulent burgher character. And the last miracle performed by Claude Monet in his old age, and which cost him his eyesight—the 'Notre-Dame in the Sunlight'—transformed the medieval Gothic of Notre-Dame into the luminous thicket of a lushly blossoming jungle. That was how the Gothic cathedral looked to the French impressionist whose aim was to depict life as he saw it.

An excellent Japanese film *Shadows of the Yoshiwara* was refreshingly pure in style, not because the buildings and costumes were authentic, but because the style of the shots, of angles and set-ups had the quality of old Japanese wood-cuts.

STYLE-CONSCIOUS FILMS

The great historical styles which were not hatched out in some workshop or studio but which were produced slowly and unconsciously by the ideologies, tastes and life-rhythm of epochs and societies—such great historical styles appear of one piece and logical only from the distance of a historical perspective, never in their own day. The Italian artists of the quattrocento had no idea that they were initiating a great new style, that of the Renaissance—they simply and modestly strove to imitate ancient Greek and Roman art. Consciousness of style develops slower than style itself and is mostly a retrospective recognition only.

One can often hear complaints nowadays that our age has no such well-defined style as for instance Gothic or Biedermeier. There are many reasons for this. But we know that the creators of these styles in their own time knew only fashions and not styles. Style was not consciously recognized as such in its own time. There is no doubt that our own epoch also has its own distinctive style which manifests itself in our tastes, way of life, clothes and manners, a style the visual unity and consistence of which we cannot see in real life, though we may see it in a film if we make a point of doing so. For the film, in reproducing with photographic fidelity the visual appearance of our life, concentrates its many forms into one picture in which the common traits that constitute a style can become manifest if angle and set-up stress them sufficiently. If the cameraman feels the style of our time, his films will tend to render us conscious of it and will thus contribute essentially to the emergence of such a style.

If the spirit of the times is reflected in the visual forms of our life and art, the film will reflect that. The film creates no primary forms, but by means of angle and set-up gives a live interpretation of the given forms of reality. It is for this reason that it can render visible their common traits and the laws that govern them. Films date very quickly. Five-year-old films already have a faintly historical tang—probably because they are more topical and time-bound than any other art.

CHAPTER TEN

EDITING

I DISLIKE THIS word and think the French expression 'montage' far more adequate and expressive, for it means 'assembly' and that is really what happens in editing. The shots are assembled by the editor in a pre-determined order, in such a way as to produce by the very sequence of frames a certain intended effect, much as the fitter assembles the parts of a machine so as to turn these disjointed parts into a power-producing, work-performing machine.

The most expressive set-up is not enough to bring on to the screen every significance of the object. This can be achieved in the last instance only by the combination of shots, their assembly in sequence, their fitting into the unity of a higher organism. The last process in creative film-making is the crowning job of editing.

The meaning of a coloured patch in a painting can be gathered only from the contemplation of the picture as a whole. The meaning of a single note in a tune, the meaning of a single word in a sentence manifests itself only through the whole. The same applies to the position and role of the single shot in the totality of the film.

The single shots are saturated with the tension of a latent meaning which is released like an electric spark when the next shot is joined to it. Of course a shot can have a meaning and significance in itself even without being joined to another. A smile is a smile, even if seen in an isolated shot. But what this smile refers to, what has evoked it, what is its effect and dramatic significance—all this can emerge only from the preceding and following shots.

INEVITABLE INTERPRETATION

Montage is the association of ideas rendered visual; it gives the single shots their ultimate meaning, if for no other reason, because the spectator presupposes that in the sequence of pictures that pass before his eyes there is an intentional pre-determination and interpretation. This consciousness, this confidence that we are seeing the work of a creative intention and purpose, not a number of pictures thrown and stuck together by chance, is a psychological precondition of film-watching and we always expect, presuppose and search for meaning in every film we see.

This is a basic, irresistible intellectual requirement of the spectator and it operates even if by some reason or other the film seen is really merely a chance collection of pictures stuck together without rhyme or reason. Seeking a meaning is a fundamental function of human consciousness and nothing is more difficult than to accept with complete passivity meaning-less, purely accidental phenomena. Our mechanism of idea association and our imagination will always tend to put some meaning into such a meaningless conglomeration, even though perhaps only in play.

It is for this reason that montage can not only produce poetry—it can also fake and falsify things more completely than any other human means of expression. Here is an amus-ing example:

WHEN THE SCISSORS LIE

Long ago, when Eisenstein's *Battleship Potemkin* was a triumphant world success, a Scandinavian distributor also wanted to buy it. The censorship thought the film too revolu-tionary, but the distributor was reluctant to forgo the profits he was certain of making with this film. So he asked permis-sion to re-edit the film very slightly. One condition of the sale was that nothing was to be added or taken away. The Scandinavian distributor had no objection to this clause—all he wanted was to lift a single scene from its place in the film and insert it in another place. Eisenstein wanted to know which scene was to go where. As those who have seen this film will know, the film begins with scenes showing how the officers ill-treat the sailors, and how the meat served out to the men is crawling with maggots. When the men respectfully protest, their spokesmen are seized and sentenced to death by drum-head court-martial. All hands are ordered on deck to witness the execution, the condemned men are brought out, a firing squad marches in—but at the last moment the firing squad turn their rifles against the officers. Mutiny. Fighting on the ship, fighting ashore. The rest of the fleet are ordered to quell the mutiny, but the crews of the other warships allow the mutineers to escape with their ship. Such is the sequence in the original film.

All the Scandinavian wanted was to take out the court-martial and execution sequence, making it appear that the sailors had mutinied and shot their officers or flung them into the sea, not because their mates were to be put to death, but because there had been maggots in the food. After this the film was to proceed unimpaired until the end, when the rest of the fleet appears. And now the execution scene was to be cut in, so that instead of the mutineers steaming away un-defeated to Rumania (as they actually did in reality) they would appear to have been shot. The connection between sav-age vindictive death-sentence and the mutiny, the refusal of the firing squad to fire on their mates—all this would have been lost—although not actually omitted—so that the conclu-sion would have been: there was an unmotivated mutiny in the ship, the officers quickly get the situation in hand, the muti-neers get their well-deserved punishment and serve them jolly well right too! And this by merely transposing a single scene! Not a shot omitted, not a title changed—just one scene shifted. Such is the power of the scissors.

PICTURES HAVE NO TENSES

Such things could of course happen only to silent films. For pictures have no tenses. They show only the present—they cannot express either a past or a future tense. In a picture itself there is nothing that would compellingly and precisely indicate the reasons for the picture being what it is. In a film scene we see only what is happening before our eyes. Why things happen as they do, of what they are the result—these are questions to which a thousand different answers could be given in the silent film.

The talkie, on the contrary, has words, words which may refer to past or future, which have a logic that determines the place of each scene in the time-sequence of events.

TIME IN THE FILM

The scenes of a film, just like the scenes of a stage play, are enacted before our eyes, that is, in real time. The photographed picture of a scene cannot last either a longer or a shorter time when projected on to the screen, than the scene itself had lasted. On the stage as much time as the author pleases may elapse between the acts, while the curtain is down. There are plays in which a century elapses between two acts. But film scenes are not separated from each other by curtains or intervals. Nevertheless the lapse of time must be conveyed, a time-perspective given. How is this done?

If the film wants to make us feel that time has elapsed between two scenes, it interpolates between these two scenes another scene enacted in some other place. When we return to the former place, time has elapsed. But how much time has elapsed can never be ascertained from the scene itself, unless one of the characters tells us.

TIME AS THEME AND EXPERIENCE

In an epic, a drama, or a film, time is just as much a theme for a work of art as is action, characterization, or psychological analysis. The reason for this is that time belongs to all of them as an organic component. There can be no story the course, significance and effect of which did not depend on the amount of time it takes up. If an event occurs twice—once slowly and once quickly, then it is no longer the same event. An explosion differs from a quiet chemical reaction only in that it is a more rapid process. One speed may take life, another speed give it. A slowly maturing action and a suddenly provoked action have widely differing psychological implications. In other words, time is an inalienable element of all human manifestations. Apart from this, the passing of time is in itself one of the deepest experiences of mortal man and an eternal theme of his poetry.

But in epic and dramatic works of art time as an experience cannot be measured by days or hours or minutes. It must be shown in perspective, in the same way as the characters, who also do not move in real space. The time effect is as much an illusion as is the space effect.

The film produces a most interesting link between time effect and space effect; so interesting, indeed, that it merits a closer analysis. Here is a fact corroborated by every experience: as has been already said, the film inserts a lapse of time between two scenes by means of cutting in a scene enacted in a different place. The experience is that the farther away the site of the inserted scene is from the site of the scenes between which it is inserted, the more time we will feel to have elapsed. If something happens in a room, then something else in the anteroom opening into it and then something in the same room a second time, we will feel that only a few minutes have elapsed and the scene in the room can go on straight away. We feel no jolt in time. But if the scene inserted between two scenes enacted in the same room leads us to Africa or Australia, then the same scene cannot be simply continued in the same room, because the spectator will feel that much time must have elapsed, even if the real duration of the interpolated distant scene is by no means longer than that of the similarly interpolated anteroom scene mentioned before.

CONTINUITY OF FORM AND ATMOSPHERE

It is difficult to avoid the use of the interpolated-scene technique and this renders it necessary to make several threads of action run parallel to one another. A film sometimes shows two or three of these parallel actions, which are plaited together into a sort of visual fugue by making each of them appear as 'interpolated scenes' in each of the others. But this method is not the only means the film possesses for the presentation of the lapse of time and of these more will be said later.

At all events the director, when he arranges the sequence of shots and determines their length, has to consider not only the contents but also the physiognomy and subtlest atmosphere of the neighbouring shots. He must not only see that a physical gesture begun in one shot should be continued without interruption in the different set-up of the next shot—mental movements must also flow smoothly from shot to shot—if they continue at all.

CREATIVE EDITING

Even the simplest narrative editing, which has no other purpose than to collate the shots into a sequence which makes the story clearly comprehensible—that it, a mere arranging the shots in their logical order—is already to some extent artistic creation. If everything the film-makers wanted us to know were already visible in the separate shots, such simple aligning, story-telling editing would have nothing more of its own to add. In this case no use would have been made of the great power, inherent in the editor's scissors, to induce associations of ideas and to help us understand the story of the film. Editing can, however, be genuinely creative and convey to us something that cannot be seen on any of the shots themselves.

A simple example: We see someone leave a room. Then we see the room in disorder, showing the traces of a struggle. Then a close-up—the back of a chair with blood dripping from it. This would be sufficient. There would be no need for us to see the struggle or the victim. We would guess it all. The editing would have given us the clue.

IDEA-ASSOCIATIVE EDITING

This technique of idea-associative montage was developed to a very high level in the days of the silent film. It provided very subtle films for a public of greater visual culture and greater sensibility. We learnt to notice and interpret the slightest details and relate them to each other. Objects not shown but merely suggested have the same sort of deeper effect as has the unspoken word. Good editing not only interprets a scene by aligning visual images—it also starts trains of ideas in us and gives them a definite direction. In this case the film only suggests, but does not show, the inner sequence of the spectators' idea-associations. But the film can also throw on to the screen a whole sequence of such ideas—associations, actually showing the pictures which follow each other in the mind and lead from one thought to the next. In such films we can see a sort of inner film of associations running within the human consciousness.

FLASHBACKS

The earliest silent films already made use of this device. Usually the pictures were soft focused, to indicate that here was not reality, but merely something passing through the memory of the character and seen with his inner eye. By this naïve device the earlier films often presented to the spectator some episode of the past which had not been shown but knowledge of which was required in order to understand the story. Of course such primitive flashbacks could never reproduce a psychological process.

Of a quite different nature are the flashbacks which Ermler used in his film *Ruins of an Empire*. The hero is a soldier who has lost his memory in the first world war, and with it his knowledge of himself. The film showed the train of ideas which restored his memory, his knowledge of himself and of the world. The spectator was made to follow a train of ideas of the sort psycho-analysis might have brought to light in a similar case. But no words could express such a train of ideas as adequately as pictures, because the rational, conceptual nature of words bars them from conveying the irrational correlation of such inner pictures. Further, the speed at which the pictures follow each other in the film can reproduce the original speed of this process of idea-association. The written or spoken word is always much slower than the inner rhythm of idea-association.

Ermler's soldier sees a sewing-machine and hears it rattle.

The rattle suddenly quickens and grows louder. Now it is the rattling of a machine-gun. Strange tatters of visions, a mosaic of bits and pieces surge up, one bringing up the other by force of some formal or tonal similarity. Nevertheless the string of associations runs in a definite direction. A rubble of war memories—wheels of a gun . . . sewing-machine needle . . . bayonet . . . convulsively gripping hands . . . The sequence irresistibly carries along the soldier's unconsciousness and drives him nearer to the breaking-point, to that spectacle of horror which made him lose memory and consciousness, in order that he may find himself again and continue his interrupted existence.

This was an example of how the film can show an inner picture-sequence of associations, reproduce a mental process. Now I would like to quote an example of the opposite process, when the sequence shown in the film does not reproduce the chain of associations in pictures, but suggests it, starts it off and directs it into a definite channel. By this means the film induces in the spectators thoughts and emotions it need not itself explicitly express.

M E T A P H O R I C A L   M O N T A G E

Griffith already used this method. For instance he showed in one of his films how the yellow press can and does ruin the reputation of a woman. He showed the immense technical plant of a newspaper with a world-wide circulation. The immense machines break into the shots like tanks advancing to the attack. This striking resemblance grows into a simile, into a train of associations. The rotaries throw out the papers like quick-firing guns their shells. This simile is evoked by the frightened face of the woman, cut in between the huge machines. Our train of ideas is already under way and the associations suggested by the montage endow the printing machines with wicked, malicious faces. The bundles of newspapers running towards us on the creepers seem an irresistible avalanche which finally buries the terrified helpless victim— whom we see again and again, cut in between the raving machines, until at last the woman is lying limp under the rollers of the rotary. Here the montage has created a metaphor.

When the battle-cruiser *Potemkin* steams into its last fight, what we see is not a great ship ploughing up the water into foam—we see what is happening inside it, in its heart. We see big close-ups of the engines, their wheels and cranks cross-cut with big close-ups of the sailors' faces. Such repeated juxtaposition compels comparison. A visual parallel inevitably conjures up a parallel in the mind. The angry, resolute faces of the sailors transfer their own expression to the wheels and cranks. Yes, they are fighting side by side in a common struggle. An almost human consciousness seems expressed in the physiognomy of the throbbing, quivering machines as they revolve at full-speed and the panting of the valves, the whirling of the flywheels seem the determined gestures of 'Comrade Machine'.

POETIC MONTAGE

Very deep subconscious idea-associations can emerge or be touched off by such editing. Sometimes the picture of a landscape is enough to conjure up the memory of a face or to characterize a situation. Such effects are certainly not 'literary', for no words can convey this non-rational correlation of shapes and images which takes place in our subconscious mind.

In Pudovkin's film *Mother* the first revolutionary demonstration of workers passes along the streets in spring, accompanied by a parallel sequence of melting snow-water which is first only a trickle, then a rivulet, a torrent, a raging flood. The streaming of the waters is time and again cut into the pictures of the demonstration and the parallel pictures are inevitably related to each other by the spectator. The spring waters glitter in the sun like a bright hope and the same hope shines in the workers' eyes. The faces of the workers, radiant with faith and expectation, are reflected in the sunlit puddles. Such a correlation of pictures is an inevitable, automatic process. Just as the contact of electrically charged objects evokes a spark, so the contact between pictures in a film evokes a mutually interpreting associative process, whether the director wishes this or not. This is an inherent power which the film-maker, if he is an artist, must hold firmly in his grip, direct and shape according to his needs.

ALLEGORIC MONTAGE

In Lupu Pick's film *New Year's Eve*, a pioneer film in its time, shots of a stormy sea tossing with varied intensity were cut in between the scenes. By a parallel between the dramatic storms and oceanic storms he wanted to increase the rhythmic and emotional effects of his scenes. Here he made that very mistake of which mention was made in the paragraph relating to allegoric set-up. Eisenstein's Cossack boots and Winter Palace chandelier were not invented merely for the sake of a simile and stuck into the film. They were real elements of the film story and only their specific presentation made them point to something beyond their own selves and thus turned them into symbols. And in Pudovkin's *Mother* the spring waters really gurgle and splash around the feet of the demonstrating workers, and are given a metaphoric significance only by dint of the montage. But Lupu Pick's film story has nothing to do with the sea. He cut the shots of a stormy sea into urban scenes merely for the sake of the parallel, the simile; it was not some organic part of the film story that was raised to symbolic significance, but an allegory brought from outside was, as it were, stuck on to the film.

LITERARY METAPHORS

On the other hand it sometimes happens that the director tries to illustrate a literary metaphor simply by means of montage. In one of Eisenstein's films two old-world Russian peasants want to divide up a heritage and they do so by sawing in two the hut which constitutes this heritage. The wife of one of them sadly watches the murderous work of the saw. A big close-up of the saw and the big close-up of the woman's face alternate so rapidly in repeated short shots that finally the spectator feels—because he actually almost sees it—as though the saw was sawing through the woman's heart. It is obvious here that a constructed literary picture has been translated into a visual image.

ASSOCIATIONS OF IDEAS

Associations of ideas induced by montage can evoke not only emotions and create an atmosphere—they can also produce in us definite thoughts, logical deductions and conclusions.

In Pudovkin's *The End of St Petersburg* we see cross-cut shots of battlefields and of the stock exchange. Stock exchange, battlefield, stock exchange, battlefield, stock exchange, battlefield. On the stock exchange a blackboard shows how the quotations are rising. On the battlefield the soldiers are falling. Stocks rising. Soldiers falling. Stocks rising. Soldiers falling. It is impossible for the spectator not to see a causal connection between the two and this is of course what the director wants. The spectator who sees a connection between the two sequences, will also know the meaning of this connection: his visual impression will turn into political understanding.

INTELLECTUAL MONTAGE

But such shots, shown in parallel, are still the real images of actual reality and are real scenes pertinent to the story of the film. Only the placing of them thus side by side puts into them an ulterior meaning, a political significance. Only this gives them their artistic justification and their sensual realism.

Directors sometimes attempt, however, to use the sequences of a film for the communication of thoughts, as a sort of hieroglyphic picture-writing, in which the pictures mean something but have no content of their own. They are like the pictures in a rebus; they mean something and the spectator must guess what it is, but in themselves, as pictures, they present no interest.

When in Eisenstein's *October* a statue falls from its pedestal, this is intended to signify that the power of the Tsar has been overthrown. If the pieces were to unite again, this would mean the restoration of that power. These are picture puzzles, not artistic effects. Eisenstein, who was perhaps the greatest master of sensuous picture effects that transcended the sphere of reason, unfortunately often fell a victim to the mistaken

' NANOOK OF THE NORTH ': The extra-social nature of the ice-pack as a social experience.

Rin-Tin-Tin in ' Jaws of Steel.'

New kinds of characters were made possible by the technical possibilities of the film.

Chaplin and Jackie Coogan in ' The Kid.'

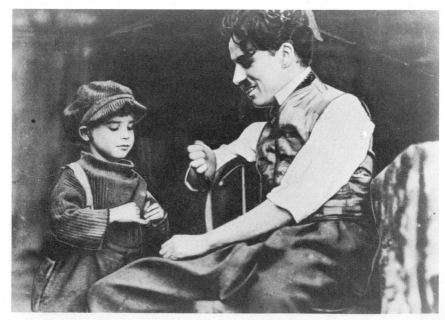

ASTA NIELSEN IN 'DIE EWEGE NATT.'

The script-writers destroyed a growing art when they gave speech to the great mutes.

LILLIAN GISH IN 'BROKEN BLOSSOMS.'

FALCONETTI IN 'THE PASSION OF JOAN OF ARC.'

The consciousness of space in the close-up.

'BATTLESHIP POTEMKIN.'

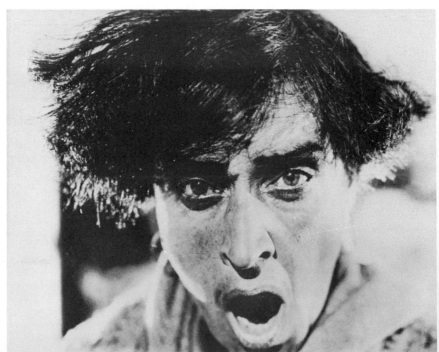

MAX LINDER: The film made a new kind of slapstick possible.

SESSUE HAYAKAWA: The 'dead-pan' countenance which showed neither feeling nor passion.

'IL SOLE SORGE ANCORA.'

The change in trend which substituted neo-naturalism for the sentimentality of Hollywood.

'VIVERE IN PACE.'

GRETA GARBO IN 'ANNA KARENINA': Her beauty bears the stamp of sorrow and loneliness.

' THE GREAT WALTZ.'

Through the camera the audience can move in the opulence and culture of other periods, other social environments.

' LADY HAMILTON.'

' BERLIN ': The characterization of a city through montage and rhythm.

' Mother.'

Eyes sharpened by revolutionary struggle saw more than just the difference between ' rich ' and ' poor.'

' Arsenal.'

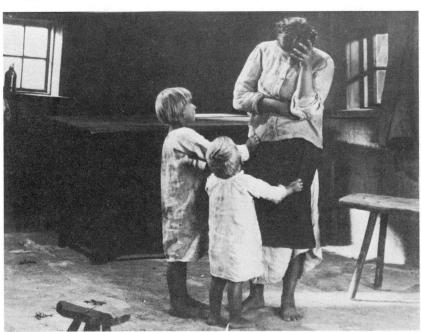

' Die Letzte Nacht.'

Each shot must be a properly composed picture.

' The Fall of the House of Usher.'

' LENIN IN OCTOBER.'

A contrast in the treatment of suspense and battle.

' THE THIRTEEN.'

'MONSIEUR VERDOUX': The Charlie mask which gagged Chaplin for so long discarded at last.

'PHILLIPS RADIO'; The mechanical monsters of the industrial age show their face.

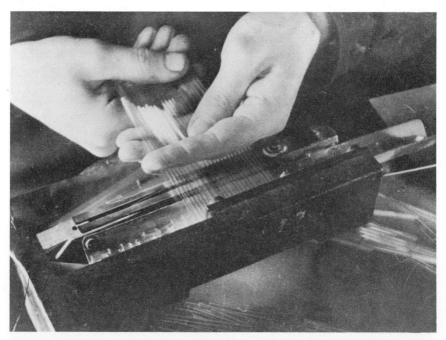

'SOUS LES TOITS DE PARIS': The visual culture of the 'avant-garde' is brought into the commercial film.

'FELIX LENDS A HAND': Here the line reached the boundaries which enclose graphic art.

'BOULE DE SUIF': The silence of this film was intentional and deliberately accepted.

'THE STREET': The picture of a city reflected through the inner vision of a young man.

'BALTIC DEPUTY':   A demonstration of the unspoken soliloquy.

'THE LADY IN THE LAKE':   The film narrated in the first person brought to its logical conclusion.

idea that the world of purely conceptual thinking could also be conquered by film art.

This is not to say that the art of the film cannot convey thoughts or achieve effects through thought. But it must not merely suggest them, it must express them explicitly, in film-language of course. The film can evoke thoughts in the spectator, but must not project on to the screen ready-made thought-symbols, ideograms which have definite, known conventional meanings, like a question mark or exclamation point, a cross or swastika; for these would be merely a primitive picture-writing, hieroglyphs, that would be less convenient than our alphabet and certainly not art.

RHYTHM IN MONTAGE

The editing gives the film narrative its style, speed and rhythm. It may flow on calmly, with long scenes played out to the end, with landscapes and settings only meant to be looked at, with weighty, slow-moving picture material. But it can also dart along with the swift rush of short-cropped detail shots. The dramatic rhythm of the story is transposed into visual picture-rhythm and the external, formal rhythm steps up the speed of the internal drama. The movement of the shots has the same visual effect as the gesturing of a narrator.

This short-shot rapid montage as expressive rhythm was much used by the early silent Soviet film. It often effectively conveyed the feverish pace of revolutionary happenings. Such accelerated cutting, in which the shots flash past our eyes in seconds,is possible only if we are able to perceive and identify the objects depicted on them. This we are able to do only thanks to our fully developed new filmic culture, our rapidly reacting sensibility for things filmic. And such rapid cutting has its own dangers: if it is not the expression of a racing internal rhythm, it easily becomes an empty formality, a banal technical trick.

SPEED OF ACTION AND SPEED OF CUTTING

These are quite independent of each other, and very subtle

effects can be achieved by various combinations of the speed of action and the speed of cutting. An instance is the picture of a race. Long shots of long duration show the whole field. The racing horses or cars run at highest speed, but the cutting is leisurely. But a director who knows his job will liven up the last few seconds of the finish with quickened cutting. The objective pace of the competitors in the race has not changed but in these last few moments the picture seems to have stopped, in order that each detail of the action may be visually dissected as it were. This increases the tension. The film may have shown a race of a thousand yards in a short sequence lasting five seconds and then give the struggle on the last hundred yards, in twenty rapidly changing close-ups, between competitors running neck and neck, panting, now gaining, now losing a few inches until at last they reach the goal. These twenty shots may last, say, forty seconds, that is, longer in *real* time than the sequence showing the first nine hundred yards of the race. Nevertheless we feel it to be shorter, our time-perspective will tell us that we have seen only a short minute, magnified as though under a time-microscope.

The scene will appear to have been shortened by the director. For it is only the last fifty yards of the race that we are seeing all the time. But the pace of the cutting has increased. Thus three kinds of time have appeared in this film: the real duration of the race; the pictured time and time-illusion of the scene shown in the film; the real running time of the film strip carrying the close-ups collated by cutting. Such films provide a rich material for research for psychologists who might like to study time-sense.

SCENE IN 'RITARDANDO', SHOTS IN 'ACCELERANDO'

The tension of dramatic scenes may be increased by using the time-honoured device of *ritardando* at the moment of the climax. But only the scene is slowed down, possibly even stopped altogether for a moment. Close-up shots of the scene may on the other hand be speeded up, rushed along in a galloping tempo in order that the external rhythm of the picture movement may convey to us the internal storms, the quiverings of internal tension. One may think in this connection of Lupu Pick's gangsters, locked up in the strongroom of a bank which has been mined. The scene is stationary, the men are waiting frozenly for the explosion to occur. But a galloping sequence of rapidly changing close-ups makes us feel the storm raging in the motionless men. Thus the cutting may convey things that are invisible and hence cannot be photographed.

To spread out the last moment so that it lasts almost through a whole act, has been the ambition of many a master of the film. The axe is raised, the fuse is lit and then . . . what happens between two battings of an eyelid? A rushing series of shots shows the feverish working of human consciousness.

LENGTH OF SHOTS

The art of cutting consists in the first place in determining the length of each shot. If a shot is a little too long or too short, it can decisively change the effect of the picture, just as a tune is completely changed if a tone is pushed up or down half an interval.

The 'length' of a shot can of course be measured only on the film strip. On the screen we can measure only its duration. And the length or shortness of that is not merely a question of visual rhythm, for the meaning and content of a scene seen on the screen is influenced by its duration. We can for instance shorten the footage of a film and yet make it appear to be dragging. The internal speed of a shot is independent of its length in feet, its duration in seconds. The inner movement is often given by just those detail shots which if omitted would reduce the footage of the scene, but make it nevertheless more lengthy. If I show an ant-heap in a long shot on six feet of film, it will be long and boring, but if I show the details of the internal life of an ant-heap in close-ups, it will not be boring even on fifty feet.

In the film every occurrence is a little like this ant-heap: it is made interesting and exciting by close-ups of detail and rhythm of cutting. A synopsis of a good novel is always less interesting than the novel itself and a long duel between two good swordsmen more exciting than the sudden stab of a dagger.

In the cinematic presentation of events only the visible movement of the smallest particles of it can give a lively tempo. The sentences of a narrative can tell the whole story and at the same time refer to a thousand details. But the picture either shows the whole, glossing over the details, or shows close-ups in which the whole is never visible but only pieced together in the cutting.

In the old silent film *Vanina,* previously mentioned, in which Asta Nielsen gave such a classic exhibition of silent speech, there is another remarkable scene. Asta has rescued her condemned lover from the death cell, but the fugitives are still running along the winding passages of the prison. These passages seem endless. But their monotonous length is not boring—on the contrary, it is most exciting, because it is precisely this monotonous length that gives them their menacing physiognomy. For we know that the fugitives have only seconds in which to make good their escape—and every door they open, as a last forlorn hope, leads not out into the open, to liberty, but into another long, grim passage. We feel the passing of the time as the running out of the sands of their lives. Each new passage faces them with a merciless, inexorable fate. We already know that they are lost. But they are still running, they have not yet been caught. Perhaps after all . . . Behind them is death. The longer the scene lasts, the greater the nervous tension.

RHYTHM OF THE SOUND FILM

The sound film brought new laws of rhythm in its train. Words have a real acoustic rhythm which cannot be slowed down or speeded up by any illusion-creating technique without changing the meaning or dramaturgic significance of the words. Sound films also have silent scenes which have their own laws of rhythm.

MUSICAL AND DECORATIVE RHYTHM IN CUTTING

An important artistic part may be played by a kind of editing which has little to do with the dramaturgic aspect of the contents of the film. It does not increase the tension of sequences, does not express internal, emotional storms. It has merely formal, musical, decorative significance. But this is a great deal.

Shots of landscapes, buildings, interiors can by cutting be given a certain irrational interrelation, like melodies in a good symphonic structure. Such musical or decorative rhythm may play an important part if combined with dramatic content. But it is dwarfed into nothingness if the attempt is made to separate it and endow it with independent life. The *avant-gardistes* and futurists made the mistake of thinking that such rhythms can become independent artistic means of expression of a special kind. Experiments in this direction led to abstractions such as were already mentioned in connection with symbolic angles and cutting.

The shots in themselves lose their primary significance when they serve as material for rhythmic effects.

What have the subtle changes and forms of rhythm in Walter Ruttmann's *Berlin* in common with the trams shown in the film? What have the shots of Montmartre streets in Cavalcanti's *Rien que les heures* in common with the *legato-staccato* of his cutting? From the viewpoint of rhythm these features are merely carriers of light and shadow, of form and movement. They are no longer objects at all. The visual music of the montage is played in a separate sphere that is parallel to the content.

Shots can be made to appear long or short not only through the rhythm but also as a result of what they depict. In editing, not only the content but the shape of shots must often be taken into account. Lines of direction and movement are usually brought into relation with one another. One of the devices used in editing is to bring details together according to the resemblance or contrast of their shapes. Narrow, per-

pendicular towers and factory chimneys may be cross-cut
with broad, heavy images, or the similarity of forms stressed
even more by matching round shapes with round shapes,
curved lines with curved lines. The contents do not always
lend themselves to such combinations. The formalists of the
'absolute' film were not interested in contents at all and even
Eisenstein, in his film *The Old and the New* (or *The General
Line)*, cut a cricket and a reaping-machine together four consecutive times, because 'they had the same line'. Such a system
of editing is only concerned with decorative features and
nothing else; it shows the world depicted as a mobile ornament.

SUBJECTIVE CUTTING

Cutting is like telling a story. The author shows us things as
he sees them. But sometimes he does not want to show things
from his own viewpoint, his own angle of vision, and the result
is a subjective, 'identifying' cut. Not only set-ups and angles
in the whole sequence are shown as one of the characters
in the film would see them. The hero starts out and the camera
follows. We see the course of events with the eyes of one of
the characters. Just as some novels are narrated in the first
person, so the film shows its story in the first person. This
technique was brought to its logical conclusion in *The Lady
in the Lake*. It is not the objects which parade in front of the
spectator—the spectator proceeds past the objects, in company with the character depicted; in such cases the editing
shows the road of the hero as well. If the film shows a landscape as, say, a wayfarer in the film would see it, then the
landscape appears as the subjective experience of a human
being, in the same order and rhythm. Such a film can be
lyrical to a high degree, even if it presents objective, 'documentary', material.

WALKING

Because in such films the rhythm of the walk of the wayfarer who looks at the landscape plays a very important part
and may determine the entire atmosphere of the scene, let us

discuss walking as a most expressive and quite specific cinematic gesture.

There is scarcely a more characteristic and expressive gesture than the walk, if for no other reason because mostly it is
not a consciously expressive movement. It can of course be
made conscious and people often intentionally show dignity,
resolution, modesty or coquetry in their gait. Gait can lie and
dissemble too. If a person is embarrassed by being observed,
it will show in his walk first of all. As the saying goes he
'would not know which foot to put forward first'. Feet give
away a great deal.

Actors on the stage rarely have an opportunity to use the
walk as a characteristic gesture, because of the lack of space.
That is why Erwin Piscator had the idea of using a conveyor
strip on his stage, so that the actor, moving in an inverse
direction to the strip would walk, while remaining in the same
spot and use the walk for characterization. Nevertheless it is
only the film that can really exhaust all the expressive possibilities of the walk, for in the film there is none of the disturbing
element brought in by the strange and unnatural walking-and-
yet-remaining-in-the-same-place of Piscator's stage device.

In preparing the atmosphere for the decisive scene, a good
director will show whether the hero is approaching the scene
of the impending climax in anticipation of what is to come
or is on the contrary 'unconscious of his doom'. Often there is
no need even to show what happened—all that needs to be
shown is the hero coming back *from* the scene of the climac-
teric event. The hero's walk will reveal what happened; his
walk will be a confession and a soliloquy expressing his
reaction to the scene just experienced, more completely and
more sincerely than if he had been shown on the spot itself.

There are walks which are not purposeful movements in a
certain direction. In such cases the person is not going somewhere, his legs are not means of transport but subconscious
means of expression betraying a certain state of mind. The
silent film often used this sort of walk as a kind of visual
soliloquy. It was called a 'passage' and many thought it a bit
of superfluous padding. Sometimes it may have been so, but
very often it was quite the reverse. For in the action itself, be

it concerned with love or with fighting or other things, the actors have to make many gestures which have a purely utilitarian purpose: they hit out, ward off a blow, put something down or pick something up, throw something away or clutch something tight. All these movements have a *purpose* and their *cause* is therefore less apparent. But after the scene itself, in the solitary walk or running, only the internal emotional causes of the movement are manifested, and hence such movements can be most expressive.

Lillian Gish once played a poor girl looking for a job. The spectator accompanied her from place to place, from street to street, upstairs and downstairs. How much hope and disappointment, how much confidence and anxiety, self-deception and dark despair were in her walk! It was a tragic poem in itself.

Can anyone who has seen it ever forget the last shot of Charlie Chaplin's *Circus,* when Charlie goes away? Once more he has been left alone, deceived by life; he has lost everything and has started out again all by himself. But the whole wide, free world lies before him, and anything might still happen, and the sun shines and the distant dreams lure him on. Charlie waddling away into the infinite was a beautiful, optimistic visual poem.

In Alexandrov's musical comedy *Jazz Comedy* the hero's walk or, more accurately, his rhythmic marching is constantly cut in, as the symbol of happy vigour. And who does not remember Conrad Veidt's romantic, panther-like walk on which so many films were built up?

Pyriev, wanting in one of his films to present the fierce competition between unemployed workers in Berlin, showed them racing wildly to be first at an address given in an advertisement offering work. The rush was a tragic symbol, in it the weak and the old were trampled down and the others ran on over their prostrate bodies.

Such presentation has, however, certain dangers too. Attention may be diverted from the essential, as for instance in the example mentioned in the preceding paragraph. Pyriev kept the race of the unemployed on the screen too long, so that the interest of the spectator took on a sporting turn. He began to see a racing field, not a crowd of unemployed, all the more so as in the end their faces bore only the familiar expression of physical effort. Finally the spectator ceased to be interested in anything save the question as to which of the racing men would win.

SPORT IN THE FILM

Because the film is the art of the visible, in other words bodily action, it is obvious that sporting, athletic or acrobatic performances can play a greater part in it than in any other art. It must not be forgotten, however, that unless the film is not a news strip, even an acrobatic performance is interesting only as long as it has a dramaturgic part to play, as long as it expresses an event, a fate, a human soul in the human story of the film. For a film is not a raree-show where we gape at everything that is exhibited—only what demonstrates a human fate is of interest to us.

If a fugitive leaps across a ditch, we are interested in the pursuit and excited by the obstacle. But if the ditch is so wide that the fugitive must break an Olympic record to jump it, then the spectator is no longer interested in the pursuit and the fate of the fugitive, but in the jump as a sporting event, quite without reference to the artistic content of the film.

Even in artistic films which have a sportsman for their hero, what is artistically interesting is not the sporting side of the performance. For instance in *Anna Karenina* (the original production with Greta Garbo) the horse-race scene only begins to be interesting and exciting when Wronski muffs his jump because he has caught sight of Anna and is thrown at the obstacle.

INEXPRESSIVE SPORT

Movements which are the correct movements for a performance in a sporting event are not spontaneous expressive gestures and for this reason they are not expressive at all. They may be beautiful because they show strength and good health and a useful flexibility. But they cannot show passion or emotion, they cannot reveal the soul. In scenes demanding physical strength and agility often only a hair's breadth separates the fighting hero from a professional boxer, or a fleeing fugitive from appearing to train for a running race. Expressive instinctive gestures have only *causes*, while the movements of a sporting performance have only an *object*. The everyday movements of life lie midway between the two.

CHAPTER ELEVEN

PANORAMA

PANORAMIC SHOTS PROVIDE changes without editing. The director does not link together the pictures of objects shot separately, but makes the camera move so that in gliding past the objects it takes pictures of them in the same order as that in which they are aligned in reality, even if this reality is only the reality of a studio set. Thus the sequence is not brought about by editing; it already exists in nature or in the studio and the rhythm and speed of change is not the work of the editor's scissors but of the camera movement which sometimes moves parallel to the row of objects to be photographed, sometimes accompanies someone who is moving along and shows what the person in question sees in passing; sometimes it turns on its heel as it were and records the surrounding objects in a circular sweep. This type of changing shot is called panoramic and modern cinematography is making increasing use of it.

Apart from other reasons, it can be used more often now because the technique of the tracking shot has developed recently to high perfection. Not only can objects moving at great speed be adequately 'tracked' but the angle and set-up can be changed during shooting. Without interrupting the continuity we can approach or withdraw, raise or lower the camera while 'tracking' or 'panning'.

The film likes to use this extraordinary cinematic possibility among other things because it increases the apparent authenticity of the picture, because in moving along with the tracking camera, it enables the spectator to remain in the real space in which the action takes place. The spectator's eye can be a witness to everything, nothing is skipped and the tracking shot cannot 'deceive' as editing can.

Such shots are used by the modern film-makers further

because they can thus show in one and the same shot a man moving in space and the space this man sees out of his own eyes. The panorama can be more subjective and lyrical than cutting.

Unfortunately the modern film uses the panorama also for another reason: because in making the characters move in real space, it can more easily return to the photographed theatre towards which the film is also perceptibly declining at the present time. Hitchcock's *Rope* is an example of this tendency.

EXPERIENCE OF TIME

It has already been said that the panorama conveys the reality of space to a greater extent than does cutting. From the linked shots we can do no more than infer that they are in the same sector of space or not. All we have to go on is the content of the shots, and logic and interrelation of events and our own memory, even if the film has once already shown us the entire space in which the scene is enacted.

But the panorama never lets us leave this space. By force of identification, we explore it in the company of the camera and our time-sense measures the real distance which lies between the various objects. Space itself, not the picture of space in perspective presentation, is what we experience here.

In Dreyer's *Joan of Arc*, we never see the entire space in which the trial takes place. The camera, moving along the rows of benches, takes striking close-ups of the heads of the judges and by this uninterrupted panoramic shot, measures for us the actual dimensions of a space we do not see. As a result, we are conscious of space all the time we are looking at the procession of close-ups. We see nothing but individual physiognomies, we look into the faces of outstanding personalities and yet never forget that here is a multitude—because we, with the camera, are there among them.

The Japanese director of *Shadows of Yoshiwara* panned from one object to the other so quickly that one could scarcely see what was in the intermediate space. The objects in between were not important for all the director wanted was to make us conscious of distance and space. For this reason he did not cut, nor skip the intermediate space. In such a film, space is not merely the place in which people and things can be shown: it achieves a reality of its own and has its own significance, independently of the objects which fill it.

Joe May, in his film *Asphalt,* showed the room of a German police sergeant. With pedantic meticulousness, the camera panned from object to object. Wardrobe, table, cage with bird, clock, enlarged photo of parents. We see everything and know everything; we see and understand the stuffy narrowness of a petty-bourgeois life—and only after this does the camera turn to the man himself. First we see his environment; not only the objects themselves, but what is more important, their stifling nearness to each other. We see the narrow confinement of this world. The reality of the panorama can convey this much better than the perspective of a long shot.

DRAMATIC QUALITY OF THE PANORAMA

It often happens in the cinema that we see by the expression of one of the characters that he has caught sight of something, though we don't know what it is—as yet we see only its effect; a smile, an expression of fear or some other reaction. We are curious to know the reason for this reaction. Then the director does not jump to another shot, but pans over and does so slowly, *ritardando,* to increase our curiosity, like a clever narrator—until at last the cause and explanation of the effect appear on the screen.

Or else: in a dialogue scene the cameras pan from one face to the other. Then one of the two does something or says something unexpected. The camera stresses this by suddenly slowing down the speed of the panning, so that it takes some time before we see the effect on the face of the other person, leaving us on tenterhooks. In such cases panning not only measures the real time that has elapsed. but may lengthen it for the sake of heightened dramatic effect. The panning is much slower than the turning of our head would be if the scene occurred in real life.

A fine example of the effect that can be achieved by this

means can be found in one of Charlie Chaplin's short burlesques, *Shoulder Arms*. Chaplin appears as a soldier in the first world war. After many tragi-comic scenes we see this comico-tragic one: Charlie in the bottom of a deep trench is standing with his comrades at the foot of the steps, waiting for the order to go over the top. The others are grim, motionless. Charlie is so frightened and trembles so much that in his clumsy fumbling he drops a little pocket mirror and it breaks. The men next to him see it and draw back from him in superstitious fear, as from one who had been marked for death by fate. Standing in a row in the narrow trench they cannot draw back very far, two short paces at most. But Charlie has understood why his neighbours drew back and looks after them like a man abandoned by his friends in the hour of peril. The camera pans, following his sad and terrified gaze, and shows a greatly increased distance between Charlie and the other men. The panning is so slow, the camera takes such a long time in turning that the few feet seem an endless, empty desert. For what Charlie sees is a great void between himself and his fellows, who have left him alone in his misfortune, an orphan left alone in the world.

We have often seen the infinities of desert and ocean, of distant horizons dipping into space in other films, but never before, in films or in any other art, such solitude in so narrow a space. This is the subtle lyricism of the panorama shot.

CHAPTER TWELVE

EXPRESSIVE TECHNIQUE OF THE CAMERA

MORE THINGS CAN be done with a camera than taking photographs. It can produce many visual effects on the screen without taking pictures, presenting some object or reproducing some shape or formation. In such cases the camera detaches itself from the object and projects its own technique on to the screen. Such efforts are the most specific subjective lyrical manifestations and the director, in identifying himself with them, can place a subtle personal emphasis on certain features in the film.

FADING

One of these effects is fading, the darkening of the scene by a slow stopping down of the iris diaphragm. This is not a shot, not a picture at all, and can yet create a most expressive atmosphere. The slow darkening of the picture is like the melancholy, slowly softening voice of a narrator and after it a pensive silence. This purely technical effect can produce in us the sadness of farewells and of the impermanence of things. Sometimes its effect is like that of a dash in a written text, sometimes like a row of full stops after a sentence, leaving it open, sometimes like a gesture of leave-taking, a mournful gaze after something that has departed for ever. But at all times it signifies the passing of time.

In the admirable *Chapayev*, Furmanov the commissar says goodbye to the partisan leader and his troop. He must leave them. The leave-taking is a short and unsentimental military affair. But the departure itself is extremely long-drawn-out, because the motor-car which takes Furmanov away from the band of partisans recedes on a perfectly straight road and dwindles more and more while still remaining visible. And the partisans stand and still keep their eyes on it. It holds their eyes and holds their hearts. And when it is so far away that it almost merges with the mist of the horizon, the picture very slowly fades out—and by this optical, technical device it takes over and continues the mood induced by the slow dwindling of the car in the distance. Up to this moment the parting friend had receded in the picture; now the picture itself recedes and fades. The sorrow of parting is here deepened into a premonition of evil, as though not only a good friend but good fortune had gone from Chapayev and his band. As the diaphragm closes, the world grows dark for them and intangibly, but none the less clearly, we feel the shadow of death fall on them. A mere technicality of the camera mechanism here induces a profound emotion such as we sometimes find in the poems of the greatest poets.

SECRET OF THE DIAPHRAGM

The iris diaphragm can produce other, no less profound psychological effects by other technical tricks. Fade-ins and dissolves also give effects only to be described as poetic. These possibilities have been known and used in practice for a long time. But what is the explanation of these effects?

As long as the film only shows objective reality in pictures, the unsophisticated spectator does not perceive the subjective part played in it by the maker of the film, the director. This part may be to a very great extent implicit in his way of showing things, but he does not show himself, just as the author of a stage play does not speak in the first person.

But when we see not only actual pictures of objects on the screen, but fades and dissolves, in other words photo-technical effects, we are no longer facing only objective reproductions of things—here the narrator, the author, the film-maker himself is speaking to us.

THE CAMERA SHOWS INVISIBLE THINGS

The strangeness of all this is that by the fades and dissolves projected on to the screen the camera in fact shows us invisible things. For instance the shot of Furmanov's departure in *Chapayev* has a profound lyrical content: the tragic darkening of Chapayev's mood, his sombre presentiment of disaster. But such things are after all not objects which can be photographed; they are invisible emotions, an invisible atmosphere which the slow darkening of the picture nevertheless expresses by visual means.

The process of thinking, the process of recalling things to one's memory is not visible. But by the slow fade-in of a picture the camera can lend it a visionary and visual character and convey to the spectator that the pictures shown are not those of real objects but of images of the mind.

TIME PERSPECTIVE

Fading out a picture can also convey the passing of time. If we see a ship slowly disappear from view on the edge of the horizon, a certain passage of time is expressed by the rhythm of the picture. But if in addition to this, the picture is also faded out, then to the feeling of time-lapse caused by the disappearance of the ship in the distance is added a feeling of further and scarcely assessable time-lapse. For now the shot shows two movements: movement of the ship and movement of the camera diaphragm. Two times: real time of the ship's disappearance and filmic time produced by the fade-out.

What we call 'filmic time' is a time effect comparable, in terms of space, to perspective. The outlines in a picture show space in perspective; certain modes of movement in the shot show time as it were in perspective. An analysis of these effects is most instructive for both film director and psychologist.

If the film is to show the passing of time by means of a cut-in shot, then the cutting-in of a motionless picture suggests the passing of more time than a picture in which motion is present. If after a dramatic scene a moving shot—even one showing some other place—is cut in and then the picture returns to the previous scene, the spectator cannot have the feeling that many years have passed in between. The reason for this is that visible movement has a real duration which gives the impression of real time. But if a motionless object, a rock, the surface of a lake or something similar is cut in between the moving scenes, it can make the spectator feel the passing of a very long, of an undetermined time. For the picture of a motionless object gives no visible measurable duration: it has no dimension in time, hence it can represent any length of it. Mountains, the sea, etc., awaken the association 'eternity' not because they show a great deal of time-lapse, but because they show none at all.

PSYCHOLOGY OF THE DISSOLVE

If a shot shows a young face and immediately afterwards the same face in old age, we feel an improbable jerk, possibly do not even recognize that the face is the same. But if the young face is slowly dissolved into the old, then this optico-technical device suggests the time that has elapsed. It does not show or reproduce the passage of time, only suggests it. Here again the narrator, the maker of the film speaks to the spectator in the first person by means of a camera mechanism.

The dissolve between two shots means a deeper connection between them. It is an accepted convention, expression, turn of speech in the language of the film, that if two pictures slowly dissolve into each other, the two are bound together by a deep, dramaturgically important, connection which may not be of a nature capable of being expressed by a series of shots depicting actual objects. The technique of the dissolve permits the placing of lyrical and intellectual emphasis where required in a film.

TIME AND SEQUENCE

In a film entitled *Homecoming*, Joe May once showed the long wandering of two escaped prisoners of war. And how did he show the devouring infinity of that journey across the endless plains of Siberia, along the endless highways of Russia? How many landscapes, how many towns and villages would he have had to show, if the spectator was to be given so much as an inkling of the endless distances and endless years? Joe May was wiser than that—he showed none at all. We saw no landscapes, not even the two prisoners, we saw only feet walking in close-up. And because we saw no landscapes, not one, there could have been a thousand of them.

For those feet walk incessantly and we see in dissolves the strong army boots go to pieces; in more slow dissolves the peasant sandals go too; then the miserable rags in which the feet are wrapped drop to tatters and finally we see only naked bleeding feet. If these shots had been placed in sequence without transition, we would have felt a brutal jerk in these four realistic shots, a symbolic presentation of four static *conditions*. The slow process of time-lapse and change is conveyed only by the dissolving of the shots into each other, although the actual projection on to the screen of a technical device does not represent any reality. The real time of projection of the shots showing the walking feet is about three minutes but our consciousness accepts the suggestion that months, even years have passed in that time.

PICTURE SIZE AND DISSOLVES

Such frequent consecutive dissolves are convincing only if the shots are close-ups. A whole human figure placed in a broad landscape impresses us too strongly with its bodily and spatial reality. This makes the illusory, thought-like weightlessness of the dissolve much less acceptable. If in the course of the four changes mentioned in the preceding we had even once seen great mountains, forests, rivers or houses dissolve into one another, the trick technique of the dissolve would have become far too obvious. A visible change in a landscape easily produces the effect of a dream, or of magic. But changes in things we do not see are no problem. Unseen landscapes can be countless and unmeasured time can be infinite. The close-up not only isolates objects in space, but seems to lift them out of space entirely and transfer them to a conceptual space in which different laws obtain.

The optical technique of dissolves very often renders unnecessary the dramaturgical technique of cut-in scenes (i.e. of parallel actions).

DISSOLVES AND SIMPLER STORIES

If a figure we have seen in one scene appears on another scene without intermediary pictures, by simply cutting them to follow each other, the spectator will consciously or subconsciously wonder how it got there. Such primitive alignment is apt to strike us as clumsy, as bad technique. But if we dissolve the first scene into the second, no one is likely to jib at suddenly seeing the same figure in another place. For in this case we are no longer passive onlookers at a spectacle; we witness the visual intervention of the film-maker in the course of the story and he, the film-maker, invites us to participate in this intervention which changes the scene and causes time to pass.

It is in many ways of advantage to get rid of the necessity of parallel actions by this means. It simplifies the progress of the story, a necessity for modern psychological films which can thus concentrate more on the main action in which the leading hero is concerned.

Dissolve technique is appropriate where the director wishes his sequences to flow in a smooth, epic stream. If the story demands sudden dramatic stresses, cross-cutting and the parallel actions it involves will be more appropriate.

DISSOLVES AND THE LINKING OF SPACE

It has been already said that a dissolve between two shots always and inevitably produces the feeling of an essential connection between them. If two scenes are dissolved into one another, the figure which appears in both provides the visual link. In such cases it is advisable to make the figure visually striking, so that its surroundings can fade away from around it as something less material than the figure itself, which seems to change its surroundings as a man changes his coat.

A frequent well-tried device for achieving this is to show the figure in the foreground in sharp focus while the surrounding scenery slowly pales and the picture narrows around the figure, thus first lifting it out of space before the iris opens again on another scene.

Narcosis

In one of my own films, *Narcosis*, there was no cutting at all because the style of the film demanded the rhythm of shots softly blending into each other. When the hero in that film was about to go on a journey, we saw a close-up of his suitcase ready packed in his room. Then the picture narrowed to show only the suitcase, while the room vanished. The suitcase slowly began to vibrate. Then the diaphragm opens up again and the vibrating suitcase which had never for an instant been lost to our view, was vibrating in the luggage-net of a railway carriage. We were on a train in motion. The camera panned from the suitcase to the seats. Our hero was already sitting on one of them and travelling.

The heroine stood deserted and disconsolate in a street. The diaphragm narrowed to her hands, which were kneading a tear-soaked handkerchief. In a slow dissolve the handkerchief turned into a white rose. The hands remained the same. When the diaphragm opened a bit more we saw that the hands were tying roses into a bouquet and when it opened fully we saw a long-medium shot of the girl serving a customer in a florist's shop. Such dissolves show not merely two situations, but can convey the broad epic flow of a human life, a human destiny. One must, however, use this method sparingly, otherwise it easily degenerates into an idle, pointless formalism.

CHANGES OF SCENE WITHOUT MOVEMENT

The most frequent form of this type of dissolve is that the last shot of a scene is a close-up in which only a single face or hand or object remains in the frame, being thus lifted out of its space. This last shot of the scene is at the same time the first shot of the next scene, which emerges as the diaphragm is opened up. The object shown in the close-up has not moved and has remained before our eyes and the new surroundings appear behind it—behind the shot as it were. By this means such a change is experienced by the spectator in his own person. We see no physical movement, we see no locomotion of any kind and so the reality of time is absent from such changes which greatly increases the non-material character of the film.

This technique also stimulates the spectator's curiosity; he waits eagerly for the next surprise in store for him when the scene—in which he already knows the hero to be—opens to view; he can even see the reflection of the new surroundings in the hero's face, while the narrowed diaphragm still conceals it from him, the spectator.

In sound films, as already mentioned, this effect can be increased by letting the sounds connected with the new scene encroach upon the unchanged close-up of the old. We thus *hear* the new surroundings before we see them.

DISSOLVE AND MENTAL PICTURE

The technique of dissolve, which can change the scene and make time and space illusory, is eminently suitable for the presentation of the association of ideas and mental pictures in memory, in dreams or in imagination.

In *Narcosis*, the life of a girl is shown as seen by her in a dream under an anæsthetic. The reason for this device was to give the scenes and shots only the emotional reality they acquired in the experience of the girl herself, without having to show the many indifferent and unimportant details of life without which it is impossible to present everyday reality so as to be readily understood.

The heroine of *Narcosis* is a schoolgirl. One day she leaves the class. (All this she dreams under an anæsthetic.) She gets to her feet, leaves the form, the camera following. We see her all the time and behold, now she is in the street, although we did not see her open a door or walk down stairs. These passages could not be left out of a presentation of reality, although they are of no importance whatsoever. In *Narcosis* the surroundings change without interrupting the flow of action. We are in the street. The street is indicated only by a row of street lamps. A light is approaching from afar. The girl does not move. A brilliantly lit shop-window, that of a bookshop. The girl dissolves through the window and is inside the bookshop. The surroundings change without the girl changing her position—because in reality she does not change it, she is

dreaming it all. Now she is standing in front of a theatre book-
ing office. She wants to buy a ticket, cannot get one. In the
theatre foyer ladies and gentlemen walk past her. She turns to
go away, but takes only one step and is walking on snow,
another step and she is walking along between snow-covered
trees in a forest. We are seeing the girl all the time but how she
'really' got out of the theatre and to the forest and when—all
this we don't see. It is thus that we see space and time in our
dreams; one scene does not change into another scene at an
improbable speed, but in such a way that the various scenes
have no consistent local character at all. We may for instance
be in a room and yet be in a forest too, all at the same time.
Such things cannot be shown or presented either on the stage
or in literature as they can be in a film. Why then do we see
such spiritual film-stories so rarely in our films ?

PHOTOGRAPHED CURTAINS

All too frequently do we see another device. When a
director wants a change of scene but does not want to show
intermediate scenes, he often has a curtain of shadow, techni-
cally termed a 'wipe', drawn across the picture. In other words
he begins a new scene by means of a device borrowed from the
stage. This admission of impotence, this barbarian bit of lazi-
ness, is so contrary to the spirit of film art that the only thing
to be said in its defence is that it is nevertheless preferable to
a picture cut in without dramaturgical motivation.

PART II

CHAPTER THIRTEEN

PROBLEMS OF STYLE IN THE FILM

THE FIRST PART of this book dealt with the transformation of cinematography from a technique into an art, the transformation of a moving picture industry, which merely reproduced stage performances, into an autonomous, independent, utterly novel art-producer which in developing its own medium of expression, developed at the same time the new sensibility, the new visual culture required for an understanding of the new art. I attempted to define in it the laws governing the new form-language of film art, especially in the period of the brilliant development of the silent film: a theory of the picture-language which at that time was as yet soundless and colourless. I dealt with this section separately because much of the visual culture created in the last years of the silent film had been lost through subsequent technical developments and I believe that the memory of this once already achieved level of culture should be preserved against the time when a new turn in the destiny of the film may enable it to be resumed again in some new form.

We have recognized as the new methods of expression provided by the film:

the division of scenes into shots, i.e. pictures of detail;
the change of angle and set-up within the same scene;
the 'identification' between spectator and camera;
the close-up;
montage (editing, cutting).

This is not to say, of course, that film art has no other specific features, nor does it imply that the value of any filmic work of art is dependent solely on these points. It does mean, however, that every other element or content of any such work of art can manifest itself only within these basic visual and acoustic forms. Colour does not constitute the only possible value of a painting, but no such value can be manifested without recourse to colour—colour is the only medium in which it can be perceived in a painting.

The dialogue is not a specific feature of the talkie; it is a far older and more essential component of both the drama and the epic. But the basic forms of film art previously mentioned, determine other, specific, new laws according to which dialogue can be used in films, and which lend the film dialogue a new specific character and produce specific effects.

PURE CINEMATOGRAPHY

Years before the sound film was invented, the means of expression of the silent film had acquired such wealth and subtlety that a tendency had arisen which advocated the discarding of all other means of expression—notably the story—entirely. At that time artists in other spheres of art were also searching for and insisting on a 'pure' style. But nowhere did such demands appear as justified as in the sphere of filmic art.

We have seen that microphysiognomy and microdramaturgy, angle, set-up and cutting had acquired a creative force which could penetrate so deeply to the core of life, reproduce so vividly the raw material of reality, as to find sufficient expressive dramatic elements in it without a need for a constructive 'plot', a preliminary literary treatment, a story, a script.

This trend established the artistic principle that the camera ought not to illustrate novels or plays written in advance (even if specially written for the purposes of the given film) but should create its works of art by the direct approach of the camera to the raw material of life. It should seek its subjects not in epic or dramatic happenings but in simple visibility, in visual existence. Approximately the same postulate had a couple of decades before eliminated the 'theme' from painting.

It cannot be denied that this demand for a 'pure style' had some artistic justification in the sphere of the film and the followers of this trend undoubtedly enriched cinematic art by certain variants of style and form. Soon however this school, known in European cinematic art as *avantgardism*, developed into a separatist art-for-art's-sake toying with mere form and ceased to exercise the fructifying influence it had at one time possessed and which manifested itself, for instance, in inspiring and developing to an important art form in its own right such things as documentaries and 'films without a hero'. It was carried away by the undertow of the decadent formalism of an expressionism by now grown quite divorced from reality and it ended up in the blind alley of the 'subjectless' 'absolute film' style. The possibilities of the means now determined the ends, and the formal intentions the contents. This trend, consistently followed, leads to the final logical conclusion of a form giving itself its own content, of words devised to designate not things but merely other words; that is, to frustration and emptiness.

I intentionally devote more attention to these trends than would be justified by their prevalence; for the film industry of the world produced a very small percentage of *avantgardiste,* 'absolute' films and they in fact remained curiosities limited to the screens of Paris, London or Berlin, and were appreciated only by small coteries of specialists, theorists and intellectual snobs.

Nevertheless their importance should not be underrated. Firstly because they were extremely productive experimental stages in a process of artistic form-seeking. Secondly because the contemporary film directors, while not themselves inclined to make pure-style *avantgardiste* films, very often made use of novel forms evolved by those who did. The ultimate development of the silent film can scarcely be explained without pointing to *avantgardiste* influences in it. Many later very successful and popular directors passed through the *avantgardiste* school and carried the visual culture developed there into their commercially-produced films. It was precisely this visual training which enabled such directors to make their films so alluring and popular. An example of this is René Clair.

Another viewpoint must however also be emphasized here. This book is intended as an investigation of the form-giving laws governing a new art, not as a Baedeker-like classification and evaluation of works of art. What is important in the first place is not how perfect a work of art as a work of art may be, but how instructive it is from the point of view of determining the laws of the art. On this point it is to be said that the phenomena connected with the decadence of so-called decadent art very often throw a more penetrating light on the æsthetic and psychological laws governing artistic creation, than the inaccessibly smooth, unbroken surfaces of a perfect masterpiece might do. Metals and rocks are recognized most easily by the characteristics of their broken surfaces. The laws of chemistry remain valid in the processes of decomposition and putrefaction, and are indeed more easily discernible there than in a healthy organism. This is one of the reasons why, in searching for the deeper chemistry of art, we devote so much attention to certain phenomena described as decadent.

Finally it is well to remember what Alois Riegl found more than once in examining changes of style in the course of art history: that a certain phenomenon may be a symptom of decadence in the art of a certain age or class and at the same time be the first manifestation of the form-language of a new class or age. I myself believe that the method of idea-association developed by the *avantgardiste* film will not really play its fructifying part in film art until some future time, when the development of the sound film and talkie will have taken a new, genuinely filmic direction. The history of art may sometimes take a leaf out of the thrifty housewife's book and keep the left-overs to dish them up again in a new form.

The *avantgardiste* movement in the film began in France together with other movements tending to 'absolutize' other specific artistic forms. The other arts rebelled against the encroachment of literature on their sphere and in the end literature, too, followed suit. Everyone wanted to reproduce 'the phenomenon pure and simple' and no one was particularly interested in the reality that manifested itself in the phenomenon. This, too, was a hangover from the psychotic conditions following the first world war; it was one of the ways in which bourgeois consciousness sought to escape reality.

FILMS WITHOUT STORY OR HERO

Such escapism very often takes roundabout ways. The psychologists know this well enough. For instance the flight from preconstructed film stories claimed that its object was to get closer to reality. The photographic 'ascertainment' of the immediate reality of life, free of literary influences, seemed more realistic than the feature films with their intricate plots. In other words, one of the directions of the flight from the film story was towards reality.

But at the same time another no less strong trend developed in another direction. Here again there was a desire to escape from the literary, epic or dramatic content of the film but the way it chose was towards the abstract shapes and formal constructions of 'pure visuality', on the model of 'abstract' painting. Thus the film attempted to get away from epic or dramatic content in two opposite directions; on the one hand towards pure reportage and the documentary film, on the other hand towards absolute visuality, the kaleidoscope of optical impressions, the purely formal capers of the 'absolute' film.

FILM WITHOUT A HERO

The first step in all this was the film without a hero. It still had predetermined events, scenes arranged in advance and a certain connection between these. It also still had a story but the story was not bound up with the person of a central character and hence such films lacked the constructed dramatic conflict and plot which arises from the struggle of two or more persons.

The adherents of this trend did not want to string the characteristic events of life on the slender thread of a single human destiny. They wanted to show a broad cross-section of life, not merely the narrow slice of it which can be seen from the viewpoint of one person and compressed into the limits of a single human being's capacity. Life as such, typical life, and not the chance life of any one man, was to be presented. Such a film, it was thought, would not appear to be artificial, a mere invention of some script-writer; it would appear natural and logical. This was the theory.

I was one of the first to make such a film. The title was *The Adventures of a Ten-Mark Note*. It was produced for the European branch of Fox in Berlin, was directed by Berthold

Viertel and the cameraman was Karl Freund. The ostensible central hero was a ten-mark banknote, which as it passed from hand to hand, was the cause of all the adventures recorded in the film. The other characters changed in every scene. The events were in casual connection with each other but the human characters moved past each other as in a mist, unaware of each other and not even suspecting that their actions decided the fate of the others. The ten-mark banknote was the only thread that held the scenes together.

The scenes of such cross-section films are just as carefully thought out as the scenes of any strictly composed drama and their sequence and linkage is even more intricate, because more subtly constructed, than the most literary of novels. But the series of scenes of such a film have no predetermined direction, no dramatic culmination, no movement towards a definite end. They move tapestry-like in one and the same plane and their number could be increased or decreased at will. Such a composition doubtless has a certain naturalistic semblance of reality through the chance character of everything that happens, but it entirely lacks the convincing power of artistic necessity.

It is characteristic that I got the first inspiration for this 'non-literary' film from a well-known literary classic: Tolstoy's *The Forged Coupon*; a story in which a coupon passes from hand to hand like my ten-mark note.

It is not surprising that the best 'hero-less' films were made in the Soviet Union soon after the 1917 revolution, when the romantic conception of the spontaneously acting 'mass-soul' was still very much in vogue. Eisenstein's mighty *October* (or *Ten Days That Shook The World*) presented the uprising in Leningrad without making a central figure even out of Lenin; only masses were shown facing masses, although of course these masses were masterfully drawn, with individual characters and characteristic physiognomies.

The basic dangers inherent in this type of film are twofold. One is that as the character and specific quality of the masses is manifested not only in their external, visual appearance but even more in their behaviour and action, such films must inevitably also have something happening in them, and these happenings are often confused, accidental and never as clearly outlined as the fate of a single hero would be.

The other basic danger arose from this: the makers of such cross-section or mass-action films imagined that they could paint a monumental picture by having no central hero and thereby avoiding the fortuitousness of an individual destiny. The trouble was that if an artist renounces individualization, what he achieves is not something of universal validity; it is on the contrary, complete disintegration. Every consciously shaped thing has its own individual physiognomy, and it is only the smallest particles that are all alike. A stone on the hillside and the stone of one of Michelangelo's sculptures are both stones. As stones, their material is more or less the same. It is not the substance but the form that constitutes the difference between them. The artist who wants to show the raw material and not the form would do better to smash his work. But it is an old canon of art that the spirit and law of a material manifests itself most perfectly in the constructed forms of a work of art and not in the raw material.

The fable, the story, is like a human portrait; only in its artistic shaping, as a closed entity, does it become expressive and it is thus that it best gives expression to its material too. But if we want to present material without reference to form, such material will have no pattern, it will be no image. Only if we smash it, can a piece of furniture again merely be a piece of wood.

TRAVEL FILMS

Travel films have grown into an interesting and important form of film art. Here are artistic presentations of reality without literary theme and script, without literary mediation, directly achieved by the new, fully-developed artistic medium of cinematography. Here are pictures, not of invented travels, but of journeys actually made and nevertheless they are works of art. Here art lies not in invention but in discovery. In the immense jungle of experienced reality the artist must find what is most characteristic, most interesting, most plastic and expressive and brings out most vividly the tendency, the ideological intention which is consciously or unconsciously but inevitably contained in every film depicting reality.

The artistic composition of such films begins with the planning of the journey, and not with the grouping of shots already made, not with the cutting. Whoever makes a journey with the intention of describing it, be it in words or in pictures, must already have a preconception of his experiences. The same applies to those who write diaries. There is a curious transitional art form here, a form which lies between a mere recording of reality and the interpreting intentions of a film director. Such intentions are often unconscious or subconscious and provide opportunities for interesting psychological studies.

A tramp sees only what chance puts in his way. But a traveller has a definite aim, just as a good writer has. The journey determines the form of the film and the itinerary already lays down the cutting plan. The actual cutting of the strip ought merely to eliminate certain residual superfluities.

Is the news film a form of artistic creation? If it is to give an honest picture of reality, its first concern should be this and not art. But it soon became obvious that even a strictly scientific instructional film cannot be made without taking artistic points into consideration and making conscious use of artistic means of expression. For in order that out of the empirical fog of reality the truth—that is, the law and meaning of reality—may emerge through the interpretation of a seeing and experiencing maker, such a maker must bring into play every means of expression available to the art of the film.

INSTRUCTIONAL FILMS WHICH HAVE A HERO

Out of the transitional form last mentioned several interesting, valuable and popular kinds of film have developed. One of the most interesting of these is the documentary film which has a central figure, a hero. In such films we see not only the neutral things of reality but in their focal point a man whose everyday life and destiny they make up and it is this man who gives meaning and functional life to that reality. Such an 'enacted' instructional film shows reality with scientific completeness but nevertheless as experienced by a human being. By this means the film is not only rendered more vivid and interesting, but also often more true. For the realities of nature are given their deepest meaning for man if presented as a social experience; even the extra-social nature of the primeval forest or the arctic ice-pack is in the last instance a social experience; the very conception of solitude is a correlative conception and acquires intellectual and emotional content only if we are aware of its opposite, non-solitude.

The first such documentaries of the silent film, showing the realities of some part of the world in the form of a human fate were *Nanook of the North; Chang,*which gave a picture of the jungle;and *Moana,* a film of the South Pacific.

In *Chang* the struggle of a poor Indian family of settlers against the jungle develops into the fierce war of an Indian village against a herd of wild elephants. It is a documentary but it is a drama built up according to all the rules of æsthetics and dramaturgy. We find even a parallel to the chorus in the antique tragedy in the band of monkeys anxiously watching the battle between men and elephants from the tops of the coconut palms. The monkey watchers are cut into the film in the same way as clever directors cut the excited crowd of fans into a sports scene. This magnificent pantomimic chorus of monkeys accompanies the struggle of the humans and stresses its every phase.

There is not one 'invented' scene in *Chang.* But every scene is 'directed'. In the way in which the scholar's lecture and explanations are rendered convincing by visual means, the artistic intention is manifested on a par with the didactic. It is quite probable that tame elephants had to be trained to play with the proper natural ferocity the part of the wild elephants before the camera. Even reality is shown more convincingly by such acting.

Another transitional film form, even more closely related to the feature film than is the documentary, is the biographical film which has recently become popular. In these there are of course many romantic, constructed scenes just as there are in the not quite strictly scientific biographical novels. Fine films have for instance been made of the lives of Edison, Pasteur,

Mme Curie; the Russian Lenin and Gorky films also belong to this category. Here, although the decisive events are not invented, the individual scenes are of course directed or at best reconstructed. Nevertheless the authentic data of the actual life-story set a limit to literary inventions.

UNKNOWN PROXIMITY

The search for the literature-free 'pure film style' led directors not only to travel with their camera into unknown distances, but also to penetrate into a yet undiscovered and unknown nearness. The first such traveller who went on a voyage of discovery into proximity was the Russian Dziga Vertov. He called it *Ciné-Eye* and his idea was to peep with his camera at the little events of our workaday lives which we incessantly see and never notice. These molecules of life become significant if we isolate them in close-up and having isolated them, draw their outlines and by doing so give them form.

These little events are genuinely captured, not constructed, reality—they are as though they had been photographed through a keyhole. A child playing—a couple of lovers kissing—a cabby grumbling—an old man having forty winks on a park seat. They never knew that they were being 'shot'. The interest of these pictures lies in their authenticity. And very often they radiate a certain latent excitement through the knowledge that we are treading on forbidden ground, that we are peeping at something we were not meant to see. Such fragments of reality can then be collated into whatever 'truth' the director chooses to demonstrate by their means. Here the scissors play the poet in good earnest and say: 'Behold! This is life!'

These entirely authentic shots of actual reality are the most subjective of all. They have no story but they do have a central figure, a hero. This hero is invisible because he is the one who sees it all out of his 'ciné-eye.' But everything he sees expresses his own personality, however unconstructed the reality in his shots may appear. It is he who is characterized and reflected in the shots which he took in preference to some other fragments of reality. Only his own subjective feeling determined the choice, the sequence, the cutting rhythm of the things he shows us. He is an artist who seems to yield himself up to objective impressions without looking for a link between them. But he himself supplies the link and his subjective self is the constructive principle on which the film is built. However faithfully he has taken his photographs, they are a deliberate selection, a selected world and this world is his own. Such 'factual' films are the most subjective of all films. They will form the most significant, the richest, the most filmic art form of that lyrical film-poetry which is yet to be born.

NEWS FILMS

We are accustomed to see them at the beginning of film shows, just before the main feature comes on. To all appearances they are an innocent form of pictorial reporting. In fact they are the most dangerous instruments of propaganda. They are not put together by poetic, artistic subjectivity, as are the reality fragments of the 'ciné-eye'—they express the intentions of the interests and power groups who pay for them. They lie even more boldly than the lying, distorting newspapers, for they appear to be objective and authentic photographic records, a sort of pictorial diary of the age. They are really interesting and instructive only if we have the opportunity of seeing side by side, or rather face to face, news films made of the same events by groups hostile to one another. They show no similarity at all, although they purport to show the same things and what is truly characteristic of them and expressive in them is what they do *not* show.

One need only edit them a little, however, and they are completely transformed. Before Hitler's seizure of power, but when the Weimar republic was already on its last legs, a workers' film society was formed in Berlin. It arranged film shows and would have shown news-reels of its own, but the censorship banned them. So they bought old UFA news-reels, which had long finished their run and had been approved by the censorship in their time. From these we cut new reels. For instance, in the 'Dogs' beauty contest', overwhelmingly glamorous ladies held expensive lap-dogs in their arms. Next to this was 'One who did not take part in the contest': a blind beggar and his 'seeing eye' dog, watching over his miserable master in the cold of winter. Then 'St Moritz': Skating rinks and the guests on the terrace of a luxury hotel. 'This, too, is St Moritz': a melancholy procession of ragged, hungry snow-shovellers and rink-sweepers. 'Brilliant military parade' followed by 'Disabled ex-servicemen begging in the streets'. There were no other captions. The police were itching to ban these news-reels but could not do so, as they were all respectable UFA news-reels, every one of them approved by the censorship. Only the order of showing had been altered a little.

Single pictures are mere reality. Only the montage turns them into either truths or falsehoods. Herein lies the immense responsibility devolving on the news-reels. Their convincing power is in the fact that the spectator feels that he is an eye-witness. The shot is accepted as a fact, a presentation of conclusive proof, although of course it is not by accident that the camera comes to a halt in front of one particular object and not of another.

EPICS OF LABOUR

If there are films which deserve the appellation of 'cultural' films, they are those film memorials to human effort, proclaiming the glory of human labour, toil which at the cost of skill and sweat is labouring to make this earth a garden. I want to mention first of all one of the finest examples of this kind of documentary: Turin's *Turksib*. All that this film shows is the building of a railway from Siberia to Turkestan. Many railways have been built before this, longer railways, railways involving more arduous technical tasks. And yet this film was such an outstanding success and exercised such an inspiring, onward-urging influence, that few feature films could be found to rival it. For the great human significance of this piece of Soviet construction was expressed by a Soviet director in a passionate and monumental pictorial epic, the appeal of which was irresistible far beyond the borders of the Soviet Union.

The building of the first railway ever to link Siberia with Turkestan is shown in this film with a dramatic tension and passionate ardour rarely matched by any feature film. First we are shown the sense and necessity of the railway by a demonstration of the mutual economic interdependence of the populations of the two regions. They cannot live while a track-less desert separates them from each other. The people suffer in the north, they suffer in the south. The murderous sand-storms of the desert destroy the caravans. These sequences are like distress signals. They show the building of the railway as a life-saving operation. This is no longer a railway, it is the very life of two peoples. The spectator watches the progress of the work with sympathy and anxiety.

Now the film shows the obstacles and difficulties. In the north a frost of 42 degrees centigrade beneath zero. In the south the parching desert. Invincible obstacles. The greatest of them the obstinate resistance of the ignorant, backward desert nomads. First this must be overcome. As in an ancient epic, human determination enters into a mythical duel with the terrifying forces of nature. Every shot is set up as a battle, every scene is directed as a struggle. The struggle is hard, per-sistent, resolute—it is fought for the good of men. This is why the film has such an irresistible appeal, this is why its end is such a triumphant apotheosis, although all it really is is just a modest be-garlanded engine puffing along a single-track road. But there are people standing along the track, waving, smil-ing, dancing, weeping for joy and exuberantly galloping on horseback, donkeyback, camelback, bullockback to race the steam engine that is bringing a new age to Siberia and Turkestan.

This film was made during the building of the railway. In the last shot the date of the planned completion of the scheme appeared in the smoke of the engine: 1930. Turksib was to be finished in 1930.

But in 1930, when I edited this film for European audiences, I had to change the date in this shot to 1929. For the railway had been completed six months before and was in operation by 1930. How did this happen?

The film, which was shot in 1928, was of course shown first of all to an audience of Turksib railway workers who having seen the importance of their own work, were so enthused that they undertook to complete Turksib six months ahead of schedule. They kept their word. Thus it happened that the dialectic interaction of life and art was palpably manifested in the story of this film. *Turksib* was a documentary and in it the reality of building was turned into art. Then when the effect of the film was to speed up building, i.e. to influence reality, art again was transformed into reality. This new reality is on the other hand again a subject for art and new works of art will again influence it. Thus life and art run parallel, inspiring, urging, directing each other's efforts.

Another splendid film is *Zuiderzee* by Joris Ivens. Men reconquer land from the sea. An invisible force is made visible in this film: the directing intelligence of man, just as an invisible wind is made visible by the bending of tree-tops.

SHOWING MAN

Thus can the documentary film fulfil its great vocation as the pictorial chronicle of mankind. For everything that happens, happens in the last resort to men and through men. You want to show a great civilization, great technical progress? Show them in the men who work; show their faces, their eyes, and then we shall be able to tell what that civilization means and what it is worth. You want to show the harvest of the fields? Only the ploughman's face will lend expression to the face of the earth. This is the decisive document among all documentary pictures. The tragedies of ocean storms can only become live experience through the microdrama of the sailors' faces.

WAR FILMS

The value and significance of documentary films will naturally depend in the first place on what sort of a reality it is which they reveal. But this book deals not with reality—its subject is the cinematic presentation of reality and therefore, however sensational the theme of a film may be, it will be discussed here only if it demonstrates the specific possibilities of the film medium. The newsreels relating to the war also interest us only inasmuch as they show something that could be shown by no other medium save the film. What concerns us here are not open-air photographs of thousands of guns, flying armadas or bursting bombs and shells but what is at the root of it all, the human face, which only the film camera can approach so intimately.

In general war-films are as primitive and brutal as is war itself. For this reason only one war film is to be mentioned here. Its artistic and moral message is such that it is worthy of being preserved for ever in some Pantheon of greatest human documents.

This film was made after the first world war and its title was *Pour la Paix du Monde*. It was produced by the French organization of the most grievously injured of all war-wounded, the name of which was 'Les Gueules Cassées'. The director who compiled the film from the strips in the archives of the armed forces was Colonel Piquard, chairman of the organisation of the 'Faceless Ones', the men who lived like lepers in an isolated, secret community of their own, because the sight of them would have been unbearable for their fellow-men. The film begins by showing these faceless ones in close-up, their mutilations covered by masks. Then they take off their silken masks and with it they tear the mask off the face of war.

Those whom the war has robbed of their faces show the true face of war to those who know nothing of it. And this physiognomy of war is of an emotional power, a force of pathos no artistic feature film about the war had ever attained. For here war is presented by its victims, horror is presented by the horrified, torture by the tortured, deadly peril by those endangered—and it is they who see these things in their true colours.

A panning shot glides over a quiet, a now quietened battle-field. The desolation of a lunar landscape. Nowhere a single blade of grass. On the mountainside gunfire has peeled the earth from the naked rock. Shell craters, trenches without end. The camera pans slowly round without stopping. Trenches full of dead bodies, more trenches and more and more and more. An immense space in which nothing moves. Corpses, corpses, only corpses. Panorama. This stolid monotony which takes hold of you and will not let go is like a long-drawn, desperate howling.

Here is another shot: a whole regiment blinded by poison gas is being driven through the streets of burning Bruges. Yes, the herd of blind men is being driven like a herd of sheep, herded with bayonet and butt to keep them from running into the burning ruins in their path. A picture for another Dante.

But there are worse things, although no human beings appear. The gardens of the Champagne after the German retreat. (It was not in the second world war that the Germans invented some of their methods.) We see a charnel-house of an ancient and lovely orchard culture. Thousands of precious, noble fruit trees neatly sawed off by power-saw, all exactly at the same height. The creation of centuries of skill and industry destroyed with machine-like accuracy. These pictures, too, have a physiognomy; the distorted faces of the tree-corpses are no less terrible than those of the human dead. But the caption to this, of course silent, shot was not: 'Behold the German barbarian!' It said 'C'est la guerre!' The noble faith of French peace-lovers did not blame the Germans even here, it blamed war. Nevertheless under the Weimar Republic the showing of this film was banned in Germany.

This French documentary of the first world war was dedicated to the six cameramen who had been killed on active service while shooting it. The Soviet war film showing the conquest of Berlin names in its credits fourteen cameramen killed while shooting it. This fate of the creative artist is also a new phenomenon in cultural history and is specific to film art. Artists in olden days rarely died of their dangerous creative work. And this has not merely a moral or political significance, but is of importance for the psychology of art as well.

This presentation of reality by means of motion pictures differs essentially from all other modes of presentation in that the reality being presented is not yet completed; it is itself still in the making while the presentation is being prepared. The creative artist does not need to dip into his memory and recall what has happened—he is present at the happening itself and participates in it.

When someone tells about past battles, these battles are already over and the greatest perils are no longer perils, once they are past and can be told by word of mouth or print.

The camera image is different. It is not made after the event. The cameraman is himself in the dangerous situation we see in his shot and it is by no means certain that he will survive the birth of his picture. Until the strip has been run to its end we cannot know whether it will be completed at all. It is this tangible being-present that gives the documentary the peculiar tension no other art can produce.

Whoever has listened to a report given over a field telephone, when the noise of battle, the rattle of shots and the screams of the wounded can be heard together with the words spoken into the microphone, will have experienced this tension in the acoustic sphere. Such telephone reports sometimes break off in the middle of a sentence and the silence that follows is as eloquent as a scream of mortal agony.

In the French war film just discussed, a sequence suddenly breaks off. It darkens and the camera wobbles. It is like an eye glazing in death. The director did not cut out this 'spoilt' bit—it shows where the camera was overturned and the cameraman killed, while the automatic mechanism ran on. In another picture we see the cameraman dying for the sake of his picture.

The significance of such shots lies not in the death-despising courage to which they bear witness. We have often heard of men who could look death in the eye. We may even have seen them. What is new and different here is that these cameramen look death in the face through the lens of a movie picture camera. This happens not only on battlefields.

Who could forget Captain Scott's film, which is almost as if he had shot his own death and breathed his last sigh into a microphone?

Who could forget Sir Ernest Shackleton's magnificent pictures of his Antarctic journey or the film taken by the Soviet Polar explorers camping beside the wreck of the ice-breaker *Chelyuskin?*

Yes, it is a new form of human consciousness that was born out of the union of man and camera. For as long as these men do not lose consciousness, their eye looks through the lens and reports and renders conscious their situation. The ice crushes their ship and with it their last hope? They shoot. The ice-floe melts under their feet? They shoot. They shoot the fact that there is scarcely room left for them to set up the camera.

Like the captain on his bridge, like the wireless operator at his set, the cameraman remains at his post to the last instant. The internal processes of presence of mind and observation are here projected outwards into the bodily action of operating the camera. The operator sees clearly and calmly as long as he is shooting in this way; it is this that helps him mechanically to preserve his consciousness, which in other circumstances consists of a sequence of images in the mind. But now it is projected outwards and runs in the camera as a strip of film, which is of advantage because the camera has no nerves and therefore is not easily perturbed. The psychological process is inverted—the cameraman does not shoot as long as he is conscious—he is conscious as long as he is shooting.

NATURE FILMS

When a film depicts human actions, it can always be confronted with a constructed or imagined or stage-managed scene. If pictures of actual happenings are shown on the screen, the spectators must be informed of this in advance if they are to accept them as such; for in pictures depicting human beings there is nothing that could serve as authentic proof of the fact that what is seen on the screen is not a picture of some artificially stage-managed scene. The technique of the film can make such constructed, stage-managed artificial pictures so deceivingly like reality that a picture of the most objective reality offers no guarantees of not having been staged in a studio.

Only pictures of nature without men bear the convincing stamp of unquestionable, authentic reality. Plants and animals do not pose or act in front of the camera, not even trained animals.

Strangely enough these absolutely authentic nature films often appear quite fantastic. Nothing could be more like fairy tales than the scientific films which show the growth of crystals or the wars of infusoria living in a drop of water. The explanation of this is that precisely their authentic reality makes the spectator feel most vividly their distance between them and the human sphere. For the farther away the existence presented in the film is from the possibility of human interference, the less is the possibility of its being artificial, faked, stage-managed. Hence the curious similarity of atmosphere between pictures of inaccessible nature and inaccessible fairyland. For although what we see is a natural phenomenon, the fact that we can see it at all strikes us as unnatural. That we can witness at closest quarters the love idylls of hedgehogs or submarine fishes or the horror thriller of a battle between two snakes, is as exciting as the eating of forbidden fruit has ever been. In watching such things we feel as if we had entered a territory closed to man. If we are shown something that human beings cannot see in normal circumstances, then, as we nevertheless see it, we have the feeling of being invisible ourselves; hence the fantastic atmosphere of such nature pictures.

CHAPTER FOURTEEN

FORMALISM OF THE AVANT-GARDE

THE LAST CHAPTER, which dealt with the attempts of the film to emancipate itself from literary content, from the story, began with the statement that this escape from the invented literary story developed in two opposite directions: towards the presentation of naked facts and the presentation of pure phenomena. On the one hand the intention was to show objects without form, on the other to show form without objects. This tendency led on the one hand to the cult of the documentary film and on the other to toying with objectless forms.

Let us consider now the play of visual forms without literary content. This trend elected to make the mere phenomenon, the bare spectacle, its sole content, even when in the beginning it screened moving still-lives, mere visual impressions which were not intended to signify anything beyond their own selves and which did not propose to convey any new reality to the spectator.

We have already shown to what extent the most objective presentation of reality in documentary films is subjective and dependent on the individual mood, philosophy and ideological intentions of its maker. We have shown how the reality of the documentary film can be made a truth or a lie at will.

But the *avantgardistes* in their films very often do not show even reality in such a way that some truth, some meaning or some law can be detected in it. Pictures of visual phenomena torn from all context no longer contain any reality at all. If we see clouds drifting and flowers nodding in the wind, does this tell us anything about the reality of wind? It tells us nothing. Hence this way of presenting reality, completely with-

out any literary constructions, in fact achieves the polar opposite of what it intends. It is not more real than any fairy-tale,
because in it bare reality is turned into pure phenomenon and
is diluted into a mere impression. Films presenting bare facts
come by inexorable logic to be the most unreal, the most
abstract of 'absolute' films. For any object by itself alone is
always a withdrawal from reality, because without explanatory
references to one another the things of reality are not real,
things being not only themselves but at the same time links in
chains of events and causalities.

There have been such masterly reality-films as Basset's
Market on the Wittenbergplatz. We saw lots of reality. The
setting-up of booths. Piles of fruit baskets. People buying and
selling. Animals, flowers, goods, garbage. The single pictures
have neither meaning, nor reference, nor actuality. They are a
spectacle of mere existence. An old woman combs her hair. A
horse dips his muzzle in a bucket of water. A wet bunch of
grapes gleams in the sunlight. We are pleased to recognize
familiar things, to be able to say 'Yes, that's just what it looks
like!' But this picture of a market is still the picture of something objectively given, the presentation of some reality existing in time and space, a reality which has its own independent
being outside the picture. Our impression is that the film has
merely shown us certain existing things. The picture has not
absorbed the object.

ABSOLUTE FILM

The Dutch film-maker Joris Ivens, one of the greatest
artists of pictorial poetry, no longer wanted to show objective
realities to the spectator. His famous impressionist films *Rain*
and *The Bridge* do not represent either objects or facts which
we might have possibly seen in their actual being. The spectator might in principle himself go to the Wittenbergplatz
market and see there everything Basset photographed, even
though possibly in less attractive form. But the rain-pictures
of Ivens could not be seen by anyone else in any rain; at most
he could recognize them after seeing the Ivens pictures and
after his eyes had been sufficiently trained by them. Ivens'

moods and impressions dematerialize their theme. Who could find the atmosphere of Claude Monet's paintings in actual nature? They do not exist outside those paintings, outside the experience which Monet painted into his work. Nor can one imagine behind Ivens' film-pictures objects that exist independently of these pictures. This is the 'absolute' film.

The rain we see in the Ivens film is not one particular rain which fell somewhere, some time. These visual impressions are not bound into unity by any conception of time and space. With subtle sensitivity he has captured, not what rain really is, but what it looks like when a soft spring rain drips off leaves, the surface of a pond gets goose-flesh from the rain, a solitary raindrop hesitatingly gropes its way down a window-pane, or the wet pavement reflects the life of a city. We get a hundred visual impressions, but never the things themselves; nor do these interest us in such films. All we want to see are the individual, intimate, surprising optical effects. Not the things but these their pictures constitute our experience and we do not think of any objects outside the impression. There are in fact no concrete objects behind such pictures, which are images, not reproductions.

Even when Ivens shows a bridge and tells us that it is the great railway bridge at Rotterdam, the huge iron structure dissolves into an immaterial picture of a hundred angles. The mere fact that one can see this one Rotterdam bridge on such a multitude of pictures almost robs it of its reality. It seems not a utilitarian bit of engineering but a series of strange optical effects, visual variations on a theme, and one can scarcely believe that a goods train could possibly pass over it. Every set-up has a different physiognomy, a different character, but none of them have anything whatever to do with either the purpose of the bridge or its architectural qualities.

This style of the 'absolute' is obviously the result of an extreme subjectivism which is undoubtedly a form of ideological escapism characteristic of decadent artistic cultures. This, however, may be admissible as a statement in the sphere of cultural history but it is certainly not a statement relating to æsthetic values.

EPISTEMOLOGY OF AESTHETICS

It is high time that an epistemology of the work of art be created. Up to now æsthetics have done very little in the direction of ascertaining how great is the share of object and of presentation respectively in the birth of a work of art. The result of such an investigation is surprising enough. It appears that it is precisely the single object, or existence quiescent in its own self, which is absorbed easily and without residue in the presented picture and transformed into an absolute visual phenomenon. For in every sequence of events there is something transcending the picture, something which does not entirely transform itself into visual presentation. This something is causality. We can see each phase of every happening as a separate entity, but that one of them causes the other is something we can only *know*, something that can never appear in the shot as a visual picture. An isolated object complete in itself, which is neither cause nor effect but merely a spectacle— such an object is divorced from time and space, as it is cut off from the chain of causality. It no longer belongs to any of the Kantian categories as an object, only as a picture. And that picture may be a spectacle or a vision and it is almost a matter of indifference which of the two it is. Here we have the immaterial theme of the absolute film.

APPEARANCE OF THE OUTER WORLD

Such impressions as Basset or Ivens put on the screen are no longer presentations of some concrete reality; but they nevertheless have real existence as visual impressions. They are mere spectacles, but they can often be seen in the external world. A mirage is only a delusion, but as such it can naturally be seen. Such visual impressions are not like the visions of a dream nor like the images evoked in the memory, which subconsciously blend into each other as figments of the mind. The pictures of Ivens are only pictures, but Ivens has seen them, some one else might have seen them too and they were optical phenomena susceptible of being photographed.

INTERNAL AFFAIRS

Walter Ruttmann's film *Berlin* is quite a different story. It does not present really visible spectacles. In it the definite shape of the pictures dissolves, and flickering, merging, blurred shapes and outlines project an inner vision out on to the screen.

Tramcars and jazz-bands, milk-floats and female legs, jostling street crowds and whirling wheels rise out of the fog of the subconscious like images seen in a half-sleep. Here the emphasis is no longer on the single self-contained spectacle, but on the total impression given by the fluctuating montage of the whole. The camera has turned inward as it were and its purpose is no longer to perpetuate an impression of the external world but project outward its reflection in the consciousness. This is no longer impressionism, it is expressionism. The impressionists, however subjectively ethereal they may have been, always wanted to reproduce faithfully the impressions they had actually received from reality. The expressionists want to project outwards the internal landscapes of the soul. Ruttmann's film could scarcely be used to guide a stranger arriving in Berlin for the first time. It summarizes far more the memories and residual moods of a traveller leaving that city. If nevertheless the film contains a characterization of the city, it is not in the shots themselves, but through their montage and rhythm.

Karl Grune was the first to show in his film *The Street*, the picture of a city as it is reflected in the inner vision of a young man thirsting for life. In the film *Shadows of Yoshiwara* someone goes blind and in the last flash of sight sees the colourful bustle of a festival. These pictures flow on to the screen without outline or shape, like the blood out of the injured eye.

This method of presentation, first used by the absolute film, was developed to a high degree of expressive power in the dream-pictures in certain artistic feature films, where they were equally not intended to reproduce realities. The absolute film approached human psychology not only in its bodily manifestations, for instance in facial expressions, but attempted to project inner conceptions of the mind directly on to the screen. Of course photographing such things is not a simple matter. They must first be conceived by the maker of the film with sufficient clarity to enable him to set it up before the camera as a 'shootable' object.

The absolute film had, however, no intention of permitting itself to be used merely as a method enabling otherwise realistic feature films to reproduce images of the soul—it had the ambition of becoming an independent variety of film art. It wanted to reproduce, not the soul in the world, but the world in the soul. Not the soul as it appeared on the surface of bodily reality in the shape of gesture, grimace, word or action, in a foreign medium, as an imperfect translation as it were; on the contrary, it strove to show introspectively the images of the outer world as reflected in the soul. Not the soul in the face but the face of the soul. And if the documentary, reality-bound films had no need for invented literary stories, neither had these mental documentaries of an internal reality.

Cavalcanti's *Montmartre*, the lovely floating landscapes of Man Ray, Renoir, Cocteau and the other *avantgardistes* were like visions seen with closed eyes. No reality, neither space nor time nor causality, were valid here any longer. The mental processes represented in the absolute film knew only one law: that of the association of ideas and it is these it cut and edited and linked together.

CONCEPTUAL FILMS

Hans Richter's *Inflation* is like a vision in a nightmare. Piles of banknotes, towers of cyphers, the empty shelves of shops, hungry and frightened faces, a panic on the stock exchange, a drunken debauch, a suicide, ticker-tape and money, money, money, are crammed topsy-turvy one on top of the other and in the turmoil of its montage there is no continuous happening, there are no scenes taking place in front of the camera, not even psychologically concrete states of mind. Internal images are here integrated into concepts, into thoughts.

Nevertheless even this film has a theme. It deals with something that exists outside the film: with the inflation in Berlin, even though the link between the shots is purely psychological, not anchored in space or time or causality.

LOGIC IS THE MEANS, PSYCHOLOGY THE END

Logic is often the vehicle for the construction of a work of art but never the theme to be presented. Logic is the scaffolding in the creation of the work, never the end in itself.

But in its psychological presentation the work also presents psychology itself. We are not only interested in what is happening in the course of a story, but even more in why and how it happens, in the psychological background of it. We are interested in the internal process of the association of ideas which led to the action. Such internal action, such internal happenings are often more important that the external.

The film can convey such associations of ideas more completely than the verbal arts, because words are loaded with too many conceptual elements, while a picture is a purely non-rational image. A sequence of such pictures needs no connecting tissue of words. But if parallel to the sequence of irrational internal images and simultaneously with it we could *hear* rational and conscious words in counterpoint; if we had two independent manifestations running concurrently side by side, the film could be given a dimension of depth which would greatly increase its possibilities. In this I see the great chance of a new third period in the evolution of the film. That is why so much attention has been devoted here to problems of the absolute film.

SURREALIST FILMS

The surrealist films of the *avantgardistes* wanted to depict internal moods and states of mind by means of a sort of pictorial hallucination. Epstein's exciting film *The Fall of the House of Usher* depicts—what? Not Edgar Allan Poe's tale, but only the haunting atmosphere of it and the moods and associations awakened in its readers. Halls without lines, uncertain flights of steps, dark and endless corridors, in which tragic shadows wander aimlessly. Doors open, curtains billow, hands stretch out, veils float on misty waters. These are not intelligible illustrations to a story, but the confused associations aroused by the dark impressions of a sinister tale.

The films of Man Ray bring to the surface the associated picture-series of a psycho-analytical examination. They not only depict the process involved in the association of ideas, but provoke it, touch it off. The film is continued in the mind of the spectator, receiving only an initial directional impulse from the pictures seen on the screen.

This kind of surrealism is a heightened form of subjectivism. The present fashionable trend of existentialism is merely a nuance of this. Artists frightened or weary of reality stick their heads into their own selves like a hunted ostrich into the sand. All these things are undoubtedly symptoms of decadence in a degenerating culture. This in itself is, however, again merely a statement of fact, not of æsthetic evaluation.

Such a classifying definition by no means circumscribes all the possibilities of a highly developed and subtle artistic method. For instance it was in vain that the æsthetes of musical theory said of atonal dissonances that they were symptoms of bourgeois decadence; they nevertheless served Béla Bartók as instruments of a new, vigorously youthful art. New palaces have often been built out of the stones of old ruins. The artistic sensibility and rich form-creating resourcefulness of the decadent French *avantgardistes* will in time serve well the new spirit and new soul of a new art. Now, in the third era of film art, in which the sound film will be enriched by the resurrected achievements of the once already so highly differentiated silent film, we shall be able to benefit much by the study of the absolute and surrealist films of the *avantgardistes*. This is why so much space was devoted to these problems here.

ABSTRACT FILM

The striving for a 'pure style' finally purged the film of every vestige of life, just as logic carried to its final conclusions makes nonsense of all human thinking. Eggeling, a Swedish painter, invented the abstract film as long ago as 1917. Abstract shapes, circles, squares, waves, gratings, moving and changing outlines dissolved into each other, no longer depicting any object existing in reality and not resembling any natural object. They existed in themselves and for themselves and if they signified anything at all, they signified only themselves.

What we saw were not the forms of life, but the liberated life of shapes, the dance, the rhythm, the mobile ornamentality of lines, planes and solids. Such a dance of shapes, which its adherents like to call visual music, could easily be linked with musical rhythms. There was no clash with the resistance of the laws of living reality, if circles and squares were made to move in perfect time with the rhythm of some piece of music.

They were the creatures of the director and he could do what he liked with them. This great ease, and especially the utterly complete, residueless, precise solutions it permitted, would in themselves have sufficed to destroy all artistic credit of such a playing with form. There was nothing here of the redemption of the chaotic material of life by forcing it into shape at the cost of a struggle, as a result of which even the most perfect form still retains a little of the raw tang of life.

SOUND ABSTRACTION

The making of abstract sound films was an obvious development. Schiffer, a Viennese, very cleverly accompanied the rhythms of Strauss with a dance of lines. It was a sort of cartoon-technique choreography and really convincing. It often brought out, and by its visual emphasis rendered more audible, the subtler, less obvious nuances of the music.

If we apply the viewpoints of our æsthetic epistemology to this art form, we find that it is not as objectless as was the silent abstract film. Its object is the music, the tonal lines of which it depicts with its graphic choreography, just as the movements and gestures of a dancer express and render visual a piece of music. It is a moving ornament which may be of great æsthetic value. Why should there not be such a form of film art? Many film-goers would derive great enjoyment from it.

FILM SUB-TITLES

Effects of the abstract film were in fact used from the inception of the silent film, in the titles. The film-makers soon discovered that the emotional effect produced by emphasis in the spoken word, can be indicated in the written word by the shape and weight of the lettering. Those who remember the titling of silent films may also remember that excitement, tension, weariness, despair or passion were made visible in the forms of lettering, in the expressive black-and-white of the titles. In the days of the silent film a special, much appreciated and well-remunerated art had developed in this field. The writers of titles were important members of a film outfit and the part played by their pen or brush was similar to that of a good announcer or narrator on the wireless at the present time. It was an accepted convention, for instance, that alerting alarm-signals rushed at us from the screen with tousled letters rapidly increasing in size. They seemed to throw themselves on us, attacking our eye as a shout assaults our ear. At other times a slowly darkening title signified a pause full of meaning or a melancholy musing. Some titles were like a dash after a sentence instead of a full stop. In the last years of the silent film no better-class film was satisfied with neutral, cold letterpress or script for its titles. The physiognomy of the pictures had to be continued in the physiognomy of the lettering, in order to preserve the visual continuity of atmosphere. This was already a kind of abstract film, because it depicted not objects but emotions. It did not photograph or draw recognizable, external things but expressed moods directly without the intervention of object images.

FALSE ANALOGY

For the sake of the completeness of epistemological analysis it is to be mentioned that the theoreticians who described this sort of abstract art as 'visual music' merely because it is not a presentation but a direct expression of emotion, were quite mistaken.

They were mistaken, because 'abstract' is a correlative concept. It has meaning and content only when contrasted with the concrete from which it is an abstraction. For instance: the apple is spherical. The abstraction of this natural shape is a circle. But of what natural shape is music the abstraction?

Nor is it an abstraction of natural noises, for those are of an entirely heterogeneous order. The circle is the abstract form of a spherical apple. But of what existing thing is music an abstraction?

A tune is no more abstract than is an expressive gesture of the limbs. It is an expressive gesture in sound. It is no more abstract than is architecture. The tones of the scale provide the concrete material out of which musical constructions are built.

Music has its abstraction though—the written music, the score. This abstract, merely visible and thinkable music, shows that there is a corresponding concrete, i.e. audible music.

Abstract symbols have another remarkable quality which should be mentioned here. Even a miniature of Mount Everest or of the ocean can convey the immensity of these objects. That is a matter for the inherent monumentality of the presentation. But abstract forms cannot possess such inherent monumentality, they cannot convey dimensions greater than their own. A circle or a triangle conveys an impression of its own actual size only, and not of any greater. For if a picture depicts something, the depicted object may be a thousand times larger than the picture itself. If it depicts nothing, just exists, then the picture can show only itself, its own size.

CHAPTER FIFTEEN

OPTICAL TRICKS, COMPOSITES, CARTOONS

IT HAS ALREADY been mentioned that the camera possesses many technical means of injecting the cameraman's subjective viewpoint and mood into the picture of the object. Fades, dissolves, slow-motion, time-lapse, soft-focus, distortion, double-exposure and many others—these camera effects can express many things but they do not depict some phenomena of reality. They are visual indications of the thoughts and emotions of the film-maker and hence they can be classed as 'absolute' film effects.

SIGNIFICANCE OF CAMERA TRICKS

For this reason the same optical trick can mean a great variety of different things. For instance the picture of a man on the screen might dissolve into a tree. This might be a scene in a fairy-tale, and in that case it would mean a miracle, or rather a piece of magic. But such dissolves are often used in the film to mark a simple change of location. Just now we have seen a man in a room and the next minute the story is continued in a forest. In such cases the dissolve means that a deeper connection is suggested between the two objects: man and tree. But if I see a man-into-tree dissolve in a dream sequence or a sequence indicating a train of associations, then I regard it only as a presentation of an associative process. Fourthly such a dissolve may be merely a form of joke and nothing else.

In the first case, that of magic, the change-over is a real happening, only it is real in a fairy-tale sense, not a natural sense. In the second case, when the dissolve is intended to convey a

185

mental process, a subconscious association of ideas, the change-over is a natural process, but not an objectively real happening. If again—this is the third case—we see such a dissolve in a realistic film, then it does not depict either a fairy-tale happening or a mental process, but just means some connection between the two objects, i.e. has a definite meaning. Finally in the fourth case, the burlesque, it indicates the exact opposite of the previous: it is absurd, nonsensical.

Every optical trick can have many meanings. Which of the many possible meanings adheres to it depends on the connection into which the strip binds it. It is always the whole which imparts a definite meaning to the details. Out of the potentially-fraught possibilities of the latent meanings in a single shot, the neighbouring shots select the one or the other. Only in editing is the shot given its definite final meaning.

MASKS

However greatly a mirror may distort a face, such distortion still remains a natural phenomenon, because it arises in accordance with known optical laws. This is true even if the distorting mirror be called 'the soul'.

But a mask is not a distorted face. It is not confronted with a supposed normal face, the face which we still see (even if in a changed form), in the distorted version. A mask does not presuppose two forms and between them a difference which expresses the tension that was the cause of the transformation of the one form into the other. A bent stick may depict the action of some force—a drawing of a semicircle cannot do this.

Puppets and silhouettes as objects for the camera are already works of art in their own right—it is not the camera that makes them so. In most cases the camera merely reproduces them—I say 'in most cases', because the camera may of course increase a hundredfold the expression carved into the puppet's face. But silhouettes or drawings cannot be developed any further by means of camera angle or set-up. In these the film is merely a technique of moving and showing what is there, although the rhythm of cutting may be more perfect than the technique of a real puppet-show would permit.

Such films do not give form to life—they give life to forms.

Good visual stories in which the characters are dolls or drawings are not 'literary', because the story does not begin with the invention of a plot but with the devising of the shapes of the visual beings who are to act in it. Their appearance already tells a story. The fairy-tale quality of such films is determined in the first instance by what the characters look like, not what they do. Visual imagination is what inspires and weaves these stories. The visual fairy-tale world which they open to us is in the main a world of shapes different from those in our own world. Here are not miracles enacted in our world, miracles which infringe the laws of our own world. Rather we are given a glimpse of another world, a world in which other laws run and other shapes are normal, a closed world in which everything happens according to rule, only that the rules are not the same as in our world.

For this reason such puppet stories must develop logically from the shape and nature of the actors. It would be out of keeping to make dolls play human parts. Dolls have the fate of dolls: if the china shepherdess tumbles off the mantelpiece, she must break to pieces and the leg of the lead soldier must melt if it falls into the fire. This is what makes such a story conform to its material.

The same applies to silhouettes. The power which rules their destinies is not psychology, not even optics, but a pair of scissors. If the story evolves smoothly from their form, then it is not 'literary'; and strictly speaking this would be the true 'absolute' film. The adventures of forms come to life have a severe logic of their own. In it cause and effect are determined by the law of form and not by the laws of nature. If one of the characters attacks another with a paintbrush and paints a hump on to its back, that character will, alas, be and remain a hunchback. And if the silhouette of a man wielding the silhouette of a pair of scissors cuts out of the silhouette of rock the silhouette of another human being, he will have created a partner equivalent to himself and in the silhouette world this is no miracle, because in the world of silhouettes the normal way of coming into being is to be cut out with a pair of scissors. So everything has happened in accordance with the formal law and logic of that formal world. In this lies its comic effect.

That is why films like the Russian Gulliver-film in which live human figures were combined with puppets, are rather problematic. This film, produced by A. Ptushko, is an allegory, just as Swift's immortal story is an allegory. In art and literature the allegory looks back on a millenary tradition and from Æsop to La Fontaine and Swift it has formed part of the classic gold fund of world literature. But these fables depict human characters and human psychology disguised under the masks of animals or what not. Although the characters are called a raven, a fox, a tortoise or a hare in the written story, this does not evoke visual conceptions in the first place and therefore the contradictions between the animals and their human psychology are not inacceptable.

If these same animals were visible as the realistic pictures of real live animals, then the complete incongruity between such beings, existing in their own right, and the things they are made to say and do in the story would be painfully evident. If on the other hand they were to be presented in a less realistic form, as mere indicative illustrations, then they would be turned into symbols, emblems standing for something else than they are, empty hieroglyphs.

An allegory can become sensory art (and all art is sensory) only to the degree in which it can approximate the naïve realism of the folk-tale. Characters in a true fairy-tale live a real life, only they live it according to the laws *sui generis* of the fairy-tale world and not according to the laws of our earthly nature. An allegory on the contrary is not realistic in any way at all. It may express a truth, but not depict a reality; neither a natural reality, nor a fairy-tale reality, nor any reality at all. It is for this reason that allegories appear bloodless, empty stereotypes which not even the profoundest truths can endow with life. This applies especially to the allegory in the sensory arts.

FILM COMEDY

The secret of the true film comedy is that in it the pheno-menon parts company with the object and leads a sort of ghost-like life of its own, free of all meaning and content. Comic films played by human actors have an inner law of their own, consisting in a complete lack of logic which is in itself comical. Even the most realistically photographed nature can suddenly be rendered funny by some optical trick. In Hans Richter's *Haunted Morning* there are six gentlemen whose hats are blown off by a wind. The hats circle in the air like a swarm of birds and cannot be caught. The same six gentlemen then steal away and hide behind a slender lamp-post and dis-appear as completely as though the lamp-post was a wall. Then we see a long perspective shot of a garden; suddenly a door opens in the middle of it, as though the garden had been a papered wall and the six gentlemen turn up again, coming through it. All this has no sense whatsoever and contains no other intention than to be funny through being nonsensical.

In another film men who are having a fight are caught up by a whirlwind and go on fighting in the air without appearing to notice that they are no longer on the ground. All this seems the work of the whirlwind, not of the camera. The camera does nothing but shoot. Its work is discreet and invi-sible. The film merely makes use of its technical facilities in order to show us a fantastic happening.

YOU CAN'T KILL A PHOTOGRAPH

When a picture is no longer a copy of something and the image no longer evokes in us a reference to some object inde-pendent of it, which it represents and which might just as well have been represented in some other way—if thus the picture appears to have an autonomous existence, a final reality, to be as it were self-contained, then it acquires that grotesquely im-material lightness which makes even the most terrible happen-ings seem entirely harmless. The hero of such a film comedy may lie down on the rails in front of an express train and we shall not be afraid, for what can happen to a picture if it is run over by another picture? All that can happen to it is that it will be flattened out like a silhouette cut out of paper. Never mind. A pal of his comes along and blows him up again like a fairground toy balloon. A bit too much of a pal, though, for he blows so hard that he makes his friend twice as fat as he was before.

This weightless, material-less freedom from danger was the essence of this old-style film comedy. For in the funniest written story there is still the possibility that a man may die, a thing may be destroyed. But a picture can only be rubbed out, painted over, dissolved or faded out, but never killed.

PSYCHOLOGY AND LENGTH

In the apsychological, mechanical hurly-burly of the old American slapstick comedy the whimsical, clever waggery of camera tricks played a great part. The figures being entirely the creations of the camera without any weight and law of their own, the camera could do with them what it pleased. On the other hand the lack of psychology in the old American slapstick is the cause and explanation of the fact that such films very rarely exceeded the length of a single reel. Mechanical action is not suitable for ringing the changes. However fast may be the movement shown in rough-and-tumbles or pursuits, there is no inner movement in them at all, for whatever may have been the cause of the fight or pursuit, it remains the same, unchanged, to the end and therefore is the manifestation of an unchanged inner condition.

The funny point in these films was always that they could suddenly and unexpectedly find a mechanical solution for some apparently insoluble situation. But such grotesquely surprising suddenness offers no opportunity for developing a slowly rising tension. The unexpected, of which we have no knowledge, cannot produce tension. Only expectation and presentiment can bind events together into a dramatic action which by its progressive unfolding keeps our interest awake for longer periods than the span of the one-reeler. On the other hand expectation and presentiment can arise in the spectator only if he feels that there is a causal connection between the scenes he witnesses. For he can only expect things to come to pass which follow from what has already been seen to happen. Only the present can causally evoke a premonition of the future. But surprise is not susceptible of degrees. Even in a fairy-tale one can to some extent tell in advance what might happen to man or beast in the course of the story. But what can happen to mere lines and patches of light and shadow is something no one can foresee.

CARTOONS

At the beginning of this book I told the story of the painter in the Chinese legend who walked into his own painting and never came back. That was a very simple case. What happened was simply that the old Chinaman had created reality with his paintbrush, not art. This was the Chinese belief: everything is what it seems, there is no difference between appearance and reality. Well-painted dragons would fly away.

The natural history of the cartoon film is not as simple as this. It first manifested itself in Felix the Cat, the ancestor of this admirable art form. Its originator was the brilliant Pat Sullivan, who created that amazing world of which the prime mover and omnipotent ruler is the pencil or paintbrush. The substance of this world is the line and it reaches to the boundaries that enclose the graphic art. Drawings such as these do not transform themselves into a natural reality, which their creator might enter like the Chinese painter his landscape. For this world is peopled only by beings drawn with pencil or pen. Their outlines do not depict a shape existing independently somewhere outside this world, but form their only actual body. Appearance is not transformed into reality here as in the Chinese story. Appearance is the sole reality here, and art is not made into reality. Indeed the Sullivan cartoons knew nothing of this duality. When Felix the Cat bends his tail into the shape of a wheel, he can already roll away on it. No need for it to turn into the reality of a wheel. A drawn wheel is good enough for a drawn cat. In Sullivan's drawn world there are no miracles; for in it there are only lines and these function according to the shape they take on.

Felix the Cat once loses his tail. He wonders what to do about it. This anxious question grows out of his head in the shape of a large question mark, demonstrating by graphic means that he is torn by doubts. Felix now gazes pensively at the beautifully curved question mark. He has a bright idea, grabs the question mark and sticks it to his rump for a new tail. The problem is solved. Someone might object to such impossibilities that the question mark was only an abstract symbol! But it appeared in the cartoon as a line and as such subject to the laws of draughtsmanship and none other. The question mark was a line, just like Felix's body, their substance was the same. In the world of creatures consisting only of lines the only impossible things are those which cannot be drawn.

In the case of drawings the creative power of angle and set-up plays an even smaller part than in the case of puppets. Looked at from different viewpoints even a mask can be made to assume different physiognomies. But drawings are two-dimensional and the film can do no more than reproduce them. What then is the nevertheless productive part played by the camera in the cartoon film?

It is that the film shows not only completed drawings but can show the coming into being of the drawing as a process, as an event. The lines emerge before our eyes, they happen. They are not graphic facts, but graphic events.

The natural style of such cartoons is the caricature, the gro-tesque. But the drawn film demands unity of style even more imperatively than does the realistic photography of some real object. A condition of such unity of style is that the draughts-man should see every figure from the viewpoint of some ideo-logy; for all the figures must be equally absurd or funny. Such a film may for instance be a political satire, but in that case it can show only the political opponents of the draughtsman's side. For the draughtsman cannot draw the figures of his own side as caricatures in the same way; if on the other hand he draws them differently, then there is a discrepancy, an infringe-ment of style in the picture.

George Grosz, the great German revolutionary cartoonist, had to struggle hard with this dilemma. His portrait-gallery of caricatures entitled *The Face of the Ruling Classes* was mag-

nificently horrible and nauseating. But if he had to put a pro-
letarian into one of his drawings, he did not know what to do.
He did not want to draw a satirical caricature of him, for that
was not how he saw and wanted to show the working man. On
the other hand could he mix his witheringly sarcastic mon-
strosities with figures drawn with a gentle, affectionate touch?

Only one solution seems possible here: to use the style of
children's drawings, a device often adopted by many a mature
master. In such drawings the distortion is motivated by the
child's lack of skill and this serves as an excuse for making
the figures which are intended to arouse sympathy just as
funny as the others.

With the coming of sound, possibilities of a new acoustic
humour and of a new extraordinary musical artistry opened
up before the cartoon film. This new form of art, of which
Walt Disney is the undisputed king, will be discussed later in
connection with the specific problems of the sound film.

CHAPTER SIXTEEN

SOUND

A TRAGIC PROPHECY

BEING A PROPHET is a hard fate. At times a prophet
can go on living and working only if he does not believe in his
own prophecies. When the technique of the sound film struck
the first blow at the art of the silent film, I said that it would
destroy the already highly developed culture of the silent film.
I added that this would be only temporary, until expression by
means of sound would have developed to a higher level. I said
that what had happened was a catastrophe, the like of which
had never occurred before in the history of any other art. But
I also said that a return to the silent film was impossible, for
the evolution of technique is the evolution of the productive
forces of mankind and the dangers it brings in its train cannot be averted by hampering its development. That would be
senseless machine-wrecking. We cannot protect people from
impending suffering by killing them.

When nearly two decades ago the first attempts at a sound
film were shown, I wrote in my book *Der Geist des Films* that
sound was not yet a gain for the film, but merely a task which
would be an immense gain once it was fulfilled. This would
be when film sound would be as docile and adaptable a
medium as the film picture already was; when the sound strip
will have turned from a technique of reproduction to a creative
art, as the picture strip had already done.

Now, two decades later, I must repeat word for word the
relevant chapter from *Der Geist des Films*. What I then fore-
told as a threat, is now already accomplished fact. On the
other hand what we hoped and expected from the sound film
has not been fulfilled. The art of the silent film is dead, but
its place was taken by the mere technique of the sound film

194

which in twenty years has not risen and evolved into an art. On the whole the film has reverted again to a speaking photographed theatre. No question but that it is often very well photographed very good theatre. The development of the new technique has served the old art well. But the new technique has not like the silent film developed into a new art, revealing new spheres of human experience and based on new principles. I said 'on the whole'. For there have been and are certain signs that the independent acoustic manifestation of the sound film is not dead yet and that this abortive great possibility of human culture, this potentiality is still seeking its own forms of expression and has broken through now and then between the pores of some recent films.

BLIND ALLEY

Was an almost useless standstill of nearly two decades really necessary in order to prove by drastic experience the correctness of this forecast? Did we have to pass along this blind alley in order to convince ourselves that it is a blind alley? Well, I believe in the continuity of development. I believe that even this was not time lost. It is the job of the theoretician to discover whether this standstill was not apparent only. But only a resumed development will be able to show what it owes to the past.

It is certain that in the reviving film culture of a Europe recovering from the second world war, the dissatisfaction with the sound film in its present state has become so universally felt that the voice of the theoretician may now meet with a better response. The time has come for an art of the sound film and hence the time has also come for a theory that is still valid to-day to attempt to render conscious and transform into will and purpose something that is now merely an instinctive urge.

PROPHECY

Two decades ago I wrote: 'In its last years the German film really began to develop rapidly. But then another departure, the sound film, stopped it before it had progressed more than half-way. The picture camera had only just started to acquire sensitive nerves and an imagination of its own. The art of set-up, viewpoint, angle and editing had just reached the stage where it could overcome the material resistance of primitive objectivity. The silent film was just about to develop a psychological subtlety and creative power almost unrivalled in any other art. Then the invention of the sound film came down on it like a landslide. The whole rich culture of the silent film which I have described in the preceding chapters, is now in danger. An undeveloped medium of expression, hitched to a highly developed one, will drag the latter back to a rudimentary condition. And it is inevitable that with the lowering of the level of expression the level of content will equally deteriorate.

'But in history there are no mortal tragedies, only crises, in matters which concern the whole human race. This, too, is a new road which has blocked up the old. In the economic sphere, too, every great new technical invention brought crises and catastrophes—but nevertheless served the advancement of humanity.

'In art every technical innovation is an inspiration. Opportunity is the true muse. It was not the painters who invented paint, and hammer and chisel were necessities before men began to carve statues. The cinematographic camera, too, was in existence before it occurred to someone to use it as the instrument of a new art and a new culture. The instrument must precede the artistic purpose it awakens. Only after such an awakening does the dialectical process of development begin, in which the now conscious purpose seeks more new technical possibilities of expression. From this point onwards it is art that determines the direction and tasks of technical development in accordance with its own needs. Why do the first sound films strike us as ridiculous and embarrassing "Kitsch"? Because we already judge by the standards not of their present performance but of their possibilities and promise. Our aversion signifies not rejection but an impatient demand.

WHAT DO WE DEMAND?

'It is this demand which grants recognition to the sound film as a new great art. The demand is that the sound film should not merely contribute sound to the silent film and thus make it even more like nature, but that it should approach the reality of life from a totally different angle and open up a new treasure-house of human experience. We do not as yet demand from the incipient sound film any technical perfection of performance, but we do demand new themes. What interests us in the first place is not how it sounds, but what it is that it endows with the power of vocal expression.

'For if the sound film will merely speak, make music and imitate sounds as the theatre has already done for some thousands of years, then even at the peak of its technical perfection it will remain nothing but a copying device. But in art only that counts for a discovery which discovers, reveals something hitherto hidden from our eyes—or ears.

'The silent film, when it became an art, discovered for us an unknown visual world. It showed us the face of things, the mimicry of nature and the microdramatics of physiognomy. In the sequence of shots produced by editing a hitherto hidden interrelation of figures and movements was revealed to us and the linking of pictures evoked new powerful trains of association.

THE ACOUSTIC WORLD

'It is the business of the sound film to reveal for us our acoustic environment, the acoustic landscape in which we live, the speech of things and the intimate whisperings of nature; all that has speech beyond human speech, and speaks to us with the vast conversational powers of life and incessantly influences and directs our thoughts and emotions, from the muttering of the sea to the din of a great city, from the roar of machinery to the gentle patter of autumn rain on a window-pane. The meaning of a floor-board creaking in a deserted room, a bullet whistling past our ear, the death-watch beetle ticking in old furniture and the forest spring tinkling

over the stones. Sensitive lyrical poets always could hear these
significant sounds of life and describe them in words. It is for
the sound film to let them speak to us more directly from the
screen.

DISCOVERY OF NOISE

'The sounds of our day-to-day life we hitherto perceived
merely as a confused noise, as a formless mass of din, rather
as an unmusical person may listen to a symphony; at best he
may be able to distinguish the leading melody, the rest will
fuse into a chaotic clamour. The sound film will teach us
to analyse even chaotic noise with our ear and read the score
of life's symphony. Our ear will hear the different voices in
the general babble and distinguish their character as manifestations of individual life. It is an old maxim that art saves us
from chaos. The arts differ from each other in the specific kind
of chaos which they fight against. The vocation of the sound
film is to redeem us from the chaos of shapeless noise by
accepting it as expression, as significance, as meaning.'

Twenty years have passed since I wrote down these conditions. The sound film has left them unfulfilled to this day. The
arts did not accede to my theoretical wishes. During its evolution the human spirit has had many a fair prospect open up
before it, which the great highroad of human culture then by-
passed and left behind. No art exploits all its possibilities, and
not only æsthetic factors influence the choice of the road that
is ultimately followed in preference to many possible others.
And I would not have repeated this my old demand if the
sound film had since advanced farther along another road. But
it has advanced nowhere. What twenty years ago was opportunity and perspective, is still perspective and opportunity to-
day. I quote:

'Only when the sound film will have resolved noise into its
elements, segregated individual, intimate voices and made them
speak to us separately in vocal, acoustic close-ups; when these
isolated detail-sounds will be collated again in purposeful
order by sound-montage, will the sound film have become a
new art. When the director will be able to lead our ear as he
could once already lead our eye in the silent film and by

means of such guidance along a series of close-ups will be able to emphasize, separate and bring into relation with each other the sounds of life as he has done with its sights, then the rattle and clatter of life will no longer overwhelm us in a lifeless chaos of sound. The sound camera will intervene in this chaos of sound, form it and interpret it and then it will again be man himself who speaks to us from the sound screen.

DRAMATURGY OF SOUND

'The genuine sound film which has a style of its own will not be satisfied with making audible the speech of human beings, which in the past has been only visible, nor will it rest content with an acoustic presentation of events. Sound will not merely be a corollary to the picture, but the subject, source and mover of the action. In other words it will become a dramaturgical element in the film. For instance, sounds will not merely be an accompaniment to a duel but possibly its cause as well. The audible clash of blades may be of less importance—because devoid of a dramaturgical function—than perhaps a song heard coming from a garden by the listening rivals and occasioning a quarrel between them. Such sounds would be essential elements of the story. There is no reason why a sound should be less apt to provoke action than a sight would be.'

The first sound films were still intent on exploiting these special possibilities of sound. At that time a film operetta was made in Berlin. In it a young composer absolutely has to produce a new valse before the end of the coming day. He racks his brains and can find nothing suitable. Then through a mistake an unknown girl comes to his room. The result of the sudden and unexpected adventure is the birth of a valse. The composer plays it on the piano and the girl sings it. But the musician's unknown muse vanishes as she had come and the composer again forgets the tune which he had no time to write down. Only the unknown girl might possibly remember it. So the composer puts a want ad. in the paper: 'The young lady, who . . .' After some naïve, even inane complications all turning on the melody, the valse finally brings the lovers together again. Here was a proper plot for a sound film. The found, lost and recovered valse had a dramaturgical, action-moving part to play.

SOUND SPEAKS UP

In the story mentioned in the preceding paragraph, the lost and found melody was, however, allotted a role such as might have been played by any other object. It was a mere 'prop' in the weft of the dramatic plot, no different than a ring or a document which might have been lost and found and around which the plot might have been woven just as well. The valse in this case is merely presented as a fact; no significance attaches to its specific acoustic quality and effect. For this reason it is the most superficial form in which sound can be given a dramaturgical function in a story.

Deeper and more organic is the dramaturgical role of sound when its effect determines the course of the action; when sound is not only made to be heard in the course of the story but can intervene to influence its course. I take an instance from an old silent film, or rather I am inventing an instance in order that light might be thrown on yet another problem in the same sphere.

In the early days of the silent film, a film was made about Paganini, with Conrad Veidt in the title role. The wizard fiddler is put in prison but he fiddles himself out again. His playing is bewitching—the enchanted turnkeys get out of his path and his violin paralyses all resistance to his escape. The crowd outside, charmed by his music, opens a path for the fiddler and his fiddle.

In this film the inaudible playing of a violin had a dramaturgical function, because it influenced the hero's fate, freed him from his prison. As a spectacle it was a fine and convincing scene, precisely because it was silent! The dumbshow of a great actor made us imagine violin-playing so enchanting that hardened jailers dropped their weapons. How great a virtuoso would have been required to play the violin in a sound film in order to achieve this? A merely visible, inaudible music, existing only in the imagination, could have a magic effect. The effect of actually heard music would depend on the public's musical sensibility and taste, a quantity susceptible of innumerable variations. But to make it credible that music did actually charm the rough jailers, it would have to have a like effect on the whole of the audience. It is not by chance that the sound film has not yet touched the Paganini theme.

Petersburg Night, made by the Russian Grigori Roshal, also has a musician hero. Here the varying effect on the audience is not due to the quality of the playing, but to the nature of the music played. The Russian violinist plays folk songs and the society ladies and gentlemen in the best seats do not like it and boo, while the poorer patrons in the gallery are enthusiastic. Just as the scene mentioned in connection with the Paganini film was possible only in a silent film, so the scene from the Russian film is possible only in a sound film, for we must hear the songs and experience their spirit in order to know why they delight one part of the audience and infuriate the other. This scene characterizes not only the music but the audience listening to it and in addition to its dramaturgical function, it also has a profound ideological significance.

SOUNDS AS DRAMATIS PERSONAE

But not only music can have a dramaturgical function in a sound film. For instance: a sailor is saying good-bye to his family. His wife, rocking a cradle, begs him to stay at home. But the sea, the great rival for his affections, is visible through the window. The sailor hesitates. Then two sounds are heard, like two rival seducers. A soft lullaby sung by the woman and the summoning murmur of the sea. In the picture one now sees only the sailor, and of him only his face, but it shows the conflict in his mind, the hard struggle within himself, evoked by these two sounds, these two calls. It is a dramatic, fate-deciding scene in which not a word is spoken. The woman's lullaby and the voice of the sea fight a duel here for possession of a soul.

INFLUENCE OF ACCOMPANYING SOUND

Sometimes the dramaturgical role of sound is indirect. A soldier is taking leave from a girl. The battlefield is near and the noise of bursting shells can be heard. The scene of leave-taking might have been shot without acoustic accompaniment. But it would certainly have taken a different turn. For the girl, starting at every shell-burst, influenced by the pictures conjured up by the danger, makes admissions which she would certainly not have made in a comfortable, safe, cosy room, or possibly not even have become conscious of them at all.

A BATTLE OF SOUNDS

The young film production of Italy uses very fine, interesting dramaturgical sound effects, showing thereby once more that it is in the first rank of those who are now striving to re-create the film as an art. In Luigi Zampa's excellent anti-Fascist film *Vivere in pace* the great central scene is built upon purely acoustic effects. A German corporal comes to the house of the Italian peasant who is harbouring a wounded American Negro soldier. The Negro must be hidden away quickly. In their hurry they can find no better place than the wine-cellar. The German is feeling very comfortable, how-ever, and stays on and on and cannot be induced to go. He asks for food and drink. He wants to have a good time. The Italian peasant and his family sit silent and yawning, trying to get rid of the German by boredom. But suddenly funny noises are heard from the wine-cellar. The Negro, tired of being shut up in the cold and dark, has broached a cask of wine and got drunk. The German pricks up his ears. Suddenly the Italian peasants break into noisy cheerfulness, in order to drown the dangerous noise. The drunken Negro smashes up everything in the cellar. The gentle, sober old peasant and his elderly wife begin to shout songs, yell, and dance and drag the German into a noisy debauch. They compete desperately with the noises from the cellar. What follows is a battle be-tween noises, a diabolical scene, which grows all the more exciting as the Negro, who has run amok in the cellar, is trying to get out of there and is kicking and battering at the door. The shadow of death falls on the breathless, feverish merriment. Finally the Negro breaks down the door and the revelry, as if cut in two, suddenly freezes into mute stiff immobility.

Even more moving is Vergano's sound scene in the film *Il Sole Sorge Ancora*. A priest, a member of the Resistance who has been condemned to death, is being taken to the scene of execution by the Germans. A crowd collects along the road. The crowd grows even larger, the ring surrounding the priest ever denser. The priest begins to pray, first softly, then more loudly, as he walks along. The camera follows with a tracking shot. The priest remains visible all the time, but of the crowd never more than two or three faces are seen, as the priest and the camera pass them. The priest is reciting the litany. Two or three of the crowd whisper the response: 'Ora pro nobis'. But as the priest walks on and on, the response grows ever louder. We see not more than two or three people, but we hear ever more and more, in an ominous *crescendo*. The shot remains a close-up all the time and can show no crowd, but more and more voices say 'Ora pro nobis'. We hear the swelling of the sound like the roaring of a torrent. It is the audible revolt of the people; its menacing power and emotion turns into a formidable acoustic symbol, precisely because we cannot see the crowd. If we saw the crowd, then the storm of voices would be explained, for the voices of so many people could scarcely be less loud. But then the sound would lose its particular significance. For never could the film show a crowd of such a size as the crowd the presence of which we are made to feel in that isolated, symbolic sound not contained by any real space. This is the voice of the nation and nevertheless we hear it in the close-up of the martyr-priest, as an answer to the mute play of his features.

I do not say that such a decisive dramaturgical role of sound is indispensable for every sound film. As the silent film has ceased to exist, the sound film must operate with many different kinds of stories. The sound film to-day is not a specific form of film, but the whole of what there is of the film and hence the specific style of one sort of film cannot be obligatory for it. It must present everything that comes along.

Nevertheless it is a pity that the sound film has almost completely dropped the cultivation of sound effects.

PROBLEM OF THE SOUND PLAY

This is a good opportunity to discuss the form problem of the sound play in general. Wireless plays are impossible without verbal explanations and descriptions of the scene. We cannot understand even words in their exact sense if we cannot see the facial expression and gestures of those who speak. For the spoken word contains only a fragment of human expression. People talk not only with their mouths. The glance, a twitching of a muscle in the face, movements of the hands speak at the same time and only all of them together add up to the exact shade of meaning intended. The word is merely one of the tones in a rich chord, so we do not understand even the word in its precise meaning if we cannot see who said it and when, in what circumstances and connection. As for the sounds of nature we know them so little that we often fail even to recognize them unless we see what is emitting them. A farmhouse may at a pinch be represented by voices of animals. But even then the listener will not be able to say whether the mooing of cows, neighing of horses, crowing of cocks, cackling of hens, barking of dogs is a sound picture of some bucolic farm or of a livestock market. Even recognizable sounds merely indicate the generality of the things they stand for. But the life of all image-art is in the concrete, exact presentation of the individuality of things.

But the rustling of a forest or the noise of the sea cannot always be distinguished—in fact the rustling of paper or the dragging of a sack along a stone floor are deceptively similar to both. Our ear is not yet sufficiently sensitive. It is the sound film that will train it, just as the silent film trained our eye. A hunter would recognize sounds in the forest which the city-dweller would not. But on the whole most of us would not even find our way about in our own homes if we had to rely on our ears alone.

For this reason radio plays always explain in one way or another what we are supposed to see, so that the sounds in it are merely acoustic illustrations of a narrated scene or a scene made intelligible by words.

THE PICTURE FORMS THE SOUND

In a sound film there is no need to explain the sounds. We see together with the word the glance, the smile, the gesture, the whole chord of expression, the exact nuance. Together with the sounds and voices of things we see their physiognomy. The noise of a machine has a different colouring for us if we see the whirling machinery at the same time. The sound of a wave is different if we see its movement. Just as the shade and value of a colour changes according to what other colours are next to it in a painting, so the *timbre* of a sound changes in accordance with the physiognomy or gesture of the visible source of the sound seen together with the sound itself in a sound film in which acoustic and optical impressions are equivalently linked together into a single picture.

In a radio play the stage has to be described in words, because sound alone is not space-creating.

SILENCE

Silence, too, is an acoustic effect, but only where sounds can be heard. The presentation of silence is one of the most specific dramatic effects of the sound film. No other art can reproduce silence, neither painting nor sculpture, neither literature nor the silent film could do so. Even on the stage silence appears only rarely as a dramatic effect and then only for short moments. Radio plays cannot make us feel the depths of silence at all, because when no sounds come from our set, the whole performance has ceased, as we cannot see any silent continuation of the action. The sole material of the wireless play being sound, the result of the cessation of sound is not silence but just nothing.

SILENCE AND SPACE

Things that we see as being different from each other, appear even more different when they emit sounds. They all sound different when they do this, but they are all silent in the same way. There are thousands of different sounds and voices, but the substance of silence appears one and the same for all. That is at first hearing. Sound differentiates visible things, silence brings them closer to each other and makes them less dissimilar. Every painting shows this happy harmony, the hidden common language of mute things conversing with each other, recognizing each others' shapes and entering into relations with each other in a composition common to them all. This was a great advantage the silent film had over the sound film. For its silence was not mute; it was given a voice in the background music, and landscapes and men and the objects surrounding them were shown on the screen against this common musical background. This made them speak a common silent language and we could feel their irrational conversation in the music which was common to them all.

But the silent film could reproduce silence only by roundabout means. On the theatrical stage cessation of the dialogue does not touch off the great emotional experience of silence, because the space of the stage is too small for that, and the experience of silence is essentially a space experience.

How do we perceive silence? By hearing nothing? That is a mere negative. Yet man has few experiences more positive than the experience of silence. Deaf people do not know what it is. But if a morning breeze blows the sound of a cock crowing over to us from the neighbouring village, if from the top of a high mountain we hear the tapping of a woodcutter's axe far below in the valley, if we can hear the crack of a whip a mile away—then we are hearing the silence around us. We feel the silence when we can hear the most distant sound or the slightest rustle near us. Silence is when the buzzing of a fly on the window-pane fills the whole room with sound and the ticking of a clock smashes time into fragments with sledgehammer blows. The silence is greatest when we can hear very distant sounds in a very large space. The widest space is our own if we can hear right across it and the noise of the alien world reaches us from beyond its boundaries. A completely soundless space on the contrary never appears quite concrete, and quite real to our perception; we feel it to be weightless and unsubstantial, for what we merely see is only a vision. We accept seen space as real only when it contains sounds as well, for these give it the dimension of depth.

On the stage, a silence which is the reverse of speech may have a dramaturgical function, as for instance if a noisy company suddenly falls silent when a new character appears; but such a silence cannot last longer than a few seconds, otherwise it curdles as it were and seems to stop the performance. On the stage, the effect of silence cannot be drawn out or made to last.

In the film, silence can be extremely vivid and varied, for although it has no voice, it has very many expressions and gestures. A silent glance can speak volumes; its soundlessness makes it more expressive because the facial movements of a silent figure may explain the reason for the silence, make us feel its weight, its menace, its tension. In the film, silence does not halt action even for an instant and such silent action gives even silence a living face.

The physiognomy of men is more intense when they are silent. More than that, in silence even things drop their masks and seem to look at you with wide-open eyes. If a sound film shows us any object surrounded by the noises of everyday life and then suddenly cuts out all sound and brings it up to us in isolated close-up, then the physiognomy of that object takes on a significance and tension that seems to provoke and invite the event which is to follow.

DRAMATURGICAL FUNCTION OF SOUND IN THE SHOT

If dramaturgy is the teaching about the laws of dramatic action, is it possible to speak about dramaturgy in connection with a single shot? Does not the most energetic action manifest itself only in the sequence, in the interrelation of varying conditions following each other? Well, the film has nothing to do with the classic problem of the ancient Greek philosophers who asked whether movement consisted of a series of distinct conditions and whether a series of static conditions could ever become motion. For although each frame of the

film is a snapshot of a separate motionless condition, our eye
does not perceive it so. What we see is motion. The motion picture is what it is because even the shortest shot shows movement. The smallest particle of action, be it internal or external
action, is always action, the optical manifestation of which is
movement—even within one and the same shot. This is how it
strikes our senses and our consciousness, and this is what
matters in art. The specific task of the film is to seize on and
localize by means of close-ups the very instants when the
decisive, initiating or direction-changing impulses enter the
action.

However extensive an event is, however vast its scale, there
has somewhere been some small spark which was the immediate cause of the explosion; a pebble must have loosened somewhere and started the landslide. These dramaturgically decisive particles of time can be presented by the film in a single
shot. It can show the one man on whom it all turned, at the
very instant which matters: that last-but-one second of hesi-
tation in a glance of the eye, the one gesture in which the final
resolve manifests itself. All this the film can separate by a
close-up from the more general picture of the scene in which
the causal course of the whole process is shown from begining
to end. In such fatal decisive close-ups sound, too, can play a
cardinal dramaturgical part.

Moments when a man is alerted by a slight noise, or hears
a word, may be of fatal significance. The close-up will show
the face and let us hear the sound too. It will show the drama
enacted on the face and at the same time let us hear its cause
and explanation. This is done in two planes, with counterpointed effects.

SOUND-EXPLAINING PICTURES

Not only the microdramatics expressed in the microphysiognomy of the face can be made intelligible by the sound which
causes it. Such a close-up-plus-sound can have the inverse
effect. The close-up of a listener's face can explain the sound
he hears. We might perhaps not have noticed the significance
of some sound or noise if we had not seen its effect in the

mirror of a human face. For instance we hear the screaming of a siren. Such a sound does not acquire a dramatic significance unless we can see from the expression on human faces that it is a danger-signal, or a call to revolt. We may hear the sound of sobbing, but how deep its meaning is will become evident only from the expression of sympathy and understanding appearing on some human face. Further, the acoustic character of a sound we understand is different too. We hear the sound of a siren differently if we know that it is a warning of impending deadly peril.

The face of a man listening to music may also show two kinds of things. The reflected effect of the music may throw light into the human soul; it may also throw light on the music itself and suggest by means of the listener's facial expression some experience touched off by this musical effect. If the director shows us a close-up of the conductor while an invisible orchestra is playing, not only can the character of the music be made clear by the dumbshow of the conductor, his facial expression may also give an interpretation of the sounds and convey it to us. And the emotion produced in a human being by music and demonstrated by a close-up of a face can enhance the power of a piece of music in our eyes far more than any added decibels.

ASYNCHRONOUS SOUND

In a close-up in which the surroundings are not visible, a sound that seeps into the shot sometimes impresses us as mysterious, simply because we cannot see its source. It produces the tension arising from curiosity and expectation. Sometimes the audience does not know what the sound is they hear, but the character in the film can hear it, turn his face towards the sound and see its source before the audience does. This handling of picture and sound provides rich opportunities for effects of tension and surprise.

Asynchronous sound (that is, when there is discrepancy between the things heard and the things seen in the film) can acquire considerable importance. If the sound or voice is not tied up with a picture of its source, it may grow beyond the dimensions of the latter. Then it is no longer the voice or sound of some chance thing, but appears as a pronouncement of universal validity. I already mentioned the 'Ora pro nobis' in that fine Italian film, which grows into such a storm of popular protest and indignation in the close-ups, that a picture of even the vastest crowd that could be photographed would only diminish the effect. The surest means by which a director can convey the pathos or symbolical significance of sound or voice is precisely to use it asynchronously.

INTIMACY OF SOUND

Acoustic close-ups make us perceive sounds which are included in the accustomed noise of day-to-day life, but which we never hear as individual sounds because they are drowned in the general din. Possibly they even have an effect on us but this effect never becomes conscious. If a close-up picks out such a sound and thereby makes us aware of its effect, then at the same time its influence on the action will have been made manifest.

On the stage such things are impossible. If a theatrical producer wanted to direct the attention of the audience to a scarcely audible sigh, because that sigh expresses a turning-point in the action, then all the other actors in the same scene would have to be very quiet, or else the actor who is to breathe the sigh would have to be brought forward to the footlights. All this, however, would cause the sigh to lose its essential character, which is that it is shy and retiring and must remain scarcely audible. As in the silent film so in the sound film, scarcely perceptible, intimate things can be conveyed with all the secrecy of the unnoticed eavesdropper. Nothing need be silenced in order to demonstrate such sounds for all to hear—and they can yet be kept intimate. The general din can go on, it may even drown completely a sound like the soft piping of a mosquito, but we can get quite close to the source of the sound with the microphone and with our ear and hear it nevertheless.

Subtle associations and interrelations of thoughts and emotions can be conveyed by means of very low, soft sound effects.

Such emotional or intellectual linkages can play a decisive dramaturgical part. They may be anything—the ticking of a clock in an empty room, a slow drip from a burst pipe or the moaning of a little child in its sleep.

SOUND CANNOT BE ISOLATED

In such close-ups of sound we must be careful, however, to bear in mind the specific nature of sound which never permits sound to be isolated from its acoustic environment as a close-up shot can be isolated from its surroundings. For what is not within the film frame cannot be seen by us, even if it is immediately beside the things that are. Light or shadow can be thrown into the picture from outside and the outline of a shadow can betray to the spectator what is outside the frame but still in the same sector of space, although the picture will show only a shadow. In sound things are different. An acoustic environment inevitably encroaches on the close-up shot and what we hear in this case is not a shadow or a beam of light, but the sounds themselves, which can always be heard through-out the whole space of the picture, however small a section of that space is included in the close-up. Sounds cannot be blocked out.

Music played in a restaurant cannot be completely cut out if a special close-up of say two people softly talking together in a corner is to be shown. The band may not always be seen in the picture, but it will always be heard. Nor is there any need to silence the music altogether in order that we may hear the soft whispering of the two guests as if we were sitting in their immediate vicinity. The close-up will contain the whole acoustic atmosphere of the restaurant space. Thus we will hear not only the people talking, we will also hear in what relation their talking is to the sounds all round them. We will be able to place it in its acoustic environment.

Such sound-pictures are often used in the film for the purpose of creating an atmosphere. Just as the film can show visual landscapes, so it can show acoustic landscapes, a tonal *milieu*.

EDUCATING THE EAR

Our eye recognizes things even if it has seen them only once or twice. Sounds are much more difficult to recognize. We know far more visual forms than sound forms. We are used to finding our way about the world without the conscious assistance of our hearing. But without sight we are lost. Our ear, however, is not less sensitive, it is only less educated than our eye. Science tells us in fact that the ear can distinguish more delicate nuances than our eye. The number of sounds and noises a human ear can distinguish runs into many thousands—far more than the shades of colour and degrees of light we can distinguish. There is however a considerable difference between perceiving a sound and identifying its source. We may be aware that we are hearing a different sound than before, without knowing to whom or what the sound belongs. We may have more difficulty in perceiving things visually, but we recognize them more easily once we have perceived them. Erdmann's experiments showed that the ear can distinguish innumerable shades and degrees in the noise of a large crowd, but at the same time it could not be stated with certainty whether the noise was that of a merry or an angry crowd.

There is a very considerable difference between our visual and acoustic education. One of the reasons for this is that we so often see without hearing. We see things from afar, through a windowpane, on pictures, on photographs. But we very rarely hear the sounds of nature and of life without seeing something. We are not accustomed therefore to draw conclusions about visual things from sounds we hear. This defective education of our hearing can be used for many surprising effects in the sound film. We hear a hiss in the darkness. A snake? A human face on the screen turns in terror towards the sound and the spectators tense in their seats. The camera, too, turns towards the sound. And behold the hiss is that of a kettle boiling on the gas-ring.

Such surprising disappointments may be tragic too. In such cases the slow approach and the slow recognition of the sound may cause a far more terrifying tension than the approach of something seen and therefore instantly recognized. The roar of an approaching flood or landslide, approaching cries of grief or terror which we discern and distinguish only gradually, impress us with the inevitability of an approaching catastrophe with almost irresistible intensity. These great possibilities of dramatic effect are due to the fact that such a slow and gradual process of recognition can symbolize the desperate resistance of the consciousness to understanding a reality which is already audible but which the consciousness is reluctant to accept.

SOUNDS   THROW   NO   SHADOW

Auditive culture can be increased like any other and the sound film is very suitable to educate our ear. There are however definite limits to the possibilities of finding our way about the world purely by sound, without any visual impressions. The reason for this is that sounds throw no shadows—in other words that sounds cannot produce shapes in space. Things which we see we must see side by side; if we do not, one of them covers up the other so that it cannot be seen. Visual impressions do not blend with each other. Sounds are different; if several of them are present at the same time, they merge into one common composite sound. We can see the dimension of space and see a direction in it. But we cannot *hear* either dimension or direction. A quite unusual, rare sensitivity of ear, the so-called absolute—is required to distinguish the several sounds which make up a composite noise. But their place in space, the direction of their source cannot be discerned even by a perfect ear, if no visual impression is present to help.

It is one of the basic form-problems of the radio play that sound alone cannot represent space and hence cannot alone represent a stage.

SOUNDS   HAVE   NO   SIDES

It is difficult to localize sound and a film director must take this fact into account. If three people are talking together in a film and they are placed so that we cannot see the movements of their mouths and if they do not accompany their words by gestures, it is almost impossible to know which of them is talking, unless the voices are very different. For sounds cannot be beamed as precisely as light can be directed by a reflector. There are no such straight and concentrated sound beams as there are rays of light.

The shapes of visible things have several sides, right side and left side, front and back. Sound has no such aspects, a sound strip will not tell us from which side the shot was made.

SOUND HAS A SPACE COLOURING

Every natural sound reproduced by art on the stage or on the platform always takes on a false tone-colouring, for it always assumes the colouring of the space in which it is presented to the public and not of the space which it is supposed to reproduce. If we hear a storm, the howling of the wind, a clap of thunder, etc. on the stage we always hear in it the *timbre* proper to the stage not in the *timbre* proper to the forest, or ocean or what not the scene is supposed to represent. If, say, a choir sings in a church on the stage, we cannot hear the unmistakable resonance of Gothic arches; for every sound bears the stamp of the space in which it is actually produced.

Every sound has a space-bound character of its own. The same sound sounds different in a small room, in a cellar, in a large empty hall, in a street, in a forest or on the sea.

Every sound which is really produced somewhere must of necessity have some such space-quality and this is a very important quality indeed if use is to be made of the sensual reproducing power of sound! It is this *timbre local* of sound which is necessarily always falsified on the theatrical stage. One of the most valuable artistic faculties of the microphone is that sounds shot at the point of origin are perpetuated by it and retain their original tonal colouring. A sound recorded in a cellar remains a cellar sound even if it is played back in a picture theatre, just as a film shot preserves the viewpoint of the camera, whatever the spectator's viewpoint in the cinema auditorium may be. If the picture was taken from above, the spectators will see the object from above, even if they have to look upwards to the screen and not downwards.

Just as our eye is identified with the camera lens, so our ear is identified with the microphone and we hear the sounds as the microphone originally heard them, irrespective of where the sound film is being shown and the sound reproduced. In this way, in the sound film, the fixed, immutable, permanent distance between spectator and actor is eliminated not only visually, as already mentioned earlier in this book, but acoustically as well. Not only as spectators, but as listeners, too, we are transferred from our seats to the space in which the events depicted on the screen are taking place.

BASIC PROBLEM OF SOUND REPRODUCTION

Our sound apparatus records sound accurately and reproduces it with tolerable fidelity. But neither our microphones nor our loudspeakers can subjectively mould the sounds as the ordinary camera can influence the visual shape of things. If two cameramen of different artistic individuality photograph the same stormy sea, the visual pictures that result may be completely different. But the acoustic reproduction of the same stormy sea will be substantially the same, the only differences that may appear being due to technical causes. The sound engineer has no possibility of presenting the same sound in different ways, according to his own artistic personality. If two cameramen shoot the same scene, their pictures may resemble one another very little, although the objects in them may be equally recognizable in both. But sound tracks recorded by two sound engineers in the same technical conditions cannot show such individual differences.

Why? Is it due only to the technical imperfections of our present-day recording apparatus or are there other deeper reasons inherent in the very nature of sound or the nature of our hearing?

When a cameraman shoots the acting of an actor, as a visual phenomenon, there emerges a synthesis of two artistic performances: to the characterization by the actor is added the presentation by the cameraman who picks the most characteristic outlines and lightings out of a thousand different possible ones. The expression of the shot, its atmosphere, enhances the expression on the actor's face, adds body and intensity to it. For this reason the cinematic shot does not merely reproduce, it also creates.

But in a sound record there is no more and no less expression than is put into it by the voice of the actor and faithfully reproduced by the sound camera. The sound engineer does nothing more than record and reproduce; he cannot project the subjectivity of his own personality into the sound picture by means of viewpoint or set-up. But only the possibility of such subjective influences would afford the sound engineer scope for artistic self-expression. The shape and outline of sounds cannot be changed by varying perspectives as the physiognomy of visible things can be changed by varying angles. Sounds have no 'angles'. The same sound coming from the same point cannot be recorded in different ways. But if the sound engineer has no free choice between many possibilities, his recording will remain a mechanical reproduction and nothing else.

SOUNDS CANNOT BE REPRESENTED BY IMAGES

What we hear from the screen is not an image of the sound but the sound itself, which the sound camera has recorded and reproduced again. It is the same sound that has been passed on to the screen. Sounds have no images. The sound itself is repeated in its original dimension with all its original physical qualities when it is echoed from the screen. There is no difference in dimension and reality between the original sound and the recorded and reproduced sound, as there is between real objects and their photographic images.

SOUND MONTAGE

The formal problems of sound montage, the acoustic and musical rules which govern the effect of sounds are purely musical and acoustic questions and it is not proposed to discuss them here. What concerns us is only the part sound montage may play in film dramaturgy.

For instance, the similarity of certain sounds may invite comparisons and evoke associations of ideas. In the film about Strauss, *The Great Waltz,* the rhythmic tap-tap of a trotting cab-horse evokes the rhythm of the waltz, to which the matutinal sounds of the Wienerwald provide the melody. In one of Ermler's films the rattle of a sewing-machine evokes in the mind of a soldier who has lost his memory the rattle of a machine-gun and thereby conjures up the whole forgotten past.

The linking of juxtaposed sub-contrasts may be more effective than the cutting together of visual contrasts. A thousand expressive effects can be produced merely by cross-cutting the sounds of sobs and laughter, groans and dance music, etc.

Silence, as a sequel to sound, may also appear as an acoustic effect in sound montage. The reason for this is that sound does not disappear from our consciousness as quickly as a vanished visual picture. It echoes in our ear for some time, thus mutely counterpointing the subsequent pictures. After a sequence of hot dance music the stillness of a sick-room affects us differently than if the preceding picture, too, had been a quiet one. Sounds which, as the saying goes, 'still resound in our ears', may deepen and interpret the silence that follows them.

SOUND DISSOLVES

The similarity of sounds renders possible the making of sound dissolves similar to picture dissolves. This is not merely a formal linkage—it may provide an essential, interpreting connection between two scenes. If the shouts 'Down tools!' 'All out!' dissolve into the rousing roar of the factory siren, the effect will be metaphoric; the siren will seem to us the angry voice of the factory. Such dissolves can become similes: if the tapping of a Morse key at the headquarters of an army in the field first grows louder, and then dissolves into the rattle of firearms, a causal, meaningful connection arises between the two sounds. The tapping of the Morse key seems in retrospect to have been the command, which is carried out by the sound of firing. Such sound similes and acoustic symbols are often somewhat too obvious and can easily degenerate into empty formalism.

ASYNCHRONOUS SOUND EFFECTS

A good traditional effect is achieved when the sounds of one scene are still heard during the next one. Instances: the jazz music of the night-club we have just seen can still be heard in the room where a dead man is lying; the roar of the open sea impinges on the sultry silence of a stuffy basement den in a great city. Or the other way round: we see a ploughman working in the fields but we can already hear in this picture the whirr and rattle of the factory machinery we are to see in the next, coming in from the neighbouring shot as it were; not a real neighbourhood, but a filmic neighbourhood, determined by the artistic composition of the film. Such anticipatory preparation increases tension and creates atmosphere.

THE MOST EXPRESSIVE INSTRUMENT

The asynchronous use of sound is the most effective device of the sound film. If recorded synchronously, sound is properly speaking merely a naturalistic complement to the picture. It simply makes the picture more like reality. But in asynchronous recording the sound grows independent of the image and can give a parallel meaning, a sort of running commentary to the scenes.

In one of the Soviet war films there was a young soldier whose nerves give way when he first comes under fire. He deserts his comrades and hides in a shell-hole. A close-up shows his face and by his closed mouth we can see that he is silent. Nevertheless we hear him talking. The monologue we hear is in his mind and we listen tensely to what he is silently saying to himself. If he had really spoken aloud and said the same words in a voiced monologue, this scene would have been unbearable. For nowadays even on the stage we find an 'unnatural' monologue difficult to accept. But isn't it even more unnatural that a human being should move across the ground with the speed of a car? As long as what we see remains close to reality, reality appears exaggerated. But if what we see is quite divorced from reality, it becomes fairy-tale or symbol. If a man has wings to fly with, he can compete even with an aeroplane; we no longer apply 'natural' standards. Asynchronous sound has no need to be natural. Its effect is symbolic and it is linked with the things it accompanies through its significance, in the sphere of the mind, not of reality. This richest and deepest possibility of artistic expression has as yet been used very little in the sound film. And yet its future development lies in this direction. It is this free, counter-pointed use of picture and sound that could deliver the sound film from the fetters of primitive naturalism and enable our filmic art to attain once again the subtlety already achieved by the silent film in the past and then lost again through the advent of sound.

In an asynchronous sound film the action can move on two parallel levels at the same time, in the sphere of sound and in the sphere of visual image. For instance: we can see what is ostensibly happening; at the same time we can hear what the persons involved in the action are thinking and feeling within themselves. Or the other way round: a narrator tells us what is happening; we need not even see it. What we do see is a sequence of thoughts, an irrational chain of associations. New art forms, the forms of the film-ballad and of lyrical film-poetry may possibly develop along these lines. We would hear the poem, accompanied by a cascade of pictures, a parallel, as it were, to a musical accompaniment but translated into the visual sphere; illustrations which have motion and which conjure up the mind-pictures of a soul moved by emotion.

ASYNCHRONOUS PICTURE, SYNCHRONOUS SOUND

If we see a close-up of a listening human face isolated in a shot and hear some other person talking to it, then the shot will be asynchronous, even though the scene may be naturalistically synchronous. The sounds exist in the same rooms, but not in the same shot. Such a split may also have its contrapuntal effects. The spectator's attention is riveted on a silent face and he sees quite different things with his eye than those about which he hears from a space outside the film frame. This again can give counterpointed effects impossible on the stage and equally impossible in the silent film.

In his first sound film (in which he did not speak), Charlie Chaplin showed us a fine example of such an asynchronous effect. His beloved is singing in a hall and does not please the audience. The crowd in the vast hall is wrapped in icy silence. Only the clapping of one isolated pair of hands is heard. The camera pans, searching the crowd for the lone applauder. It searches for a long time among cruelly indifferent faces. But the applause grows louder. The camera is drawing closer. Finally it lights on Charlie, clapping away alone in a corner of the hall, fighting single-handed against the indifference of the crowd and against fate.

In *Party Crowd,* a film made by Pyriev, the Soviet director, there is another fine instance of such an effect. The heroine is expelled from the party by a show of hands at a committee meeting. We see her alone in close-up. We cannot see the hands raised in the vote and so we cannot at the first glance ascertain whether the majority is for her or against her. But we can hear the tellers count: 'One, two, three . . .' The heroine bows her head more and more. 'Four, five, six . . .' the figures crash down on the bowed head like hammer-blows. But we cannot see the final result, which we would of course have seen at a glance if the shot had been a longer one instead of a close-up. Only hearing the count permits us still to go on hoping, and because we can't see the teller, his voice is magnified to the dimensions of an impersonal, inexorable destiny.

CHAPTER SEVENTEEN

DIALOGUE

W H E N T H E T A L K I E made its appearance, there was a panic among the producers, directors, actors and script writers. This was another thing that had never happened before in the history of any other art; that the technical development of the medium of expression should have so embarrassed the artists who practised the art.

The anxiety and uncertainty had many reasons. The talking film seemed to threaten the international validity of the silent film and by rendering export much more difficult, endanger the financial and business interests which had invested in it. Many directors and actors lacked the required ability to deal with speech. It is characteristic that no one objected to the appearance of sound in the film. Charlie Chaplin was prepared on the spot to use the craziest sound effects. In his first sound film he accidentally swallows a whistle which begins to whistle at the most inopportune moments. It was only speech against which the almost universal objections were raised. Artists and theoreticians mobilized the traditional laws of art, philosophy and æsthetics against the talking film, just as they had done against the silent film—and with the same lack of success.

How silly the resistance to the talking film was can be gauged if we imagine what would have happened if the Lumières had constructed a sound camera at the same time as the silent camera—a supposition which is not impossible in principle. Had they done so, no one would have conceived the crazy idea of presenting dramatic scenes in dumb-show. Everyone would have condemned such an idea as inartistic, unnatural and ridiculous. To show people talking without sound, mouthing the words without saying them! And then they disappear and we read what they were supposed to say, in the form of a caption! Then we see the same man again talking soundlessly! Absurd!

Well, let us admit this was a very naïve and primitive method, by which we attempted to remedy the imperfections of our technique. Nevertheless, we gave it the status of an æsthetic principle. This was a necessary and extremely fruitful thesis. After all, the silence of the pictures could not be changed—we got it as the material with which we had to work whether we liked it or not, and every artistic possibility of it had to be exploited to the full.

In the beginning everyone saw only a disturbing element in speech and the best directors exerted their imagination and skill to the utmost to avoid having to make their characters speak. At all cost they wanted to get round using the new technique. If anything could condemn the present state of the sound film, it is certainly the fact that this situation has changed little to this day and dialogue is still regarded as a necessary evil. In other words the sound film is an art which regards its essential means of expression as a nuisance. It is much as if a painter began to paint with the intention of doing without colours as much as possible.

Stroheim got round the problem in his first sound film by using a ventriloquist character. Even René Clair in his *Sous les Toits de Paris* made his characters talk behind a window or in such noise that one could only see the movement of their mouths but not understand what they were saying.

This resistance to dialogue, this refusal to accept the historical fact of the talkie, this infertile, conservative attitude was nevertheless more artistic and productive than the decadence of the last decade of the sound film, when it resigned itself to the American conception of the pure talkie and thereby sank back to the stage of photographed theatre which had once already been left behind by the silent film. Those who still sought to rescue what they could out of this debacle were trying to save the pictorial culture evolved through the silent film, a culture which the spoken word nullified. But the newer American film industry and film business harbours no such artistic anxieties. They have by now quite forgotten the great art which had its cradle in Hollywood and is now dead. They blithely make their characters talk in close-ups from start to finish. It is cheaper and quicker that way. It is photographed theatre again as it was at the very beginning.

But now we have come to the threshold of the second period of film art, when Europe will rediscover the film, the sound film, the talkie, the colour film and stereoscopic film, which nevertheless will not be a copy of the theatre but an autonomous new art using every one of its media of expression in a way differing from the methods of the theatrical stage. This art will not regard the dialogue as a nuisance but use it according to its own new and autonomous methods.

In my *Der sichtbare Mensch* I outlined the æsthetics of silence in film art. This was no error on my part, for the sound film was no organic continuation of the silent film, but a different form of art. In the silent film of the silent days, silence was in fact an essential element.

It is nevertheless true that the silent film would never have emerged in the form in which it did emerge, had the sound camera been developed at the same time as the ordinary cinematographic camera. Every phenomenon of history has its reason, but not every phenomenon is necessary for all that. The essential difference between visual culture and the intellectual culture of words, of which I wrote in *Der sichtbare Mensch,* does in fact exist, but that does not mean that it must continue to exist for ever as a gulf that cannot be bridged.

It is true also that the talkie has thrown a developed pictorial, visual culture back to a primitive stage. But it would be dogmatic and pedantic to magnify a technical crisis into an impassable essential gulf between pictorial and verbal presentation.

In the silent film, too, there was in fact a contradiction between the picture and the written word, because the picture, the visual scene had to be interrupted in order to let the public read the captions. Picture and writing, two basically different dimensions of the mind, had thus constantly to alternate with each other. The rhythm of the cutting was constantly held up. Looking at it to-day this appears an intolerable crudity.

In the sound film the sequence of the pictures is never interrupted in this way. The visual montage is never stopped by a caption written only to be read. The speech is incorporated in the picture itself, not in expressionless written words the emphasis on which the reader has to supply as he reads them. And not only is the spoken word heard together with the seeing of the picture—the expression of sound and image merge into an organic unity when they depict the emotions or state of mind of the characters.

Thus the objection to words was legitimate in the silent film because the written caption was always an alien element in the sequence of pictures. The absolute ideal of the silent film would have been a completely captionless film and it has often been attempted to produce such films. These attempts were in fact protests not against speech, but against the necessity of reading—which is also an optical process, but not a process of the same nature as the other optical process of watching pictures. Seeing people talking in some dramatic scene was never considered undesirable. Nor would the hearing of speech have been disturbing if the picture had not been interfered with. We would have all been delighted if we had not been forced to break the picture sequences with written explanations. But the silent film could reach perfection only as a silent film.

SPEECH SEEN AND SPEECH HEARD

In spite of all such logical considerations, it was precisely men of better taste who protested loudest at first against the speaking film, although it seemed at the beginning as if the sound film could preserve such artistic achievements of the silent film as the close-up which revealed the microphysiognomy of the actors and the face of things; the living soul of landscapes; the rhythm of cutting; the change of viewpoint and set-up. What was it then that was so offensive to so many at first?

It was a bitter disappointment, a painful revelation in fact, when the public heard and understood for the first time what the film stars were saying on the screen, after having for so long only seen them talking. Not the fact that they were talking but what they said was a shock. The things they were saying were so trite, so inane, that the public of a higher level of taste longed to have the silent film back again. Thus it happened that the objection to the platitudes and silliness of the dialogue turned into a prejudice against dialogue as such.

The authors of the silent films were very seldom great writers and the quality of their dialogue was in accordance with their own qualities as writers. The mimic dialogues of great actors were often more expressive, more profound and more moving than the dialogues of even the best film writers of the day. In the silent film we understood the speech of the eyes even without words. A glance from Asta Nielsen or Lillian Gish or Charlie Chaplin spoke volumes—more than the words of many a good writer. The mute dialogues of such actors often moved us even if the story of the film was as silly as could be.

But when these great mute speakers actually began to speak, something terrible happened. The incredible triviality of their audible words overlaid the human depths of their glances and gestures. For now it was no longer these great artists who were speaking to us in the language of hand and eye, but the scriptwriters! A great illusion was destroyed.

Strangely enough to this day the public and the critics treat the dialogue in sound films with far greater indulgence than dialogue on the stage. But in those old days no one so much as conceived the idea that the film might have anything to do with serious literature and that the dialogue of the sound film might have possibilities, tasks and problems that are deeper than those of the stage dialogue, and, what is more, are completely new, completely of our own time.

SILENCE IS ACTION

Even to-day the watchword is still 'speak as little as possible'. And yet it is wrong to represent the characters in a film at all cost as always less talkative than the actors in the theatre. After all, the characters in the silent film also spoke but we did not hear what they were saying. The titles of course told us no more of the mute dialogue than was absolutely indispensable for the understanding of what was going on.

But in the sound film, if no talking is to be heard, no talking may be seen either. For it is of course impossible that the public should hear every noise save only human speech; it is equally impossible to render audible only two 'important' sentences and let the public merely see the rest as soundless mouthing, the way it was in the days of the silent film. Hence if in a sound film no speaking is to be heard, then the characters must in fact not talk.

But the silence of human beings is not merely a passive negative. The act of keeping silent is often an intentional, dramatically expressive act, and always an indication of some quite definite state of mind.

In the silent film every shot is silent but it very rarely depicts silence. Silence is either a characteristic trait of a character or must have some dramaturgical motivation. In the film no more than on the stage can characters fall silent simply 'in order that there may be less talking'; if it is done without inner motivation, a meaningless void is created.

Talking much or little is not merely a matter of quantity. Here quantity very soon turns into quality and the formal acoustic effect grows beyond itself into a dramaturgical factor. Speaking much or little is a difference in characterization.

In Ostrovski's famous play *Storm*, the heroine, Catherine, is a chatterbox, who never stops babbling. This restless, unceasing talking outlines her undecided, unstable, volatile character, recalling the fluttering of a bird. Only such a chattering, silly child could be the victim of such a tragedy as the one which overtakes Catherine. But when a producer, Petrov, in his aversion to much talking presented Catherine as a taciturn woman, he changed her character; she was now a sober, quiet and resolute woman who could not have possibly experienced the fate which was natural and necessary in the case of Ostrovski's original Catherine.

The speech of human beings is not a progress report given to some audience—it is an instinctive expression of their emotions and is just as independent of rational intentions as is laughing or weeping. Live men and women don't say only things that have reason or purpose and it is not their rational utterings that are most characteristic of them. We must not

forget, even in the sound film, that speech, apart from everything else, is a visible play of features as well.

A U D I B L E   G E S T U R E   O F   S P E E C H

In the American films of recent years people talk a great
deal, far too much in fact. This is one of the symptoms of the
decadent relapse of the American film towards the photographed theatre. Often this happens merely for technical
reasons, in order to reduce the cost of production. And yet
precisely in these dialogue scenes there is something specifically filmic.

In discussing the silent film we have already analysed speech
as expressive movement, which can show the most delicate
shades of emotion even if we cannot understand what is being
said. Now in the present-day sound film we understand the
words and therefore very often understand that their meaning
is unimportant. But all the more important is the tone in which
they are said: the cadence, the emphasis, the timbre, the husky
resonance, which are not intentional, not conscious. Vibrations
of the voice may mean many things that are not included in
the meaning of the word itself—it is a sort of accompaniment
to the words, a verbal gesture.

Loquacity is often merely a vehicle for such extra-rational
expression and the easy, fluid speaking manner of the modern
film is very suitable for such vocal manifestations. In this
manner the words glide out from between the lips with a
fleeting, feeble smile, or a scarcely noticeable shadow of grief
in the eyes. The micromimicry of the close-up turns such
speech into an audible play of features.

Modern actors in modern stage plays also speak without
rhetorical emphasis. But the stylized framework of the stage
settings, the position of the footlights and the distance from
the audience nevertheless do not permit such weightless
speech. Then there is the sound connected with mere breathing, which we ourselves do not even perceive as intentional
action, but merely as the acoustic aura of a human being,
something like the scent of skin or hair. Herein lies a specific
opportunity for the sound film. The ever-completely open

whole space of the theatrical stage damps down the emphasis of the spoken word; the film close-up renders such emphasis as unnecessary as it does the violent grimacing, the lurid make-up or the sweeping gesture.

WHY LANGUAGE DUBBING IS IMPOSSIBLE

One of the most acute problems of film production to-day is the question of exports to areas speaking a foreign language. This problem affects especially small nations very seriously. The inner market is insufficient to pay for production costs and the great nations who can satisfy the demand of their own inner market by their own production, very seldom buy films, the foreign dialogue of which has to be conveyed to the public by means of titles. It is well known that half the effect is lost in this way.

Why then is dialogue not dubbed in various languages? This was done a good deal in the first years of the sound film and this technique has also made great progress since that time. There must be a serious reason for the film industry's abandonment of this practice and with it much of the possibility of earnings in foreign countries.

The reason is that by now it has become impossible to dub in the dialogue of a sound film. This is a result of the developmen of film culture to a higher stage. The sound film has educated the public to see and hear the profound connection between speech and facial expression. The public to-day understands not only the meaning of the spoken word but also the sound-gesture that goes with it (which was discussed in the preceding chapter) and can hear in it the parallel to gesture and facial expression. A thus sophisticated public immediately feels the contradiction between, say, French facial expression and an English voice subsequently dubbed on to it. In the old days when we as yet paid attention only to the conceptual meaning of the dialogue, it was conceivable that someone in a film should say in English with an English calm, cool intonation 'I love you' and accompany the words with passionate Italian gestures. It strikes the present-day public as irresistibly funny if it notices—and it does notice—a discrepancy of temperament between word and gesture. This is a consoling thought because it proves that the sound-film culture of the public has developed greatly since the dubbing days, even though this development made dubbing impossible.

AESTHETIC LAW OF IMPERMEABILITY

We know that the Shakespearian stage had no scenery. No visual impression distracted the attention of the audience from the words of the play. Shakespeare's colourful language filled the stage with a rich baroque imagery. But æsthetics have a law which is related *per analogiam* to the law of impermeability known to physics. According to this the sound film is so full of visual images that there is little room in it for words. This is the exact opposite of the position on the Shakespearian stage. The sound film consists of a series of pictures and the words sound within the picture—they are just as much an element of the picture as any line or shadow. They will always only complete or stress the impression made by the picture. For this reason the words must not become too prominent in it. The sound film demands a style of weightless words.

THE FILM SHOT AND THE WORD

It is an artistic postulate that each shot should be a properly composed picture. The words must not be allowed to burst the bounds of this composition. Words can assist the film's visual pictoriality by permitting the leaving-out of many transition shots which would be needed only to make what is happening easier to understand, which can be adequately narrated in words, and which it would not be worth while to show pictorially. The talkie can even give optical emphasis to words, can underscore them visually, for instance by making the character say the crucial sentence in a close-up and thereby lifting it out above the rest. Another device is to have it said in a suddenly enlarged shot taken by the camera moving quickly closer to the speaker. Camera technique thus makes it possible to emphasize a word or a phrase without the speaker actually having to do so. On the stage, only the actor can put stress on a word. If he wants to give it prominence he must speak it in a different tone from the other words, even though this is not otherwise indicated or desirable. In the talkie the actor can speak with an unchanged, uniform lack of emphasis and not he but the suddenly changed set-up (which is a matter for the director) will cause the public to note the importance of a certain word. The character into whose mouth such words are put may not even know that these particular words are key words. Their significance is established not by the actor but by the set-up. Hence the dialogue of a sound film need not be as well-constructed, logical and so completely revealing as the dialogue in a stage play. For the picture—and not only the things depicted in it, but its whole atmosphere—may express much of what the words do not say.

On the other hand the words must fit into the composition of the picture in such a way as to enhance acoustically and not counteract the visual effect of the former. For instance the words must not attract our attention just when the visual picture is expressing something important.

The strength of sound and the tone of the lighting also have to be in harmony with each other. Further, if the spoken words have a sound background (background music or noise), then, if something is visible of pictorial background, the word should not stand out more from the *acoustic* background than the speaking figure stands out against the *visual* background.

SPEECH AS AN IRRATIONAL SOUND EFFECT

It has already been said that the spoken word is not merely the reflection of a concept—its intonation, its *timbre,* at the same time make it an irrational expression of emotion. It has further been said that the sound film with its close-up is more suitable than the theatrical stage for capturing these underlying acoustic colourings which express not only the logical thoughts of the speakers but the unconscious moods which at the same time are reflected by their facial expression. It is the business of poets to capture in writing the moods which hover, as it were, between the words. But it is one of the paradoxes of irrational expression that one can 'read between the lines' only where rationally readable lines are avail-able. The unspoken word can find a voice only as a sort of consonant of the spoken word. Between two clearly intelli-gible words we can seize, as between the points of delicate forceps, that something for which there is no word. But words which have no rational content can never conjure up the aura of irrational moods. They can be only inarticulate sounds of passion, such as screams, sobs, laughter, which cannot express subtly differentiated shades of feeling. The irrationality of such sounds gives no deeper meaning to words but deprives them on the contrary of all meaning.

CHAPTER EIGHTEEN

PROBLEM OF THE SOUND COMEDY

THE CONCEPTUAL, RATIONAL quality of the word makes the sound-film comedy a rather special problem. The distortion of visual forms appears as a distortion only if we remember the original form of which it is a distortion and recognize it in the caricature. Unless this is so, we would be seeing just another form with no relation to any other living thing. The caricature is the more effective, the more it resembles its original. But a sound, as we have already said, is not capable of varied angles. Any change in a sound simply produces another sound which has no connection with the previous one.

Of course the analogy to a shape is not a single sound but a sound picture or melody, and caricatures of melodies are within the range of possibility. But how can one distort the voice of a living being or the noises of nature in such a manner as to keep them still recognizable?

Are improbable sounds, fantastic or grotesque noises possible at all? We can imagine fairies or witches or ogres or dragons and other fairy-like characters and draw them too—but fairy-tale sounds, fairy-tale voices and noises . . . what are they like? We can invent all sorts of non-existent and impossible things but we cannot invent impossible sounds, that is sounds which could not be heard in reality, for we must produce them if we invent them. A picture being an image, an illusion, may be the image of something non-existent and merely imagined. The sound in a film is on the contrary not an *image* of a real sound, but a repetition, a re-voicing of the real sound itself. In other words it is impossible to invent an impossible sound.

IMPROBABLE SOUNDS

A sound itself cannot in itself be improbable. But the source of a sound may be improbable or inadequate. The roaring of a lion is not in itself grotesque, but it becomes so if it comes out of the mouth of a mouse. A sound in itself does not appear distorted if we do not see it together with a picture to which it is unsuitable. On the other hand the sight of an unsuitable source of sound may be very funny and this device has been used a great deal by the American cartoons. When Mickey Mouse spits, the gob makes a noise on the floor like a bass drum.

It is no less improbable and hence fairy-tale-like when things which normally have no voice at all suddenly begin to speak. Or if for instance a spider begins to play the harp on the threads of its web and the threads do really emit the sounds of a harp. The threads of the web can have some resemblance to the strings of a musical instrument and this visual resemblance is the basis for the sound-association. If we see a skeleton dancing and someone tapping its ribs with a thigh-bone, as a xylophone player does the xylophone keys, and if the sound heard is like that of a xylophone, this strikes the listener as convincing.

It is a well-known phenomenon that certain visual impressions arouse acoustic associations. Poets very often mention such things. Who has not heard of the silver tinkle of moonbeams or the jingle of the harebell? The cartoon film had only to take the most trivial metaphors literally in order to obtain funny but perfectly convincing sound-pictures.

SPEECH GROTESQUES

Possibilities in this field are much more limited owing to the conceptual and rational nature of words. We may exaggerate or distort a mannerism of speech for instance and produce a funny effect. Intonation and cadence can be thus exaggerated even without intelligible words. But the limits to which words can be distorted are fixed by the limits of intelligibility. Words and sentences which are quite unintelligible cannot be funny.

If we see something incomprehensible, perhaps in darkness or in a dream, such a thing may still be uncanny and frightening. But if words are incomprehensible, they are robbed of every possibility of being terrifying. They turn into empty, conglomerates of sound which convey nothing and rouse no associations of any kind in us.

Convincing historical proof of the great difficulty of talkie comedies is the fact that with the emergence of the talkie the already very well developed American slapstick comedy almost completely disappeared. None of the world famous great masters of this genre could retain their popularity in the world of sound. Neither Buster Keaton nor Harold Lloyd survived because they were unable to distort their voices and speech to harmonize with the funniness of their visual appearance. Charlie Chaplin is an exception and he will be discussed later in this connection.

PROBLEM OF THE MUSICAL GROTESQUE

The basic principle of the musical grotesque is also that a sound is made grotesque by the fact that its quality is at odds with the nature of the instrument producing it. In Alexandrov's film *Jazz Comedy,* a musical farce, the shepherd taps the peasant jugs and plays on them as on a musical instrument. But the melody he thus produces is not at all grotesque. What is grotesque is the surprising fact that he is able to produce such a not-at-all-distorted, even pleasant melody, by tapping earthenware jugs. If we were not shown the funny source of this music, we would see nothing funny in it at all. Thus a beautiful melody may strike us as funny if it emanates from objects which do not seem suitable to produce it. The musical clowns of the circus ring have used this effect from time immemorial. When a clown takes a broomstick, a pig's bladder and a piece of string and turns them into a string instrument from which he evokes the mellow sounds of a violoncello, then what is funny is not the sound of the cello but the fact that it is produced by a broomstick and a pig's bladder.

Another basic principle of sound distortion is that the fact and intention of distortion should be manifest. This is possible only if the original sound, the sound which is to be shown distorted, is either universally known to the public or can be heard by it at the same time as the distorted sound. A frequent musical joke for instance is when musical instruments imitate human or animal sounds—it is much in use in jazz. The saxophone laughs, the clarinet crows like a cock, and that is amusing as it would not be if a member of the band actually laughed or a real cock were made to crow.

FILM MUSIC

To-day even the most serious composers write music for the film and regard it as a distinct form of art, like the opera. This has been rendered possible by the sound film. The silent film did not provide much inspiration for the composers, although it was throughout accompanied by music. The main reason for this was that few cinemas had a good orchestra of their own and that the films were shown, and hence the music played, for only a very short time. The sound film, unlike the silent, preserves permanently the good performance of a piece of music just as a gramophone record does.

In the last years of the silent film serious music was nevertheless composed frequently for certain especially important productions. Because such music accompanied silent pictures, it was natural that it should be used to indicate the absent sounds and hence was more or less programme music. The roaring of the sea, the thunder of machinery and other such naturalistic sounds were exactly recorded in the score as musical components of the composition, which were evoked at the waving of the conductor's baton, as if they were issuing from some novel noise-producing instruments.

The sound film made such naturalistic imitation of sounds by music unnecessary. In the sound film the sea itself can roar as it pleases and no longer needs the assistance of the orchestra, the machines can thunder, cocks can crow, and the music need not imitate anything—it can remain pure music. Of course the composer must take into account the volume of sound which the recording apparatus records as the natural noises of life and must compose his music to fit it, in order that the final acoustic impression may be all of one piece.

Thus the sound film in its most recent development no longer seeks to illustrate the passions seen in the pictures, but to give them a parallel, different, musical expression. The visible reflection in the picture and the audible manifestation in the music of the same human experience thus run parallel without being dependent on each other. It is natural for music to accompany the main turning-points of the action of the film, but it need not translate its every motive into rhythm— such servile following of the action would lend the film a ballet-like or pantomime-like quality.

The composer working for the sound film must also be able to remain silent when required. For silence is an important medium of expression in the sound film. It can be like the holding of one's breath in a moment of intense tension. It can help to establish an atmosphere. But frequently it is precisely the music which expresses the great experience of silence, of quiet. The great spiritual experience of silence cannot be adequately expressed by the mere negative of an absence of sound; it is expressed in the face of one who is silent, in a gesture or in a music which is the voice of silence. Perhaps the most perfect example of this is the scene in Wagner's *Flying Dutchman*, when the Dutchman first meets Senta. They stand facing each other for a long time in silence. They themselves are silent, but the music is not. Such a long, frozen silence would be unbearably empty on the stage if the silence were complete, if the music did not express the passions ravaging the hearts of the mute characters.

CHARLIE CHAPLIN'S SECRET

Charlie Chaplin was against the talkie from the start. He had no objection to sounds and noises and used them from the beginning. He did not even mind if the other characters in his films talked, as long as he himself could remain silent. This conservative attitude began to make even the visual picture-technique of his films dangerously out of date, for in dramatic scenes he could not bring the characters into close-up, for in close-up the public would have to hear what they were saying;

now, in the days of the sound film, it would have appeared that the sound apparatus had broken down. Nowadays the silence of a film would never be regarded as artistic intention, but only as a technical lapse. It was for this reason that Chaplin's *Modern Times* was more primitive, more out of date in its camera-work than his last silent films had been.

What we have lost in no longer being able to see close-ups of Charlie's face can be measured only by those who remember the heart-rending close-ups of his older films, those sad and wise child-like eyes, that roguishly charming smile and the tragic expression of frustrated goodwill in eyes overflowing with kindness.

If Chaplin's last films were nevertheless great artistic achievements, they were so not because of their silence but in spite of it. There was nothing in these films which would have justified their silence as an artistic necessity. So Charlie's silence remained a mystery right up to the time he made *Modern Times*, when at last he found his tongue—but only to sing. And in that singing scene it was at once clear why Charlie did not want to speak before.

Not that his voice is unpleasant. On the contrary, he has a perfectly charming voice. But how was Charlie to speak? How does such a funny little man speak, who wears such a funny bowler hat perched on the top of his head, whose pants are so wide and wrinkled, who walks with such a funny little cane, on such funny boat-like feet, with such a funny waddling gait? Such a funny figure must have a correspondingly funny voice and manner of speech. But what would such a voice and manner be like? How does a caricature talk? How does a mask talk? What is its voice like? What manner of speech would be as funny and touching, as clumsy and agile, as good-natured and cunning, as Charlie's visual image? Can this improbable, yet convincing, this true and yet unnatural being talk naturally, without affectation?

Charlie, the funny little man, would have had to invent some specific manner of speech which would have been as different from the speech of other men as his appearance was different from the appearance of other men. We know that the actors of the ancient Greek theatre did not talk naturally but used a kind of megaphone to recite their verses. Their language and voice were not natural. The masques of the ancient Japanese theatre also had their unnatural style of speech. The Charlie-image would also have had to have an artificial voice and language, an acoustic mask to match his visual make-up.

Charlie had to be silent, for he was locked into his own grotesque mask, a mask which he had invented for himself and the success and popularity of which imprisoned him like an iron mask and would not let him go.

Then why did Chaplin nevertheless break silence in his *Modern Times*? Because there he sang and a text that is sung is not natural and tolerates a funny distortion no less than does a visual image. In that singing scene Chaplin loses his cuff on which he noted the words of the song he was to sing. Why? In order that he need not pronounce sensible, natural words. He begins to gabble, he sings meaningless, non-existent words and the result is a grotesque caricature in the sphere of sound which harmonizes well with his visual appearance and manner, because it is as unnatural as these.

This was, however, merely a resourceful evasion of the problem and not a solution. But it is already obvious that Chaplin is working hard to escape from the prison of the old Charlie mask. His figure is developing and gaining in depth and stature both socially and psychologically. The inevitably stereotyped character of a grotesque mask no longer satisfies him. The Charlie mask, that figure of unprecedented popularity throughout the whole world, the mask which has so long gagged Charles Chaplin the great artist and great man, was in fact eventually discarded in *Monsieur Verdoux*.

Modern Times was the first step in this direction. Charlie now rarely wears his little bowler, the little cane has left his hands, the shoes on his waddling feet are not so long. And those who watched the last shot of the film with attention, will remember that the Chaplin sitting in the ditch with the girl no longer wears the old mask and is no longer funny, but a clean, earnest-faced man. It was obvious then that in his next film Charlie would speak.

In *The Great Dictator* Chaplin was already speaking. And he even had his little moustache shaved to be less like Hitler.

There is another very interesting difference between the old Chaplin and the new, between the old grotesque figure and the new, many-faceted personality. In the last shot of *Modern Times* Charlie for the first time does not go his ways alone but with a girl friend. The silent Charlie was not only silent, he was also always alone and lonely!

PERSPECTIVES OF THE SOUND FILM

It has already been said that the sound film was not an organic continuation of the silent film, but another art in its own right, just as painting is not a more highly developed form of black and white graphic art but a different art altogether. We can easily imagine that they might have emerged in inverted sequence. If the sound film had been invented first, someone might still have had the idea of using dumb-show silent pictures to create a separate new art, the silent film. It might have been an artistic tit-bit for the select few, a collector's piece for the highbrows in contrast to the more widespread and vulgar art of the sound film. But it might also have been much more. I could imagine, I might even dare to initiate (now that the sound film has become paramount) a new kind of silent film which would really present only those most specifically visual experiences which cannot find room in the sound film. I can also imagine quite concretely, and would like to initiate, a new kind of film lyric which would be a hitherto unknown synthesis of the silent and sound films. Its content would be not a story but a lyrical poem. One would hear the words of the poem and the images of a parallel-running picture film would form a silent accompaniment to these words, not as illustrations but as free associations of ideas, the two interpreting one another in counterpointed simultaneity, just as in a *lied* the melody and accompaniment are a complement to the words. The music of silent pictures would widen the film poem into a work of art in three voices, in which words, music and pictures would be merged into one organic whole.

SPARING USE OF SOUND

I have previously complained that the sound film did not develop into a revelation of a new world of acoustic experience as we had expected and as it at the outset actually set itself to do. On the contrary it in part grew silent again where it had already sounded once. At first we heard the splash and rippling of every running water, we heard the thud of every footstep, the creaking of every door, the tinkling of every glass. The sound film seemed noisier than noisy life itself. The sound film of to-day uses sound much more sparingly and rightly so, for where sound is only a natural complement, it is as coarsely superfluous as would be the painting of a statue with the purpose of making it seem more lifelike. Sound is justified only when it has artistic significance; that is, when it has some dramaturgical part to play or if it is required to establish an atmosphere.

RULE OF THE WORD

What is the cause and explanation of the fact that the world of noises, the presentation of the acoustic *milieu,* has been relegated to the background even as a theme, although the technique of sound recording seemed to be the very thing for reproducing these effects and experiences? In the course of its development the sound film reverted to a stage more primitive than that reached by the silent film and again came closer to the style of the theatre.

The cause and explanation is the word. For the sound film is also a talking film. The silent film, in which the word could play no constructive part, developed the expression of emotional, non-rational experiences in a visual form-language. The sound film, with its acoustic form-language, could not develop the non-rational side of emotional experience in the same way. For in it the rational word had to be allotted its proper place, otherwise it would have been a sound-accompanied silent film, or a film of mutes. The conceptual interpreting force and content of the word, its ability to recall the past and forecast the future not only rendered superfluous many roundabout visual and acoustic devices developed for this purpose by the silent film, but completely crowded them out of the film by force of the æsthetic law of impermeability already mentioned.

All these are realities of the evolving history of the film about which it would be vain to argue. No theory could alter this practice. But we maintain that the power of theory to render conscious what is instinctive can grow into a material force and while it is itself a result of evolution, can dialectically react on evolution and influence it. This return of the sound film to a previous stage is not inevitable and final. Without reducing the importance of the word, the expression and artistic forming of acoustic experiences can (and I am certain will), again develop to a higher stage. I am sure that our sound-film makers will soon realize that in the sound film the use of the word offers quite different possibilities and is therefore faced with quite different tasks than the dialogue on the theatrical stage.

FILM NARRATOR

I believe there is a great future for the narrated film, in which the story is narrated by an invisible author-narrator. This device would free the visual presentation from having to show unimportant details merely in order to render the story intelligible—for we shall hear the words of the narrator telling us what has happened. While he is doing so the pictures can show the internal happenings in a counterpointed association of ideas and thus open a depth-dimension to the film which it did not possess before.

This kind of sound film, the birth of which is imminent, will again be able to use, and thus save for us, the high degree of visual culture once already attained by the silent film.

CHAPTER NINETEEN

REMARKS ON THE COLOUR FILM AND STEREOSCOPIC FILM

THE TECHNICAL PROBLEMS of the colour film have no interest for us. Colour in the film has artistic significance only if it expresses some specifically filmic experience. If it merely wanted to compete with the artistic effects of painting, it would be doomed to defeat from the outset and could never be anything but a primitive and trite parody of the greatest and most ancient art. The artistic reason for colour cinematography can lie only in the experience and expression of colour in motion.

MOVING COLOURS

One of the dangers of the colour film is the temptation to compose the shots too much with a view to a static pictorial effect, like a painting, thus breaking up the flow of the film into a series of staccato jerks. On the other hand the filming of colours in movement, provided our technique is sensitive enough to record them and our sensitivity sufficiently developed to absorb them, could open up a vast domain of human experience which could not find expression in any other art, least of all in painting. For a painter may paint a flushed face but never a pale face slowly being warmed to rose-red by a blush; he can paint a pale face but never the dramatic phenomenon of blanching.

Why does the beauty of a painted sunset often strike us as trivial, although in nature a sunset is always exciting and interesting? Because in reality a sunset is an event, not a static condition, it is a change of colour, a transition from one spectacle to the next which is often rendered a mere formula by the rigid abstraction of a painting.

242

In the first colour film made by the Russian director Ekk we see a boorish foreman pursuing a girl with unwelcome attentions. The girl rebuffs him indignantly and we see the gentle blue of her eyes darken and an angry glint come into them. Colours can by their changing express emotions and passions which mere facial expression without colour could not convey. Changes of colour add shadings and delicacy to the play of the features. For a change of colour can be most expressive even if not a muscle moves in the face. Here is a possibility of extending microphysiognomics by means of colour.

The movement of colour is sometimes so delicate as to be imperceptible but nevertheless effect a change in atmosphere. A landscape shown at noon in summer, although it appears motionless, yet makes quite a different impression in a colour film than on the best painting. For however skilfully a good painter can convey the effect of vibrating hot air, he can never match the effect of the colour film in which the dark-blue sky really vibrates, and thereby, however imperceptibly, changes the impression made on us by the landscape.

COLOUR CUTTING

The cutting of colour films also brought new problems and tasks. Not only must the colours following upon each other be in harmony—there is also the point that the black-and-white picture was much more homogeneous, much more of one material. The difference in colour differentiates things and figures much more sharply than the old grey films did. The formal rules of dissolves are much influenced by this fact. The coloured forms appear more massive and merge into each other far less easily than the less weighty grey light-and-shadow photographs—unless they happen to dissolve into their dominant colour. The dissolve based on similarity of form, much used in the silent film, can seldom be used in colour films, because here the most characteristic feature of a figure is not its shape but its colour.

Thus the similarity or contrast of the colour plays a very important part in the editing of a colour film, and that not only for formal reasons, but because colours have an extraordinary symbolic effect, an intense power of evoking associations of ideas and inspiring emotions.

Another difficulty in the cutting of colour films is due to the fact that colour lends depth and perspective to the shots. No longer do two-dimensional images slide into each other on the same plane. Colour enables us to distinguish things in the background which in a similar black-and-white film would have been a mere greyish fog. In a black-and-white picture the impression of distance is a negative effect: it consists in our not seeing things clearly. In a coloured background, however, we see quite clearly that such and such an object is far away, and we find it more difficult to withdraw our gaze again and again as the pictures change.

STEREOSCOPIC FILMS

The stereoscopic film will naturally make the problem of editing even more difficult. One of the essential effects of the old film was the effortless ease of change, rendered possible by the depthless shadows of the black-and-white film. It is difficult to imagine that in the coloured, stereoscopic sound film which will give us a complete illusion of palpable three-dimensional reality, the shots could follow upon each other in rapid succession, with the speed of thought-association. We must also remember that the stereoscopic film which produces the illusion that the figures on the screen are three-dimensional and protrude into the audience, will break up even more that traditional closed composition of the picture which was from the birth of the film a specific trait of the new art. In this respect the stereoscopic film will be even more 'filmic' than the two-dimensional film. But so far as the rhythm of the cutting is concerned, it will demand a very different set of rules, quite new rules.

Colour and particularly the change of colour can play a dramaturgical part, can influence the course of the action. It may also have a symbolic significance. In the film by Ekk, already mentioned, the last shot shows the girl waving a white cloth from a tower as a signal. But she is wounded and the white cloth, stained with her blood, is transformed into a red flag. This has a decisive effect on events. The workers in the factory see a red flag waving from the tower.

However, colour, unlike the more decisively significant word, cannot essentially change the dramaturgical structure of a film; it can only sometimes enhance the significance of certain scenes.

COLOURED CARTOONS

The quickest and most final victory of colour was its conquest of the cartoon world. Not only because it offered fewer technical difficulties, but because, for the time being, it was easier to produce artistic effects here, where the colours could be chosen and painted, and did not have to be photographed. The artistic presentation of the movement of colours has been so little able to approach our natural experiences that a well-photographed sunset or sunrise will still be richer in colour shadings than any colour cartoon, however skilfully painted.

CHAPTER TWENTY

THE SCRIPT

NOT SO VERY long ago it was still difficult to convince the Philistines that the film was an independent, autonomous new art with laws of its own. To-day this is scarcely ever questioned and it is also admitted that the literary foundation of the new art, the script, is just as much a specific, independent literary form as the written stage play. The script is no longer a technical accessory, not a scaffolding which is taken away once the house is built, but a literary form worthy of the pen of poets, a literary form which may even be published in book form and read as such. Of course scripts can be good or bad, like any other literary work, but there is nothing to prevent them from being literary masterpieces. That the literary form of the film script has not yet had a Shakespeare, a Calderón, a Molière, an Ibsen is no matter—it will have some day. In any case, we do not even know whether there may or may not have been some great masterpiece lost among the thousands of film scripts to which we paid not the slightest attention. We never searched for masterpieces among them, often even denied the very possibility of one being found in such an unlikely place.

Most cinema-goers do not realize that what they are watching is the staging of a film script, very much as they would be watching the staging of a play in the theatre. And even in the theatre, how many spectators think of this? If the newspaper reviews did not discuss the play itself and the performance of it as two distinct subjects, few theatre-goers would think of the literary creative work that has to precede every stage performance of a play.

That public opinion distinguishes more easily between play and stage performance than between script and screened film is due to the fact that a play can be performed in many ways in many theatres, thus demonstrating that the play has an existence of its own apart from the performance. The film on the contrary mostly absorbs the script completely so that it is not preserved as an independent object which could be used again for a different film production. In most cases it is not available in print; it is not yet an accepted custom to publish scripts for reading.

The film script is an entirely new literary form, newer even than the film itself, and so it is scarcely surprising that no books on the æsthetics of literature mention it as yet. The film is fifty years old, the script as a literary form only twenty-five at most. It was in the twenties of this century, in Germany, that specially interesting scripts first began to be published.

In this again the film slavishly copied the development of the stage. There had been highly developed and popular theatre, there had been great playwrights for centuries before plays began to be written down and made available for reading outside the theatre. In ancient Greece, in the Middle Ages and in the Renaissance the written play was always a product of a later differentiation. The drama began with ritual or improvisation, or was born on the stage itself out of the permanent characters of the *commedia dell' arte*. The stage is a much older thing than the play. It is well known that Shakespeare's plays were pieced together later from the parts written out for the actors.

In the same way the film is much older than the script. 'Much' here means about twenty years—but that is nearly half of the whole history of the film.

When the film began, there was no script; the director improvised each scene on the set, telling each actor what to do during the next shot. The sub-titles were written and cut in later.

The film script was born when the film had already developed into an independent new art and it was no longer possible to improvise its new subtle visual effects in front of the camera; these had to be planned carefully in advance. The film script became a literary form when the film ceased to aim at literary effects, planted itself firmly on its own feet and thought in terms of visual effects. The picture sequences of the photographed theatre could be written down in the form of a stereo-typed stage play; but a film using specific visual effects could no longer be pressed into the form of the drama, nor of the novel. A new form was needed. Its terms of reference and its novelty were determined by the paradoxical task it had to fulfil, which was to present in words the visual experiences of the silent film, that is, something that could not be adequately expressed in words.

The first scripts were in fact mere technical aids, nothing but lists of the scenes and shots for the convenience of the director. They merely indicated what was to be in the picture, and in what order, but said nothing about how it was to be presented.

In the days of the silent film the importance of the literary script grew in the same measure in which the adventurous film stories were simplified and the films themselves given a deeper meaning. The type of imagination the adventure-story writers possessed was no longer suitable; a special filmic imagination was required, subtle visual ideas without intricate plots. The intensity of the close-up drove out the complicated story and brought a new literary form into being.

Such a simplification of the story did not, however, simplify the film at all. There was less adventure, but more psychology. The development turned inward and script-writing was now a task worthy of the pen of the best writers.

It should be said here that this decline of the adventure story was not the only trend in the development of the silent film. There was at the same time a leaning towards the most exotic romanticism—and both these trends can be traced to the same origins. They were both escapist trends, but running in opposite directions. On the one hand the film provided escape into exotic, romantic adventure, on the other escape to some particle of reality entirely isolated from the rest.

With the birth of the talkie the script automatically came to be of paramount importance. It needed dialogue, as a play did, but it needed very much more than that. For a play is only dialogue and nothing else; it is dialogue spoken, as it were, in a vacuum. The stage, though indicated by the author's directions, is not presented in literary form. In the abstract spiritual space of the drama the visual surroundings of the *dramatis personae* were a mere background which could not influence their state of mind and hence could not take part in the action. But in the film visible and audible things are projected on to the same plane as the human characters and in that pictorial composition common to them all they are all equivalent participants in the action. For this reason the script-writer cannot deal with the scene of action by means of a few stage directions. He must present, characterize, depict the visual aspect as well as the rest, express it by literary means, but in much greater detail than for instance the novelist, who may leave a great deal to the imagination of his readers. In the script the script-writer must define the part played by the images of things every bit as carefully as all the other parts, for it is through them that the destinies of the human characters fulfil themselves.

Thus the now fully developed and mature film art had borne a new fruit, a new literary form, the film script. By now many scripts are available in print and soon they may be more popular reading than the more abstract stage play. It is difficult to say how much time must elapse before our literary critics finally notice this new phenomenon born before their eyes; for this reason we shall try to define the laws governing this new literary form.

The problem is: in what respect does the film script differ from the stage play or the novel? The question is put in this form because it will be easiest to define the specific principles and laws of the script by defining the essential qualities which distinguish it from the other forms most closely related to it.

The present-day script is not an unfinished sketch, not a ground-plan, not a mere outline of a work of art, but a complete work of art in itself. The script can present reality, give an independent, intelligible picture of reality like any other form of art. True, the script puts on paper scenes and dialogues which later are to be turned into a film; but so does the drama put on paper the stage performance. And yet the latter is regarded as a literary form superior to the former.

Written music is only a symbol of the music to be produced by the instruments, but nevertheless no one would call a

Beethoven sonata 'unfinished' or a 'sketch' because of this. We even have film scripts now which are intended for reading and could not be shot—just as there are 'book' plays which could never be staged. Nevertheless such scripts are not novels or short stories or stage plays—they are film scripts. They belong to a new literary form.

The basic fact which underlies every form of film and determines the laws governing the script is that the film is an audible spectacle, a motion picture, i.e. an action played out in the present, before our eyes.

One of the things that follow from this basic fact is that the script, like the drama, can present only 'real time'. The author cannot speak for himself in the script, just as he cannot in the drama. The author cannot say 'meanwhile time passed . . .', he cannot say '. . . After many years . . .' or '. . . after this . . .'.The script cannot refer to the past, cannot tell us about something that happened long ago or in some other place, it cannot summarize events, as the epic forms can. The script can only present what can be enacted before our eyes, in the present, in a space and time accessible to our senses; in this it is similar to the drama.

How, then, does the script differ from the **drama?**

In the film, as on the stage, the action is visible and audible, but on the stage it is enacted in real space (the space of the stage) by live human beings (the actors). The film on the other hand shows only pictures, images of that space and of those human beings. The film does not present some action played out in the imagination of a poet, but an actual event enacted in real space by real human beings in nature or in a studio, but presents only a picture, a photograph of these events. Thus it is neither a figment of the brain nor immediate reality.

The upshot of this is that the script as a literary form can contain only what is visible and audible on the screen. This appears to be a truism if we do not examine the bounds set by this rule. But it is on this that everything turns.

In one of the finest Soviet films, *Chapayev,* the political commissar attached to Chapayev's partisan troop arrests one of the partisan leaders for stealing a pig. But why lock him up on the farm where they are staying? There is only a dilapidated barn with a broken door that cannot be locked. We see this because the giant partisan more than once pushes his tiger-like head through the door. He could of course come out at will. What prevents him from kicking down the whole tumbledown contraption? That Furmanov, the political commissar, has placed a sentry to guard the door? But the sentry is even more decrepit than the barn; he is a hollow-chested short-sighted, pitiful little figure, a clerk who scarcely knows one end of his rifle from the other. The giant, savage partisan could blow the funny little man away with a breath of his mighty lungs. But he does not do so. It is thus made obvious that what holds the giant captive is not physical force but a moral influence. And we can *see* this moral influence, it is quite unmistakably manifested in a pictorial effect.

Then Chapayev himself comes to release his friend. But the ridiculous, miserable little private who is guarding the prisoner, bars his way. Whose way? The way of the commander, the tremendously strong, fierce, dangerous Chapayev, who rages, flings his sword away—but does not shove the ridiculous little soldier out of the way. Why? Here again it is not physical force that stops Chapayev, but a moral power rendered evident by the visible, pictorial presentation; a moral force incarnated in the hollow-chested, short-sighted, clumsy little man put there on guard by the representative of the Party. It is the authority of the Communist Party which even the undisciplined, unruly, fierce partisans respect and which endows the ridiculous little sentry with a conscious dignity.

Here the authority of the Party, although it may seem an abstract idea, has been rendered visible in a dramatic scene, and thus something that can be photographed. It is to be particularly noted that in this example there are no symbolic or 'metaphorical' shots, they are all quite real, ordinary, pictures with nothing improbable about them and yet they radiate a 'deeper meaning'.

LESSING AND THE FILM

In analysing the basic difference between the drama and its stage presentation, Lessing outlined the difference between the film script and the film a century and a half before their time. His definition of the nature and laws governing the stage were so brilliant that now, 150 years later, they helped us to define the different laws and the different nature of a different although not entirely unrelated art.

At the beginning of his *Hamburgische Dramaturgie* he speaks of plays made from novels and says: 'It is not at all difficult . . . to expand single emotions into scenes . . . but to be able to transpose oneself from the point of view of a narrator to the true point of view of each character and instead of describing their passions make these come into existence under the eyes of the spectator and develop without a break in an illusory continuity—that is what is needed here.' In this passage all is said about the most essential difference between drama and epic. The same difference exists between the film script and the epic. Like the drama, the script does not describe the passions but makes them come into being and develop under the eyes of the spectator. But in this same passage Lessing also defined the difference between the drama and the film script and has helped us to understand one of the basic principles of film art. He says that the drama presents the passions without a break, in an illusory continuity. And truly this is the specific quality of the drama; such continuity is a necessary consequence of the fact that the drama is written for the stage. For a character coming on to the stage is under our eyes in uninterrupted continuity, without a break, until it leaves the stage again.

PARALLEL ACTIONS

The novelist can take his readers into a large gathering and then deal with only one person of all the company. He can tell the whole life-story of that one person without informing the reader of what the other people present were doing all that time. The reader may easily forget that they are there at all. In the epic forms such 'jumps' are possible and the illusion of an unbroken continuity of scene is not imperative as it is on the stage. This is the basic difference between epic and dramatic forms.

In this respect, however, the film script is related to the epic rather than the dramatic form. The film, like the epic, is not bound to maintain the illusion of unbroken continuity, —such continuity is not even possible. In a film scene all the persons present at the same place not only need not all be visible in every shot but to show them all, all the time, would even be contrary to the style and technique of the film. The public has the illusion that the participants in the scene are present, but they are not always all of them visible. In ceaselessly changing short shots and close-ups we see only those whose face or words happen to be needed just then. The film can lift such a figure out of the greatest crowd and devote special attention to it, penetrate deeply into its emotions and psychology. In this the film and the film script are related to the epic.

The film can interrupt the continuity of a scene not only by not showing all the persons in a scene all the time—the whole scene itself can be interrupted, the film show a different scene enacted in quite a different place, and then the previously interrupted scene can be continued. This is inconceivable on the stage. The possibility of showing in parallel sequence more than one simultaneous action is a quite specific feature of the film and hence a specific possibility of the film script as an art form.

The unity of space thus binds the film even less than the least form-bound of dramas. For the drama cannot in the middle of a scene show another scene enacted in quite a different place and then return to continue the original scene. The law of the unity of space does not apply to the film at all. But the unity of time all the more so. For even if we interrupt a scene and the interpolated scene is enacted *elsewhere,* it must not be enacted at another *time.* It must happen neither sooner nor later, but at the same time, else the audience would either not understand what was going on or would not believe it.

TECHNICAL CONDITIONS AND
ARTISTIC PRINCIPLES

The question now arises: if there are several characters on the stage but only one or two of them are really engaged in speech or action, do not the others pale into mere lifeless properties? (This is what the technique of the film enables us to avoid.) In a good play this cannot happen, because a good play always has a central problem which organically binds together all the *dramatis personae*. Whatever is said on the stage, whoever says it, always concerns questions vital to all the characters and therefore they all remain alive and interesting. Thus the technical requirements of the stage determine the literary structure of the drama.

As we have seen, the technical requirements of the film are different and therefore the literary structure of the script is different too. The single central problem, the grouping around a single central conflict, which characterizes the structure of the drama, is contrary to the nature of the film, the technical conditions of which are different. The visual nature of the film does not tolerate a structure consisting of a few long scenes. The reason for this is that while long scenes without a change of setting are possible if they are full of internal movement and people can talk in a room for hours if their words express some internal movement or internal struggle, the film, in which the decisive element is always the visual, cannot be content with such long-drawn, merely internal—and hence non-visible— events. The film requires an external, visible, 'shootable' picture for every internal happening. For this reason the film script—again like the novel—does not centralize the conflicts but faces the characters with a series of problems in the course of the story.

One of the laws governing the form of the film script is its prescribed length. In this it resembles the drama, the length of which is determined by the duration feasible on the stage. Of course there are also dramas which are not intended to be performed and which disregard this condition. In the same way it is possible to write fine film scripts intended only for reading and not for shooting as a film.

The film, too, has by now developed a standard length, partly for business reasons, to enable the motion picture theatres to give several shows daily; but there are also physiological reasons which have limited the length of films. For the time being, films longer than ten thousand feet tire the eye.

These are merely external, technical considerations. But it often happens in art that external technical conditions harden into laws governing the internal artistic composition of the work. The short story was created by the predetermined length of the newspaper feature and this art form then brought forth such classics as the short stories of Maupassant or Chekhov. Architectural forms dictated many a composition of sculpture.

The predetermined length may also determine the content. The prescribed length of the sonnet determines its style. No one is forced to write sonnets or film scripts. But if one does, the predetermined length must not become a bed of Procrustes which curtails or draws out the required content. The theme, content and style of the film script must be inspired by the predetermined length of it. This predetermined length is in itself a style, which the script-writer must master.

By now the script has come to be an independent literary form. It was born of the film as the drama was born of the stage play. In the course of time the drama gained precedence over the stage play and now it is the drama that prescribes the tasks and style of the stage, and the history of the stage has long been merely an appendage to the history of the drama.

In the film there is as yet no trace of a similar development. But it will come in time. Up to now the history of the film script has been merely a chapter in the history of the film. But soon the script may in its turn determine the history of the film. Present developments certainly point in this direction.

In discussing the specific laws of the film script as a literary form there is, however, need for some further remarks. No art and no art form consist exclusively of specific elements, because the reproduction of reality has certain basic principles which are universally valid for every art. These principles, however, can be readily found in any text-book on æsthetics. Nevertheless, all things can be characterized the most precisely by means of the specific peculiarities which differentiate them from all other things. It is this specific trait which determines the varying forms of manifestation taken in each art by elements basically common to them all. For instance, painting can express not only experiences 'purely' and 'absolutely' pertaining only to the art of painting—it can also express motives borrowed from literature, philosophy, psychology—in fact every kind of thought and emotion. But whatever may be the content it expresses, such content will have to be made apparent in the specific material of painting, that is, in the form of visual impressions—otherwise it would not be made manifest at all. Hence if we talk of painting, we must first define its specific material.

The art of the film does not consist solely of specific film effects (any more than painting consists of colour effects alone) —however fiercely the fanatics of the absolute film championed such a limitation. In it, as in other art forms, we can find elements of dramatic presentation and of psychological characterization. But one thing is certain: in the film these elements can appear only in the form of moving and talking pictures, that is, they must conform to the specific laws of film art.

It has been said that the content determines the form. But things are not quite so simple as all that, and one need not take this rule to mean that for ages writers had been hatching film themes, film stories and film characters which could not be presented in novels or plays; that these poor authors had to wait decade after decade for the possibility of visual expression, until finally they went to the Lumière brothers and ordered a cinematograph, the new form to fit the new content.

History tells us that the reverse is what actually happened. Lumière had been photographing stage performances for a dozen years before a truly filmic, genuinely specific film story could be born. The hammer and the chisel were not invented by sculptors for their own ends. The technique of the film was known for some time. But it did not develop into a new form-language until a new content, a new and different message was added to it. The hammer and chisel would have for ever remained the tools of the stonemason, if there had been no human being who had experiences which could be best expressed by hewing stone into shape with hammer and chisel. But if a form of art has once developed, then its specific laws determine by dialectic interaction the suitable, specific themes and contents. The script-writers must make their contents conform to the laws governing the fully developed art form of the film.

Then new contents, too, may for a long time be contained in older forms, setting up tensions and causing slight changes in them until after a certain, perhaps a long, time, the new content bursts the old form and creates a new one. But this, too, is done within the bounds of the art form in question. The drama still remains drama, the novel novel, the film film. Only once in our history have we experienced the birth of a completely new art—the art of the film.

The dialectic interrelation of form and content can be compared with the interrelation of a river and its bed. The water is the content, the river-bed the form. Without a doubt it was the water that at one time dug itself this bed—the content created the form. But once the river bed is made it collects the waters of the surrounding countryside and gives them shape. That is, the form shapes the content. The power of mighty floods is required before the waters, over-flowing the old bed, dig an entirely new bed for themselves.

CHAPTER TWENTY-ONE

ART FORM AND MATERIAL

I T I S A N accepted practice that we adapt novels and plays
for the film; sometimes because we think their stories 'filmic',
sometimes because the popularity they have gained as novels
or plays is to be exploited in the film market. Original film
stories are very few and far between, a circumstance which
undoubtedly points to the undeveloped state and imperfections
of script-writing.

There is little point in discussing the practical aspects of
this question. Shall we demand original film stories when even
all the adaptations taken together are insufficient to satisfy
the demand? In practice the law of supply and demand decides
the issue. If there were a greater supply of good original film
stories, there would probably be less adaptations from other
forms.

We however are at the present moment interested in the
laws of art and not the law of supply and demand. The method
of adapting novels or plays may obey the latter law—
but does it not contravene the laws of art? Must not such
pandering to a practical demand necessarily be detrimental to
the interests of art and the æsthetic culture of the public?

'Necessarily' is the key word here, because on it depends
whether the problem is one of principle. For if such adaptations can be good *in principle* then it is for the film critics to
decide in each case whether they are well or ill done and
there is no theoretical problem.

There is, however, an old—one could almost say classic—
æsthetic viewpoint which rejects on principle all adaptations
on the grounds that they are necessarily inartistic. Here is a
problem that is of the greatest interest for the theory of art
because, although the opponents of adaptations base themselves on an undoubtedly correct thesis, they are nevertheless

258

wrong. The history of literature is full of classic masterpieces which are adaptations of other works.

The theoretical reason on which the opposition to adaptations is based is that there is an organic connection between form and content in every art and that a certain art form always offers the most adequate expression for a certain content. Thus the adaptation of a content to a different art form can only be detrimental to a work of art, if that work of art was good. In other words, one may perhaps make a good film out of a bad novel, but never out of a good one.

This theoretically impeccable thesis is contradicted by such realities as these: Shakespeare took the stories of some of his very good plays from certain very good old Italian tales and the plots of the Greek classical drama were also derived from older epics.

Most of the classical dramas used the material of the old epics and if we turn the pages of Lessing's *Hamburgische Dramaturgie* we will find that the very first three reviews in it deal with plays adapted from novels. It should be mentioned that the author of the immortal art philosophy contained in *Laokoon,* whose concern was precisely to find the specific laws governing each form of art, found much to criticize in the plays which he reviewed, but had no objection to their being the adaptations of novels. On the contrary, he proffered much good advice as to how such adaptations could be more skilfully done.

The contradiction appears so obvious that one must wonder why no learned æstheticist ever bothered to clear up this problem. For if the objection on principle to adaptations were merely a theoretical error, the matter would be simple. But it is not an error; it is a logical conclusion from the undeniably correct thesis about the connection between content and form.

It is obvious that the contradiction here is only apparent—an undialectic nailing-down of partial truths. It may be worth while to probe deeper for the source of the error.

To accept the thesis that the content or material determines the form and with it the art form, and nevertheless to admit the possibility of putting the same material into a different form, is thinkable only if the terms used are used loosely, that is if the terms 'content' and 'form' do not exactly cover what we are accustomed to call material, action, plot, story, subject, etc. on the one hand, and 'art form' on the other. There can be no doubt that it is possible to take the subject, the story, the plot of a novel, turn it into a play or a film and yet produce perfect works of art in each case—the form being in each case adequate to the content. How is this possible? It is possible because, while the subject, or story, of both works is identical, their *content* is nevertheless different. It is this different *content* that is adequately expressed in the changed form resulting from the adaptation.

The unsophisticated and naïve believe that life itself provides the writer with ready-made dramas and novels. According to this view every event has an *a priori,* immanent affinity to a certain form of art; that life itself determines what happenings are suitable for a play, for a novel or for a film; the writer is given, as it were, a pre-determined material as a definite subject susceptible of being used in only one way, in only one art form. If a certain subject takes his fancy, he cannot use the art form he pleases—that has been already decided by the artistic predetermination inherent in reality itself.

The world outside us, however, has an objective reality which is independent of our consciousness and hence independent of our artistic ideas. Reality has colours, shapes and sounds but it can have no immanent affinity to painting, sculpture or music, for these are specifically human activities. Reality does not of itself curdle into any art form, not even into subjects suitable for definite art forms, and waiting like ripe apples for some artist to pick them. Art and its forms are not *a priori* inherent in reality but are methods of human approach to it, although of course this approach and its methods are also elements of reality as a whole.

These methods of approach are naturally neither arbitrary nor is their number unlimited. In the cultural sphere of civilized humanity several such methods of approach (or art forms) have evolved as historically given objective forms of culture, and although they are merely subjective forms by means of which human consciousness approaches reality, they nevertheless appear to the individual as being objectively given. The parallel of the dialectic interaction of river and river-bed could again be quoted here as the model for the mutual relationship of material and art form.

Hence, if there is a 'dramatic' theme or subject which appears specific because it already shows the peculiar characteristics of the dramatic art form, then it is already *content* (which really determines the form it can take) and no longer mere 'material' i.e. merely the raw material of living reality, which cannot as yet determine its art form and could be the content of any of them not yet being content in its own right.

Such specific themes (or contents) are no longer mere fragments of reality—they are an approach to reality from the viewpoint of a certain form of art. One might call them 'semi-fashioned' for they are already prepared to fit into a certain art form. If we call them 'themes' 'subjects' or 'stories', we are already using a correlative term which cannot be conceived in itself, but only as the theme of something, e.g. a drama, as the subject of a novel, as the story on which a film is based. Such can be found only in a reality already regarded from the angle of one or the other of the forms of art.

What is the conclusion from this? That the raw material of reality can be fashioned into many different art forms. But a 'content', which determines the form, is no longer such raw material.

Are there not writers who write nothing but plays or nothing but novels? They, too, regard the entire reality of life, but only from the viewpoint of their own form of art, which has become an organic part of their approach. There are others who work in more than one art form; writers who regard life now with the eye of the novelist, now with the eye of the dramatist. So it may happen that they see the same bit of reality more than once; perhaps once as a drama and once as a film. But if this does happen, they would not be adapting their own drama for the screen. They would have gone back to their own basic experience and formed the same raw material once as a play, once as a film. It is quite certain that there are few outstanding events in history which have not served as material for ballads, plays, epics or novels. But a historical event is in itself only material, not theme. Material can still be regarded from the angle of various art forms. But a theme is already something regarded from the viewpoint of one or the other art form, lifted out of a multiform reality and developed into a dominant *motif*. Such themes can be adequately expressed in only one art form; they determine their art form, for they have themselves been determined by it. Such a theme, such a reality, such a material is already 'content' and determines its form.

Take a portrait. The reality of the model is as yet only raw material. It can be painted or drawn in black-and-white or modelled in clay. But if a true painter looks at the model, he will see colours in the first place, the colours will be the dominant characteristic and once this has happened the colours will no longer be raw material—they will be a theme for a painter, a content which determines the form, which is the art form, which is painting. A black-and-white artist will see the lines of the same model. Here, the same material will provide a different artistic theme, and this theme will be the content determining the art form, which will be drawing or etching or some other line technique. A sculptor may see the same model, and yet not the same model, for in his case it will be a model for a sculpture. The same material will provide for him a theme of plastic shapes, and thereby determine the adequate art form, sculpture.

The same applies to the literary forms. One writer may feel the atmosphere, the fleeting moods in a subject and take that for his theme; probably he will make it a short story. Another will see in the same subject a central conflict, an inexorable problem which demands a dramatic approach. The raw material of life may be the same, but the themes of the two writers will be different. And the different themes will give rise to different contents and demand different art forms. A third writer might come across the same event and see in it not the event itself but the inner adventures of human beings interacting with one another and showing the web of their destinies like a multicoloured carpet of life. This third writer would probably write a novel. Thus the same event as raw material regarded from three different angles can result in three themes, three contents, three forms of art. What mostly happens, however, is that a subject already used in one form of art is adapted to another form—in other words, it would not be the same model sitting to three different artists but rather a drawing made after a painting, or a sculpture after a drawing. This is much more problematic than the other case.

If, however, the artist is a true artist and not a botcher, the dramatist dramatizing a novel or a film-script writer adapting a play may use the existing work of art merely as raw material, regard it from the specific angle of his own art form as if it were raw reality, and pay no attention to the form once already given to the material. The playwright, Shakespeare, reading a story by Bandello, saw in it not the artistic form of a masterpiece of story-telling but merely the naked event narrated in it. He saw it isolated from the story form, as raw life-material with all its dramatic possibilities, i.e. possibilities which Bandello could never have expressed in a *novella*.

Thus although it is the raw material of a Bandello story that was given new form in a Shakespeare play, there is no trace of the main content of the play in the Bandello story. In that story Shakespeare saw a totally different theme and therefore the content that determined the art form of his play was also totally different.

I would like to mention here a less well-known adaptation, for the reason that the poet who was its author was at the same time an accomplished theoretician who could explain how and why the adaptation was made. Friedrich Hebbel, the German playwright, wrote plays based on the mighty epic material of the Nibelung saga. It would be quite impossible to accuse Hebbel of insufficient respect for the eternal greatness of the Germanic epic and its peerless formal perfection. Hebbel had no intention of improving on the Nibelung saga, nor can any intention of a popularization for money-making purposes be ascribed to this very serious writer. What then were his motives and his purpose in undertaking such an adaptation?

Hebbel himself gives the reason in his famous diary: 'It seems to me that on the foundation of the Nibelung saga one could build a purely human tragedy which would be quite natural in its motivation.'

What, then, did Hebbel do? He kept the mythical foundation, that is the skeleton of the story. But he gave it a different interpretation. The actions and events remained largely the same, but were given other motives and explanations.

Thus the same event, being given quite different emphasis, was turned into a different theme. The theme and content of Hebbel's Nibelung trilogy is not identical with that of the Nibelung saga. For although in Hebbel's drama Hagen kills Siegfried, as he does in the saga, he does so from entirely different motives and Kriemhild's vengeance, as depicted in Hebbel's drama, is a tragedy of a quite different order than the same event in the Germanic epic.

Nearly every artistically serious and intelligent adaptation is such a re-interpretation. The same external action has quite different inner motives, and it is these inner motives which throw light on the hearts of the characters and determine the content which determines the form. The material, that is the external events, serve merely as clues, and clues can be interpreted in many ways—as we know from the detective stories.

It often happens that a writer uses a second time, in another art form, the material he himself has once already used in a certain art form. We know that nowadays, especially when it is a question of adapting novels or plays for the films, this is mostly done for financial reasons. A successful novel can be adapted first as a play and then as a film, and thus make money for its author several times over. But sometimes such adaptations are made with quite serious artistic intentions.

Let us take a case in which no suspicion of financial motives can arise. We know that Goethe wanted to make a play out of his very interesting story 'The man of fifty', which is a part of his *Wilhelm Meister*. The plan of this play has been preserved—it gives, already divided into acts and scenes, the content of the projected play, which is the content of the story, only told in a different way. This different way very instructively shows why Goethe felt the need of re-writing in another art form the material once already used. We can see in detail how in the projected play he stresses aspects which are scarcely or not at all perceptible in the short story, how he tries to bring to the surface a totally different layer of reality. The course of events is similar, but their significance is different and it contains a quite different inner experience. The reality from which he borrowed his material included this inner experience; but when he shaped his material into a short story, he had to pass by this inner experience; it was for this reason that he felt the urge of dipping once more into the depths of the same life-material by means of another art form.

It may at first sound paradoxical to say that it is often a respect for the laws of style that govern the various art forms which makes adaptations justifiable and even necessary. The severe style of the drama, for instance, demands the omission of the multiple colours and changing moods of real life. The drama is the art form suited to great conflicts and the wealth of detail which a novel may contain finds no room in its severe structure. But sometimes the author is loath to let all the wealth of mood and detail go to waste and so he puts it into a novel rather than impair the pure style of the drama. And if an author wants to pour into a film the colours of life which are barred by the severe style of the drama, he does so not because he does not respect the style of the various art forms, but because he respects them absolutely.

CHAPTER TWENTY-TWO

PROBLEMS OF STYLE

THE FORM-LANGUAGE OF film art, although it has acquired an extraordinary power of expression, seems to have remained almost stationary in the past two decades during which more attention was given to content than to form. Now, after the end of the second world war, the as yet unexploited formal possibilities of the sound film seem to be entering on a new development.

After the first emergence of a filmic form-language, distinct styles and art forms began to develop within the framework of film art. The problems connected with the film styles are particularly interesting and important because their social roots and significance are revealed more openly than in any other medium of art.

THE EPIC

This problem came to the fore in its most conscious form in the Soviet film, where general questions of principle always received much attention. The problem of the epic was among others the subject of heated arguments. Some demanded of the Soviet film that in conformity with its Socialist spirit, it should not depict intimate private affairs, but present only problems that concern the whole community—in other words that it should be of epic proportions. This not unjustified demand had its dangers, which soon showed in Soviet scripts; too little attention was given to the psychology of individuals and the films were sometimes less studies of human beings than historical panoramas painted with a certain sociological pedantry and limited to generalizations.

Contrasting the epic and the intimate in this way poses the question incorrectly. Until the beginning of the nineteenth century this mutually exclusive choice was never thought of at all. Can there be anything more private and intimate than the conversation of two lovers in each others' arms? The situation itself demands isolation, retirement, concealment. And yet the amorous dialogue of Romeo and Juliet is one of the most epic scenes in the dramatic literature of the world, for in this most intimate, private dialogue a historical turning-point is reached: the revolt of individual personal love against the fetters imposed by the feudal, patriarchal family and the tribal laws.

That Antigone loves and respects her brother is a private family matter, but in Sophocles' tragedy it becomes an epic because it is made problematic by the dominant social order.

In former times art knew nothing of the contrast between the epic and the intimate, the great and the small, the universally valid and the merely private. Such differentiation between private experience and socially significant event in the mode of presentation is a phenomenon specific to bourgeois art. This brought about on the one hand the purely introspective 'chamber' art devoid of all social connections and on the other the decorative generalizations of the epic form which glosses over all individual traits. It is obvious from this that this problem could not survive very long in Soviet art and the Soviet film, and that the style of the newer Soviet forms was precisely the historical perspective manifested in private, individual human destinies.

Monumentality in art is not a question of quantity. Neither numbers nor dimensions decide it. Defoe's Crusoe, alone on a desert island, is undoubtedly one of the most epic tales in world literature. It is a well-known fact that it is impossible to estimate the dimensions of a painting or a piece of sculpture from a photographic reproduction of it. Some of these, although small, give the impression of monumentality, and *vice versa*. What is decisive is the principle that in art only man can be great or little. The large size of an elephant or of a mountain is without significance in art for it is an external, natural quality; a matter of chance, which does not express any inner greatness. Only man's living image can give us the real epic quality and this impression is the mightier, the more individual even, the more personal the image. The reason for this is that we well know the dimensions of normal men and unaccustomed largeness is therefore all the more striking. The colossi of ancient Egypt impress us as monumental because in their faces, in the corners of their eyes and lips, there is something individual, an almost intimately alive human expression. Without this they would be merely rocks resembling human beings, and rocks can be any size. As it is, they are human beings which resemble huge rocks and they impress us as superhuman because we can identify the human being and human proportions in them. If the outlines of a mountain remind one of the outlines of a human body, the mountain will appear smaller than its actual size. But if the statue of a man reminds one of a mountain through the weight of its forms, then it appears larger than its actual size—or in other words it will be monumental. The secret of the monumentality of the Ravenna mosaics is that they appear as individual portraits, although in reality they are huge architectural shapes formed out of stone.

A film can never be made 'monumental' by the number of extras in crowd scenes or the size of the set, but only by the weight of its theme or the personality of its hero. The most intimate human experiences can be the result and reflection of great historical events. The question is only whether the author can see and show them as such without any pedantic explanations.

STYLE AND STYLIZATION

The question of stylization in the film is exceptionally complicated because the technique of photography had from the start determined unstylized naturalness as the basic principle of filmic presentation. But there is no art which could evolve its styles without stylization. Nevertheless there is a difference between style and stylization.

We designate as style the formal characteristics of every art. The peculiarities of the artist's personality and those of his people, his class and his time are all reflected in the formal style of the work of art. As there is no work of art in which the personality of the artist, the ideology of his class, the traditions of his people and the taste of his time are not to some extent reflected, there is no work of art without style, even if the style is unconscious or insignificant.

It is important, however, that the work of art expresses the synthesis of all these influences in a unified style, in other words that the personal style of the artist, the style of his time and the style of his class and nation will all be manifested in the forms of a single style. In addition to this, every work of art worthy of the name has an *ad hoc* style of its own, in which its own content and tendency finds expression. It must also be remembered that the great historical styles came into being unconsciously and without theoretical intentions; they were born out of practice, almost imperceptibly, as mere fashions at first and only later, when they had already faded out, was it possible to recognize them as comprehensive, epoch-making 'styles'. Sometimes styles were born out of a false consciousness, based on false theories, such as the early Renaissance style,which was intended only as a modest imitation of the ancient Greek style and regarded itself as such. Or a style could be born under the influence of some moral trend devoid of any æsthetic ideas, as for instance the severe simplicity of the *directoire* style,which was an expression of the puritan spirit of the revolutionary bourgoisie as opposed to the aristocratic *rococo*. If we regard style as the general character of artistic forms, then even completely unstylized naturalism is a style; even an eclectic mixture of styles can be a style. The word style does not in itself imply any sort of value judgment.

So much for style. Stylization is quite another thing. The difference between style and stylization might best be illustrated by the example of literature. Every literary work—it need not even be a work of art—has some sort of style in the sense that it formulates what it has to say in some characteristic manner. But not every work of literature is stylized. For instance, plays written in natural colloquial dialogue are not stylized, but all poetry and rhythmic prose is.

There is thus a mutually exclusive contrast between naturalist, or near-naturalist, 'natural' works and works which intentionally deviate from the natural, are deliberately formed and tied, or in other words are stylized. Nevertheless stylization and realism are not mutually exclusive. There are plenty of great realists among the poets who write in verse. For the truth and law resident in nature can be reproduced not merely by a servile imitation of nature but even more faithfully by a stylization which exaggerates and stresses certain points. The natural presentation may perhaps reproduce reality, but the stylized image expresses the truth.

This problem of style interests us now only inasmuch as it concerns the film. Is stylization possible in the film? Can photography give a picture of life which would correspond, say, to a story told in verse? In other words, can the film tolerate a presentation the formative principle of which is not mere similarity to nature but some abstract law of rhythm and form? Can we make people talk in verse in a film without causing a disturbing contradiction to arise between stylized speech and the unstylized naturalness of the picture?

We know that the film began seeking possibilities of stylization from the very beginning, photographic technique notwithstanding. The directors strove to achieve the picturesque by composition, light effects, close-ups, soft focus, distortion and especially through the medium of angle and set-up. Swedish films especially sought poetic pictorial effects. Fritz Lang, Murnau and Robert Wiene, the creator of the expressionist *Cabinet of Dr Caligari*, did much fine work in this direction in the days of the silent film and in Russia. Moskvin, the greatest pictorialist among cameramen, created together with Eisenstein (whose guiding artistic principle was precisely stylization) the most interesting and valuable stylized film in *Ivan the Terrible*. The real content of this demoniacally monumental musical-pictorial symphony is not the story of Ivan the Terrible but a revelation of the terrifying medieval Pravoslav-Orthodox Gothic spirit and superstition in pictures that are like old icons come to life. In this film the stylization has reached a culminating point.

Nevertheless there is something that *always* requires to be natural in the film and which does not tolerate stylization. This does not apply to forms, which have often been successfully stylized, but it does to movement. On the stage we accept and often do not even notice the unnatural gestures of the actors. The same applies to the film if we see the figures as on the stage, that is in a long shot, from a distance. Strangely enough it becomes intolerable, however, if a human being whom we see in close-up isolated from the environment, moves unnaturally. An exception to this rule is a dance when the unnaturalness of movement is motivated. In a long shot the figure is fitted into the visible setting and its stylized movements are in keeping with the style of the whole picture. We accept an unnatural line if it is balanced by a similar line on the other side of the frame. But if a figure or a face is so near to us that it is no longer merely a component of a larger composition, and we see the smallest detail in the play of features, the curve of lip, the narrowing of an eye, that whole natural picture of the microphysiognomy which is not amenable to stylization, then an unnatural stylization of the poise of the head, the gesture of the hands, the movement of the feet will make an unpleasant impression on the spectator or strike him as funny. The stylization of outline contradicts the natural truth of the inner details.

This explains why the film is difficult to stylize. The microphysiognomy of the close-up, the intimate play of features, is not susceptible to stylization, and yet it is the very soul of the film. The most beautiful stylized long shots are unmasked by the intimate life of the close-up. The mask slips and the human being peeps out from behind it. It is for this reason, too, that we have no films in verse. Tied speech seems to contradict the natural movement of even a stylized film.

The question does not arise, of course, in the case of the animated cartoon. There, on the contrary, it is complete naturalness that is almost unattainable and the stylization which is a necessary corollary of the animating technique determines the whole style of the film. If drawings talk in verse, no one is shocked.

How is it possible then that we accept the singing film, the certainly unnatural film operetta and opera? The reason is that singing is a natural function of human beings. Thank goodness we can see and hear people singing everywhere, and very rarely may we even hear someone reciting a poem. But it is quite improbable that any human beings should discuss matters concerning their everyday lives with each other in the form of rhyming or rhythmic dialogue. When we watch and listen to a film opera, we know that it is an artistic presentation and is not supposed to be nature. This point will be discussed in greater detail in another chapter.

SUBJECTIVE AND TRADITIONAL STYLIZATION

In that synthesis of objective impression and subjective interpretation which is the basic process in every artistic work of creation, style and stylization undoubtedly come from the subjective side. For stylization is always a deviation from authentic, objective reality. The same object can be presented in a great variety of styles, according to subjective interpretations, even if the style is not an individual style but a national or class style. For even these will have to manifest themselves through the art of some individual creative artist. It is not the community of the people who produce works of art but single individuals belonging to this community.

But here we find ourselves faced with a paradoxical problem. If style is a subjective element of presentation, how is it then that the traditional folk styles have always been the most impersonal, most generally valid elements of art? What is the relationship between the arbitrarily stylizing, reality-deforming formalism of extreme subjectivism and the naïve stylizing tendencies of folk art which so often result in abstract ornamentation? Why is the one arbitrary subjectivism and the other impersonal, universally valid, objectively valuable?

It has already been said here that the most original and ancient folk style can manifest itself only as the personal taste and artistic intention of some individual. And yet this personal taste and artistic intention will not be merely individual. Every artist who is vitally bound up with the society in which he lives will consciously or unconsciously represent in his ideology and feeling the people whose superpersonal traditional style he quite naïvely regards as his own.

Traditional folk styles are objective historical facts although stylization itself is a subjective process. If an artist can live and express in his works, as his own subjective experience, this historical tradition transformed into objective phenomena, the result will be that happiest of coincidences, when the artist can create objective, general works of historical validity through his own most subjective, personal manifestations. This is one of the rare cases when an art may be stylized to the limit and yet not be arbitrarily subjective.

In the western cultural sphere such a contingency is almost unimaginable to-day, for ancient and primitive folk styles are not suitable for the presentation of modern industrialized life. And is there anywhere a traditional folk style which is not primitive and not antiquated, which could therefore be used to express present-day experiences?

Citizens of Western Europe or America would certainly be startled if Homer or one of the singers of the Kalevala were suddenly to appear in a French literary café and it would be no less strange if someone were to sing of the fights between modern aeroplanes in the ancient rhythm and melody of the rhapsodies. And yet such strange things are happening now among the national minorities in the Soviet Union. The most surprising and striking evidence of this are the products of Central Asian folk poetry. But the same can be observed in the films made by the people of Soviet Asia, in the interesting productions of the Kazakhstan, Tashkent, Uzbek and Turkmen film studios.

As everyone knows, the people of Central Asia awoke to the consciousness of their own national and folk culture only as a result of the cultural policy of the Soviet government. Until then it was merely a dwindling tradition, a memory in the minds of the old people. But under the Soviets not only was the almost forgotten tradition awakened to new life, but its revival and continuation stimulated and encouraged. Among the peoples of Central Asia the tradition of the old minstrels was still alive because the minstrels themselves still existed. Grey-haired old rhapsodists roamed the country from *aul* to *aul* with their two-stringed *dombra,* singing the ancient epics which were passed on from mouth to mouth and had never been written down. The Soviet government not only had these glorious old epics written down but saw to it that this last generation of the *akins* (as they were called in the Kazak language) turned their attention to the present-day life of the Soviet Union and sang not only of the old heroes but of the new exploits of the Red Army, while still preserving the old folk style and language. In doing this, the *akins* strongly influenced the style of the younger generation of writers in these parts of the Soviet Union.

Something that is almost a miracle has happened in our days in Soviet Asia, something that in the future may have a decisive influence on western art: modern life has been presented in the style of a folk art which has an ancient tradition and is nevertheless still alive to-day. Such things are not limited to the sphere of literature. Kazak and Tartar, Uzbek and Turkmen, Kirghiz and Yakut film directors, actors and scriptwriters, working in modern, well-equipped film studios and skilfully handling the latest technical means of film production, have grown up in the traditions of a still living folk art and have enjoyed the unique, enviable good fortune that they did not invent individual styles for themselves at the cost of immense effort, for the torrent of a live, great folk style swept them along.

CHAPTER TWENTY-THREE

MUSICAL FORMS

IT IS OBVIOUS that the film of an opera and a film opera belong to different forms of art. This is not a play on words. Bizet's *Carmen* or Verdi's *Rigoletto* and every classical opera can be shot as a sound film and thus a superlative performance may be perpetuated and popularized. Such films are necessary and valuable reproductions and are very useful in improving the musical taste of the public. But it has little to do with the problems and tasks of film art. The film opera on the other hand, which is intended and directed and composed for the film from the start, is a new musical form of art with new problems and new tasks.

If the object is to adapt an already existing opera for the film, the work can be motivated by two intentions. One of them is to popularize high quality music in its unadulterated, original, classical form. The other motive may be that the subject and musical *motifs* of the opera seem to offer material for film presentation. In the first case we cannot treat the opera as novels or plays can be treated when adapted for the film—that is to say, we cannot regard it as raw material and remodel it in filmic style. The reason why this cannot be done is that the music, which is to be filmed and which must not be changed in any way, ties the adaptor to the existing order of scenes and acts. The music, crystallized around the action, must necessarily transfer the action unchanged to the film. The result is that such action will appear even more stiff and unnatural in the film than on the operatic stage. For we have in the course of time become accustomed to this style on the operatic stage, it has become traditional and conventional and is in harmony with the 'unnatural' stylization of stage, scenery and visible orchestra. In the unstylized, photographed 'natural' world of the film the operatic style of acting (which, however, is determined by the music) will in most cases impress the audience as an impossible, a ridiculous contradiction. For this reason, when filming a classical opera, it is mostly advisable to present it as a reproduction of an ordinary operatic performance. In this case the most operatically stylized performance will still give a realistic picture, because it will be the faithful reproduction of a familiar reality, and gestures and deportment which would strike us as ridiculous if seen in a real street, do not appear ridiculous, and are perfectly acceptable, if we see the stage on which they happen.

Of course even in such operatic films, technique can do much to loosen up the old-fashioned rigidity which is scarcely tolerable even on the stage to-day. For even though what is being photographed is not nature but a stage performance, close-ups, changing set-ups and angles, and good editing can do much dramatically to enliven the opera and make it more palatable to the present-day spectator.

From the beginning films often contained scenes enacted on the stage or platform, especially if the hero of the film was an actor. Such scene were scenes of real life no less than any street scene and their unnatural style was natural, for everyone knew that here was a stage and that this was what stages were like. Nevertheless such scenes were shot with every trick of the trade and a good director would make use of the specific media and technique of the film with which to stress the theatrical quality of the stage, very often in a satirical vein. René Clair was never more specifically filmic than when he parodied the grotesquely unnatural character of stage style in his films.

But even if a film is intended to present the operatic performance seriously in all its classical, original style, it should still do so in the language of the modern film. The original style must be preserved in the first place because, as has already been said, the music demands it. Classical music may be cut if need be, but cannot be changed. But the classical operas were written to old, much-stylized libretti, the archaic dramatic structure of which they must thus immutably preserve. If on the operatic stage two mortal enemies stand face to face with drawn swords and instead of going for each other hammer and

tongs, sing about their mutual hatred for half an hour, that is
bearable only on the operatic stage, where an ancient and
noble cultural tradition protects them from ridicule. And after
all it is the singing that is the most valuable in the scene just
mentioned. But it does not follow from this that such a scene
must absolutely be photographed in a setting of painted
scenery. After all, operas are often performed in open-air
theatres, in a natural setting. But even if the setting is natural,
it must nevertheless be scenery and the public must know that
it is scenery and that it is watching an operatic performance,
even if the performance is staged in a real wood. If this is
done, the outdated stylization of the action and acting (which
cannot be avoided because the music requires it) will not be
out of keeping with the natural environment.

By this device operas can be shown in the film with
far greater decorative freedom than on the best of operatic
stages. In the open-air theatre all of nature can be used for
scenery.

However, in the operatic film the question of natural and
unnatural presentation is not only a question of setting and
scenery, but of direction and acting as well. Little can be
changed in a dialogue inlaid with classical music. However
ornate and long-winded it may appear to our taste, neither
single sentences nor the whole dialogue can be cut without
damaging the classical music. In a film depicting real life,
such a dialogue would be impossible. In a film depicting
scenes from an opera, it is natural.

Another problem which must be solved is the grimacing of
singers. Those who sing consider in the first place the ears of
the public, not their eyes. The talkie already posed a difficult
problem when it compelled the actor to speak in a way intelligible to the ear, not the eye. The movement of a singer's mouth
in close-up is a problem even more difficult of solution. The
accurate forming of vowels and consonants made the movements of the lips empty and grotesque. How much more does
this apply to singing! All this is less objectionable from the
distance of the stage, but the nearness of the close-up can
make it very unpleasant. This difficulty may be at least par-
tially overcome by using the technique of the 'play-back', i.e.

the actors may be photographed merely mouthing their words, their singing being dubbed on to the film later.

The technique of the film also puts us in the position of being able to listen to a long *aria* without having to look the singer in the mouth all the time. The camera can meanwhile wander around and show, for instance, the things to which the *aria* refers: the object of love, or a landscape, or a dwelling or a threatening danger. The stage must remain stage and the public must be always conscious of this, but it need not be incessantly before our eyes in the close-ups. If this is done properly, rigidly immobile scenery and groups of extras will not bother us. For they may be immobile but the camera is not; it moves and the rhythm of the shot-sequence also moves, and this rhythm, adapting itself to the rhythm of the music, can emphasize and interpret it.

The technique of the film and especially the colour film will fulfil an important mission by popularizing the classical opera. In most cases operas will still have to be cut, for films running for more than two hours are as yet difficult to set before a public, though this difficulty will disappear in time. Such cutting must be governed by musical considerations and hence it is the music that should be cut first, and the dramaturgical cut must follow it. This can rarely be done by means of simple omission—single scenes and often even the course of the action have to be re-aligned. All this will not affect the spirit of the opera as long as the music safeguards it. But here are no easy tasks and the shooting of an operatic film is scarcely less of a venture on the part of director, actors and technical team than making an original film.

FILM OPERA

In speaking of the film opera, that is an opera intended and composed for the film, we must unfortunately discuss an art form which has not yet been realized. Attempts have been made, but without much success. The reasons for this provide an interesting problem, because in theory and principle the possibility of a film opera can be quite easily proved.

In operettas, musical comedies, revues and all other musical stage productions (hence in the popular film variants of these art forms) the players sing songs. In certain dramatic situations the characters express their feelings by means of a song. In this in itself there is nothing unnatural or stylized, for even in everyday life people sing when they are in a certain mood. Hence this in itself is not improbable. But in the opera, in the film opera as in all other operas, the characters not only sing songs, they also converse with each other by singing and this is what is unnatural, stylized, improbable.

In the operetta and any musical drama an inset song may have a dramaturgical part to play. For instance the song may be the signal for something to happen; the characters may recognize each other by means of the song; someone who has lost all hope may be cheered and reinvigorated by a song. But in such cases the song is a finished, closed piece of music and is used almost in the way a prop is used. The same dramaturgical part might be played by a light signal for instance. Such a song may bring about a dramatic situation, but the song itself will not be the result of such a situation, it will not be born before our eyes, out of the situation. The song is already in existence as a finished thing and is merely used or applied in the given situation. A song thus used may start off a whole chain of action, but the action is not carried forward in the song itself. The song expresses a certain state of mind, but the evolution of the soul does not manifest itself in the music. The song may express a stage in the story, but the story is not continued in the music as it is in the opera.

Music was from the beginning much more closely linked with the film than with the stage. It is organically and structurally as much a part of the film picture, as are light and shadow. Music was an indispensable element of the silent film and is no less indispensable in the sound film.

On the stage, background music always gives the scene a certain melodramatic, festive or lyrical character and background music is rarely used in the theatre save for specially stressing some mood prevalent in a scene.

The music accompanying the silent film did not in normal circumstances produce any special festive or lyrical effect unless the pictures that went with it expressed such moods. But we always feel the need of music with the silent film, even with the most objective, instructional or informative film.

A silent film seen without musical accompaniment makes the spectator feel uncomfortable, a phenomenon which has a psycho-physical explanation. The explanation is that for the silent film the music was not merely an additional instrument for expressing a mood but to some extent a sort of third dimension added to the two dimensions of the screen.

As long as the spectator hears music, he does not become conscious of the fact that the grey film-pictures have only two dimensions and lack real depth; he accepts the image on the screen as a true picture of live reality. But as soon as the moving pictures really become silent, they at once appear flat, the flickering of suddenly bloodless shadows. It is a fact confirmed by much experience that the greater part of the public is not conscious of hearing music in the cinema. They immediately notice, however, when the music ceases. The psychological reason for this is that we never perceive reality by means of one sense alone. What we merely hear or merely see, etc. has no three-dimensional reality for us.

The conclusion to be drawn from this is that music in the film has not only an artistic part to play—it is required in order that the pictures may give the impression of being alive and natural; music gives the pictures atmosphere and represents, as it were, a third dimension. The music provides an acoustic background and perspective. It must never become music for music's sake—as soon as this happens the music detaches itself from the picture and destroys its life.

Every problem of the film opera can be traced back to this nature of film music.

As has already been said, the 'sung' dialogue and 'sung' dramatic action are not natural; they are strongly stylized forms. Very real feelings can be most realistically expressed in sung dialogues. But the medium of expression will not be natural—it will be stylized and hence out of keeping with the essence of the film. For similar reasons films with rhymed or rhythmic dialogue have not been a success. It has been repeatedly shown in these pages why the illusion of naturalness is more indispensable in the film than on the stage. The film may show us the real nature of fairyland, but must never depict our workaday world by means of painted scenery. It has already been said why a similar illusion is required to make the acting seem real.

In the film opera, which will also not tolerate stylization, the most difficult problem to be solved will not be the scenery and direction but the music itself. The reason for this is that musical expression, expression in words and expression in feature-play and gesture, are of unequal duration. The most profound and complicated emotions may appear all at once in a single movement of facial muscles or one gesture, taking up only a second or two of time—or to put it in film language, a few feet of film. To express the same emotion or state of mind in words would take more time and more footage. But while the character in question is talking about his feelings, he preserves them precisely by speaking of them, and the accompanying facial expression may remain on his face all the time he speaks of the same emotion.

To express the same emotion in melody takes longer. Even a few bars take more time and footage and by the time the film gets through with it, the character, if it moves at a natural speed, would long be expressing a different mood by means of a different facial expression and gesture. It was not without good reason that Wagner, in directing his operas, made his singers move much slower than would have been natural. The tied stylized periods of the antique drama were spoken by actors on thick-soled buskins, which also slowed down movement; it is a known fact that opera was born in the sixteenth century out of the attempt to find a style and manner suitable for the staging of the antique tragedy and the singing of the recitatives seemed a suitable means of slowing down the action.

Why such stylized slowing-down is possible on the stage and impossible in the film has another deeper reason as well.

When Senta and the flying Dutchman first meet in Wagner's *Flying Dutchman*, they stare at each other in motionless silence. This spell of motionless silence, which lasts nearly twenty minutes, escapes being a lifeless patch on the stage, because the music of the orchestra expresses the dramatic movement of their thoughts and emotions. This is possible on the stage but in the film a musical movement cannot take the place of a visual movement. The rhythm of detail shots and cross-cutting can bridge for a time the always damaging effect of a pause in the picture sequence. But not for long. On the stage the motionless figures retain their life because the public knows that they are alive, hence supposes and accepts that something is happening in their hearts, however rigidly motionless they appear to be. But the rigidity of a photograph is not semblance—it is reality. The immobility of a good painting is the quintessence of motion and never dead, but the film can only stop by showing a single frame as a snapshot—and in that instant is dead.

This does not mean that a film opera is beyond the bounds of possibility—only that the shots must be as stylized as possible. This, as we know, is possible to a very great extent by the technical means at our disposal. Such stylization will be most convincing if it takes the content for its starting-point. For in the case of fairy-tales, legends or fantastic stories, no one is surprised if the formal aspect of the presentation is not natural but stylized. The miraculousness of a miracle is not surprising—what would be surprising would be a non-miraculous miracle. Fairyland landscapes are the more strange the more accurate the photographs are in which they are shown, and singing speech goes well with singing gestures.

CHAPTER TWENTY-FOUR

HEROES, BEAUTY, STARS AND THE CASE OF GRETA GARBO

THE HERO, THE paragon, the model and example is an indispensable element in the poetry of all races and peoples, from the ancient epics to the modern film. This is a manifestation of the natural selection of the best, of the instinctive urge towards improvement, a postulate of biology, not of æsthetics. In the course of the cultural history of man, changing, increasingly discerning tastes modified merely the *beau ideal* of the hero according to the interests of the class, the wishful thinking of which determined the hero's qualities and beauty.

The physical being of the hero, the ideal of beauty, was a signpost for more than biological selection and evolution. From the beginning it also appeared in literature and art in sublimated form, as the physiognomic expression of spiritual and ethical values. In the age of conceptual culture initiated by the invention of printing (of which mention was made earlier on) the bodily visibility of human values lost its significance. Beauty was no longer a dream and an experience of great masses. The revival of visual culture with the advent of the film has again made physical beauty an important experience of the masses. If to-day every illustrated paper of the world is full of the pictures of beautiful women, this does not mean that all mankind has grown less serious-minded. Illustrated papers existed long before the films, but they were at that time not galleries of physical beauty. On the other hand in ancient Athens, where there were no illustrated papers, the streets and squares were full of ideal images of human bodies in the guise of gods and goddesses and pregnant women came to look at them in order that the fruit of their wombs would be as beautiful as those images. For images of beauty were the manifestations of the primeval desire for improvement. In this age of film culture, when man has again become visible, he has again been awakened to consciousness of beauty, and the visual propaganda of beauty is again an expression of deep-seated biological and social urges.

The physical incarnation of the hero or heroine is beauty of a kind which exactly expresses the ideologies and aspirations of those who admire it. We must learn to read beauty, as we have learned to read the face. A scientific analysis of what we now call sex appeal, for instance, would greatly enrich our knowledge of social psychology.

Periods and classes which had no epics, and no ideal of beauty, were ever decadent periods or classes. A society which loudly proclaims the idea of a new humanity will always seek for the ideal physical type of this new man as well as other qualities. And what is meant by this are not some profound beauties of the soul which show in the face, nor that other 'beauty' which is merely an inexact term for the expressive power of a work of art. What is meant by beauty in the following is simply and literally the natural beauty of the body which plays so great a part in film art.

Art snobs often affect to despise the beauty of film stars and tend to regard beauty as a disturbing secondary effect which rouses base instincts and has nothing to do with 'real art'. But such a universal cultural phenomenon as the film must not be measured solely by the standards of a purely artistic production. For beyond this the vital instincts and social tendencies of mankind manifest themselves in so significant a form in the film that they cannot be disregarded.

The film stars who have been most successful did not owe their popularity to their histrionic gifts, even if they happened to be excellent actors. The most popular of them did not act at all, or rather acted only themselves. Not only Charlie Chaplin remained always the same Charlie in every film, without changing mask, costume or manner. Douglas Fairbanks, Asta Nielsen, Lillian Gish, Rudolph Valentino and others of the greatest also remained the same. They were no creators of characters. Their names, costumes, social positions could be changed in their various parts, but they always showed the same personality and this personality was their own. For the dominant element in the impression they made was their personal appearance. They turned up as old acquaintances in each new film and it was not they who assumed the mask of the character they played—on the contrary, the parts were written for them in advance, were made to measure for them so to speak. For what the public loved was not their acting ability, but they themselves, their personal charm and attraction. Of course to possess such charm is also a great thing. But as an art it most resembles lyrical poetry, which also expresses the poet's heart and not things external. These great film stars were great lyrical poets whose medium was not the word, but the body, the facial expression and gesture; the parts they played merely chance opportunities of exercising this their art.

Such world-wide adulation as that which surrounded these legendary stars cannot be evoked by the most brilliant stage performance in itself. There are very many excellent and even great actors in the world. Many of them have been, and are, far better actors than those demigods of the film in whom many millions of fans saw the incarnation of their own dreams, and whose art consists only in the ability to express their own personality with complete intensity. But such a personality must be more than just interesting and attractive. There are very many interesting and attractive people in the world. If Charlie Chaplin came to be the best-beloved darling of half the human race, then millions of men and women must have seen in his personality something that means much to them; Charlie Chaplin's personality must have expressed something that lived in all of them as a secret feeling, urge or desire, some unconscious thought, something that far transcends the limits of personal charm or artistic performance. The golden-hearted, shiftless, blundering, cunning little tramp, the victim of mechanization and capitalism, who hits back with grotesquely resourceful pinpricks—Charlie, with his melancholy optimism, expresses the opposition of all of us to an inhuman order of society.

Up to now Greta Garbo was the most popular star in the world. This is said not on the basis of æsthetic considerations. There is a better, more exact, indeed absolutely accurate standard. This standard is the amount in dollars which was the reward of her popularity.

It was not the actress Garbo who conquered the hearts of the world. Garbo is not a bad actress, but her popularity is due to her beauty. Though even this is not so simple. Mere beauty is a matter of taste, of sex appeal, and for this one reason alone cannot have the same effect on many millions of people in the whole world to the same degree. And then there are so many perfectly beautiful women that the harmony of Garbo's lines could not in itself have ensured such a unique privileged position for her.

Garbo's beauty is not just a harmony of lines, it is not merely ornamental. Her beauty contains a physiognomy expressing a very definite state of mind.

Like the face of all other actors, Greta Garbo's face changes during a scene. She, too, laughs and is sad, is surprised or angry, as prescribed by her part. Her face, too, may be once that of a queen and once that of a bedraggled drab, according to what character she has to play. But behind this variety of facial expression we can always see that unchanged Garbo face, the fixed unchanged expression of which has conquered the world. It is not mere beauty, but a beauty of peculiar significance, a beauty expressing one particular thing, that has captured the heart of half mankind. And what is this thing?

Greta Garbo is sad. Not only in certain situations, for certain reasons. Greta Garbo's beauty is a beauty of suffering; she suffers life and all the surrounding world. And this sadness, this sorrow is a very definite one: the sadness of loneliness, of an estrangement which feels no common tie with other human beings. The sadness of the inner nobility of a reticent purity, of the shrinking of a sensitive plant from a rude touch is in this beauty, even when she plays a down-and-out tart. Her brooding glance comes from afar even then and looks into the endless distance. Even then she is an exile in a distant land and does not know how she ever came to be where she is.

But why should this strange sort of beauty affect millions more deeply than some bright and sparkling pin-up girl? What is the meaning of the Garbo expression?

We feel and see Greta Garbo's beauty as finer and nobler, precisely because it bears the stamp of sorrow and loneliness. For however harmonious may be the lines of a face, if it is contentedly smiling, if it is bright and happy, if it can be bright and happy in this world of ours, then it must of necessity belong to an inferior human being. Even the usually insensitive person can understand that a sad and suffering beauty, gestures expressing horror at the touch of an unclean world, indicate a higher order of human being, a purer and nobler soul than smiles and mirth. Greta Garbo's beauty is a beauty which is in opposition to the world of to-day.

Millions see in her face a protest against this world, millions who may perhaps not even be conscious as yet of their own suffering protest; but they admire Garbo for it and find her beauty the most beautiful of all.

INDEX

Tolstoy, 160
Turin, 166
Turksib, 166-168

Valentino, Rudolph, 284
Vanina, 69, 132
Veidt, Conrad, 78, 136, 200
Verdi, 275
Vergano, 203
Vertov, Dziga, 164
Vidor, King, 86

Viertel, Berthold, 159-160
Vivere in pace, 202

Wagner, 236, 281
Westerns, 25
Wiene, Robert, 106, 270

Yoshiwara, 116, 140, 178

Zuidersee, 168
Zampa, Luigi, 202

A CATALOGUE OF SELECTED DOVER BOOKS
IN ALL FIELDS OF INTEREST

A CATALOGUE OF SELECTED DOVER BOOKS
IN ALL FIELDS OF INTEREST

WHAT IS SCIENCE?, *N. Campbell*
The role of experiment and measurement, the function of mathematics, the nature of scientific laws, the difference between laws and theories, the limitations of science, and many similarly provocative topics are treated clearly and without technicalities by an eminent scientist. "Still an excellent introduction to scientific philosophy," H. Margenau in *Physics Today*. "A first-rate primer . . . deserves a wide audience," *Scientific American*. 192pp. 5⅜ x 8.
60043-2 Paperbound $1.25

THE NATURE OF LIGHT AND COLOUR IN THE OPEN AIR, *M. Minnaert*
Why are shadows sometimes blue, sometimes green, or other colors depending on the light and surroundings? What causes mirages? Why do multiple suns and moons appear in the sky? Professor Minnaert explains these unusual phenomena and hundreds of others in simple, easy-to-understand terms based on optical laws and the properties of light and color. No mathematics is required but artists, scientists, students, and everyone fascinated by these "tricks" of nature will find thousands of useful and amazing pieces of information. Hundreds of observational experiments are suggested which require no special equipment. 200 illustrations; 42 photos. xvi + 362pp. 5⅜ x 8.
20196-1 Paperbound $2.00

THE STRANGE STORY OF THE QUANTUM, AN ACCOUNT FOR THE GENERAL READER OF THE GROWTH OF IDEAS UNDERLYING OUR PRESENT ATOMIC KNOWLEDGE, *B. Hoffmann*
Presents lucidly and expertly, with barest amount of mathematics, the problems and theories which led to modern quantum physics. Dr. Hoffmann begins with the closing years of the 19th century, when certain trifling discrepancies were noticed, and with illuminating analogies and examples takes you through the brilliant concepts of Planck, Einstein, Pauli, Broglie, Bohr, Schroedinger, Heisenberg, Dirac, Sommerfeld, Feynman, etc. This edition includes a new, long postscript carrying the story through 1958. "Of the books attempting an account of the history and contents of our modern atomic physics which have come to my attention, this is the best," H. Margenau, Yale University, in *American Journal of Physics*. 32 tables and line illustrations. Index. 275pp. 5⅜ x 8.
20518-5 Paperbound $2.00

GREAT IDEAS OF MODERN MATHEMATICS: THEIR NATURE AND USE, *Jagjit Singh*
Reader with only high school math will understand main mathematical ideas of modern physics, astronomy, genetics, psychology, evolution, etc. better than many who use them as tools, but comprehend little of their basic structure. Author uses his wide knowledge of non-mathematical fields in brilliant exposition of differential equations, matrices, group theory, logic, statistics, problems of mathematical foundations, imaginary numbers, vectors, etc. Original publication. 2 appendixes. 2 indexes. 65 ills. 322pp. 5⅜ x 8.
20587-8 Paperbound $2.25

CATALOGUE OF DOVER BOOKS

THE PRINCIPLES OF PSYCHOLOGY,
William James
The full long-course, unabridged, of one of the great classics of Western
literature and science. Wonderfully lucid descriptions of human mental
activity, the stream of thought, consciousness, time perception, memory, imagination, emotions, reason, abnormal phenomena, and similar topics. Original
contributions are integrated with the work of such men as Berkeley, Binet,
Mills, Darwin, Hume, Kant, Royce, Schopenhauer, Spinoza, Locke, Descartes,
Galton, Wundt, Lotze, Herbart, Fechner, and scores of others. All contrasting
interpretations of mental phenomena are examined in detail—introspective
analysis, philosophical interpretation, and experimental research. "A classic,"
Journal of Consulting Psychology. "The main lines are as valid as ever,"
Psychoanalytical Quarterly. "Standard reading . . . a classic of interpretation,"
Psychiatric Quarterly. 94 illustrations. 1408pp. 5⅜ x 8.
20381-6, 20382-4 Two volume set, paperbound $6.00

VISUAL ILLUSIONS: THEIR CAUSES, CHARACTERISTICS AND APPLICATIONS,
M. Luckiesh
"Seeing is deceiving," asserts the author of this introduction to virtually every
type of optical illusion known. The text both describes and explains the
principles involved in color illusions, figure-ground, distance illusions, etc.
100 photographs, drawings and diagrams prove how easy it is to fool the sense:
circles that aren't round, parallel lines that seem to bend, stationary figures that
seem to move as you stare at them — illustration after illustration strains our
credulity at what we see. Fascinating book from many points of view, from
applications for artists, in camouflage, etc. to the psychology of vision. New
introduction by William Ittleson, Dept. of Psychology, Queens College. Index.
Bibliography. xxi + 252pp. 5⅜ x 8½.   21530-X Paperbound $1.50

FADS AND FALLACIES IN THE NAME OF SCIENCE,
Martin Gardner
This is the standard account of various cults, quack systems, and delusions
which have masqueraded as science: hollow earth fanatics. Reich and orgone
sex energy, dianetics, Atlantis, multiple moons, Forteanism, flying saucers,
medical fallacies like iridiagnosis, zone therapy, etc. A new chapter has been
added on Bridey Murphy, psionics, and other recent manifestations in this
field. This is a fair, reasoned appraisal of eccentric theory which provides
excellent inoculation against cleverly masked nonsense. "Should be read by
everyone, scientist and non-scientist alike," R. T. Birge, Prof. Emeritus of
Physics, Univ. of California; Former President, American Physical Society.
Index. x + 365pp. 5⅜ x 8.   20394-8 Paperbound $2.00

ILLUSIONS AND DELUSIONS OF THE SUPERNATURAL AND THE OCCULT,
D. H. Rawcliffe
Holds up to rational examination hundreds of persistent delusions including
crystal gazing, automatic writing, table turning, mediumistic trances, mental
healing, stigmata, lycanthropy, live burial, the Indian Rope Trick, spiritualism,
dowsing, telepathy, clairvoyance, ghosts, ESP, etc. The author explains and
exposes the mental and physical deceptions involved, making this not only
an exposé of supernatural phenomena, but a valuable exposition of characteristic types of abnormal psychology. Originally titled "The Psychology of
the Occult." 14 illustrations. Index. 551pp. 5⅜ x 8. 20503-7 Paperbound $3.50

FAIRY TALE COLLECTIONS, *edited by Andrew Lang*
Andrew Lang's fairy tale collections make up the richest shelf-full of traditional children's stories anywhere available. Lang supervised the translation of stories from all over the world—familiar European tales collected by Grimm, animal stories from Negro Africa, myths of primitive Australia, stories from Russia, Hungary, Iceland, Japan, and many other countries. Lang's selection of translations are unusually high; many authorities consider that the most familiar tales find their best versions in these volumes. All collections are richly decorated and illustrated by H. J. Ford and other artists.

THE BLUE FAIRY BOOK. 37 stories. 138 illustrations. ix + 390pp. 5⅜ x 8½.
21437-0 Paperbound $1.95

THE GREEN FAIRY BOOK. 42 stories. 100 illustrations. xiii + 366pp. 5⅜ x 8½.
21439-7 Paperbound $1.75

THE BROWN FAIRY BOOK. 32 stories. 50 illustrations, 8 in color. xii + 350pp. 5⅜ x 8½.
21438-9 Paperbound $1.95

THE BEST TALES OF HOFFMANN, *edited by E. F. Bleiler*
10 stories by E. T. A. Hoffmann, one of the greatest of all writers of fantasy. The tales include "The Golden Flower Pot," "Automata," "A New Year's Eve Adventure," "Nutcracker and the King of Mice," "Sand-Man," and others. Vigorous characterizations of highly eccentric personalities, remarkably imaginative situations, and intensely fast pacing has made these tales popular all over the world for 150 years. Editor's introduction. 7 drawings by Hoffmann. xxxiii + 419pp. 5⅜ x 8½.
21793-0 Paperbound $2.25

GHOST AND HORROR STORIES OF AMBROSE BIERCE,
edited by E. F. Bleiler
Morbid, eerie, horrifying tales of possessed poets, shabby aristocrats, revived corpses, and haunted malefactors. Widely acknowledged as the best of their kind between Poe and the moderns, reflecting their author's inner torment and bitter view of life. Includes "Damned Thing," "The Middle Toe of the Right Foot," "The Eyes of the Panther," "Visions of the Night," "Moxon's Master," and over a dozen others. Editor's introduction. xxii + 199pp. 5⅜ x 8½.
20767-6 Paperbound $1.50

THREE GOTHIC NOVELS, *edited by E. F. Bleiler*
Originators of the still popular Gothic novel form, influential in ushering in early 19th-century Romanticism. Horace Walpole's *Castle of Otranto*, William Beckford's *Vathek*, John Polidori's *The Vampyre*, and a *Fragment* by Lord Byron are enjoyable as exciting reading or as documents in the history of English literature. Editor's introduction. xi + 291pp. 5⅜ x 8½.
21232-7 Paperbound $2.00

BEST GHOST STORIES OF LEFANU, *edited by E. F. Bleiler*
Though admired by such critics as V. S. Pritchett, Charles Dickens and Henry James ghost stories by the Irish novelist Joseph Sheridan LeFanu have never become as widely known as his detective fiction. About half of the 16 stories in this collection have never before been available in America. Collection includes "Carmilla" (perhaps the best vampire story ever written), "The Haunted Baronet," "The Fortunes of Sir Robert Ardagh," and the classic "Green Tea." Editor's introduction. 7 contemporary illustrations. Portrait of LeFanu. xii + 467pp. 5⅜ x 8.
20415-4 Paperbound $2.50

EASY-TO-DO ENTERTAINMENTS AND DIVERSIONS WITH COINS, CARDS, STRING, PAPER AND MATCHES, *R. M. Abraham*
Over 300 tricks, games and puzzles will provide young readers with absorbing fun. Sections on card games; paper-folding; tricks with coins, matches and pieces of string; games for the agile; toy-making from common household objects; mathematical recreations; and 50 miscellaneous pastimes. Anyone in charge of groups of youngsters, including hard-pressed parents, and in need of suggestions on how to keep children sensibly amused and quietly content will find this book indispensable. Clear, simple text, copious number of delightful line drawings and illustrative diagrams. Originally titled "Winter Nights' Entertainments." Introduction by Lord Baden Powell. 329 illustrations. v + 186pp. 5⅜ x 8½.   20921-0 Paperbound $1.00

AN INTRODUCTION TO CHESS MOVES AND TACTICS SIMPLY EXPLAINED, *Leonard Barden*
Beginner's introduction to the royal game. Names, possible moves of the pieces, definitions of essential terms, how games are won, etc. explained in 30-odd pages. With this background you'll be able to sit right down and play. Balance of book teaches strategy — openings, middle game, typical endgame play, and suggestions for improving your game. A sample game is fully analyzed. True middle-level introduction, teaching you all the essentials without oversimplifying or losing you in a maze of detail. 58 figures. 102pp. 5⅜ x 8½.   21210-6 Paperbound $1.25

LASKER'S MANUAL OF CHESS, *Dr. Emanuel Lasker*
Probably the greatest chess player of modern times, Dr. Emanuel Lasker held the world championship 28 years, independent of passing schools or fashions. This unmatched study of the game, chiefly for intermediate to skilled players, analyzes basic methods, combinations, position play, the aesthetics of chess, dozens of different openings, etc., with constant reference to great modern games. Contains a brilliant exposition of Steinitz's important theories. Introduction by Fred Reinfeld. Tables of Lasker's tournament record. 3 indices. 308 diagrams. 1 photograph. xxx + 349pp. 5⅜ x 8.20640-8 Paperbound $2.50

COMBINATIONS: THE HEART OF CHESS, *Irving Chernev*
Step-by-step from simple combinations to complex, this book, by a well-known chess writer, shows you the intricacies of pins, counter-pins, knight forks, and smothered mates. Other chapters show alternate lines of play to those taken in actual championship games; boomerang combinations; classic examples of brilliant combination play by Nimzovich, Rubinstein, Tarrasch, Botvinnik, Alekhine and Capablanca. Index. 356 diagrams. ix + 245pp. 5⅜ x 8½.   21744-2 Paperbound $2.00

HOW TO SOLVE CHESS PROBLEMS, *K. S. Howard*
Full of practical suggestions for the fan or the beginner — who knows only the moves of the chessmen. Contains preliminary section and 58 two-move, 46 three-move, and 8 four-move problems composed by 27 outstanding American problem creators in the last 30 years. Explanation of all terms and exhaustive index. "Just what is wanted for the student," Brian Harley. 112 problems, solutions. vi + 171pp. 5⅜ x 8.   20748-X Paperbound $1.50

SOCIAL THOUGHT FROM LORE TO SCIENCE,
H. E. Barnes and H. Becker
An immense survey of sociological thought and ways of viewing, studying, planning, and reforming society from earliest times to the present. Includes thought on society of preliterate peoples, ancient non-Western cultures, and every great movement in Europe, America, and modern Japan. Analyzes hundreds of great thinkers: Plato, Augustine, Bodin, Vico, Montesquieu, Herder, Comte, Marx, etc. Weighs the contributions of utopians, sophists, fascists and communists; economists, jurists, philosophers, ecclesiastics, and every 19th and 20th century school of scientific sociology, anthropology, and social psychology throughout the world. Combines topical, chronological, and regional approaches, treating the evolution of social thought as a process rather than as a series of mere topics. "Impressive accuracy, competence, and discrimination . . . easily the best single survey," *Nation*. Thoroughly revised, with new material up to 1960. 2 indexes. Over 2200 bibliographical notes. Three volume set. Total of 1586pp. 5⅜ x 8.
20901-6, 20902-4, 20903-2   Three volume set, paperbound $9.00

A HISTORY OF HISTORICAL WRITING, *Harry Elmer Barnes*
Virtually the only adequate survey of the whole course of historical writing in a single volume. Surveys developments from the beginnings of historiography in the ancient Near East and the Classical World, up through the Cold War. Covers major historians in detail, shows interrelationship with cultural background, makes clear individual contributions, evaluates and estimates importance; also enormously rich upon minor authors and thinkers who are usually passed over. Packed with scholarship and learning, clear, easily written. Indispensable to every student of history. Revised and enlarged up to 1961. Index and bibliography. xv + 442pp. 5⅜ x 8½.
20104-X Paperbound $2.75

JOHANN SEBASTIAN BACH, *Philipp Spitta*
The complete and unabridged text of the definitive study of Bach. Written some 70 years ago, it is still unsurpassed for its coverage of nearly all aspects of Bach's life and work. There could hardly be a finer non-technical introduction to Bach's music than the detailed, lucid analyses which Spitta provides for hundreds of individual pieces. 26 solid pages are devoted to the B minor mass, for example, and 30 pages to the glorious St. Matthew Passion. This monumental set also includes a major analysis of the music of the 18th century: Buxtehude, Pachelbel, etc. "Unchallenged as the last word on one of the supreme geniuses of music," John Barkham, *Saturday Review Syndicate*. Total of 1819pp. Heavy cloth binding. 5⅜ x 8.
22278-0, 22279-9 Two volume set, clothbound $15.00

BEETHOVEN AND HIS NINE SYMPHONIES, *George Grove*
In this modern middle-level classic of musicology Grove not only analyzes all nine of Beethoven's symphonies very thoroughly in terms of their musical structure, but also discusses the circumstances under which they were written, Beethoven's stylistic development, and much other background material. This is an extremely rich book, yet very easily followed; it is highly recommended to anyone seriously interested in music. Over 250 musical passages. Index. viii + 407pp. 5⅜ x 8.
20334-4 Paperbound $2.25

CATALOGUE OF DOVER BOOKS

THREE SCIENCE FICTION NOVELS,
John Taine
Acknowledged by many as the best SF writer of the 1920's, Taine (under the name Eric Temple Bell) was also a Professor of Mathematics of considerable renown. Reprinted here are *The Time Stream*, generally considered Taine's best, *The Greatest Game*, a biological-fiction novel, and *The Purple Sapphire*, involving a supercivilization of the past. Taine's stories tie fantastic narratives to frameworks of original and logical scientific concepts. Speculation is often profound on such questions as the nature of time, concept of entropy, cyclical universes, etc. 4 contemporary illustrations. v + 532pp. 5⅜ x 8⅜.
21180-0 Paperbound $2.50

SEVEN SCIENCE FICTION NOVELS,
H. G. Wells
Full unabridged texts of 7 science-fiction novels of the master. Ranging from biology, physics, chemistry, astronomy, to sociology and other studies, Mr. Wells extrapolates whole worlds of strange and intriguing character. "One will have to go far to match this for entertainment, excitement, and sheer pleasure . . ."*New York Times*. Contents: The Time Machine, The Island of Dr. Moreau, The First Men in the Moon, The Invisible Man, The War of the Worlds, The Food of the Gods, In The Days of the Comet. 1015pp. 5⅜ x 8.
20264-X Clothbound $5.00

28 SCIENCE FICTION STORIES OF H. G. WELLS.
Two full, unabridged novels, *Men Like Gods* and *Star Begotten*, plus 26 short stories by the master science-fiction writer of all time! Stories of space, time, invention, exploration, futuristic adventure. Partial contents: *The Country of the Blind, In the Abyss, The Crystal Egg, The Man Who Could Work Miracles, A Story of Days to Come, The Empire of the Ants, The Magic Shop, The Valley of the Spiders, A Story of the Stone Age, Under the Knife, Sea Raiders,* etc. An indispensable collection for the library of anyone interested in science fiction adventure. 928pp. 5⅜ x 8.
20265-8 Clothbound $5.00

THREE MARTIAN NOVELS,
Edgar Rice Burroughs
Complete, unabridged reprinting, in one volume, of Thuvia, Maid of Mars; Chessmen of Mars; The Master Mind of Mars. Hours of science-fiction adventure by a modern master storyteller. Reset in large clear type for easy reading. 16 illustrations by J. Allen St. John. vi + 490pp. 5⅜ x 8½.
20039-6 Paperbound $2.50

AN INTELLECTUAL AND CULTURAL HISTORY OF THE WESTERN WORLD,
Harry Elmer Barnes
Monumental 3-volume survey of intellectual development of Europe from primitive cultures to the present day. Every significant product of human intellect traced through history: art, literature, mathematics, physical sciences, medicine, music, technology, social sciences, religions, jurisprudence, education, etc. Presentation is lucid and specific, analyzing in detail specific discoveries, theories, literary works, and so on. Revised (1965) by recognized scholars in specialized fields under the direction of Prof. Barnes. Revised bibliography. Indexes. 24 illustrations. Total of xxix + 1318pp.
21275-0, 21276-9, 21277-7 Three volume set, paperbound $8.25

HEAR ME TALKIN' TO YA, *edited by Nat Shapiro and Nat Hentoff*
In their own words, Louis Armstrong, King Oliver, Fletcher Henderson, Bunk Johnson, Bix Beiderbecke, Billy Holiday, Fats Waller, Jelly Roll Morton, Duke Ellington, and many others comment on the origins of jazz in New Orleans and its growth in Chicago's South Side, Kansas City's jam sessions, Depression Harlem, and the modernism of the West Coast schools. Taken from taped conversations, letters, magazine articles, other first-hand sources. Editors' introduction. xvi + 429pp. 5⅜ x 8½. 21726-4 Paperbound $2.00

THE JOURNAL OF HENRY D. THOREAU
A 25-year record by the great American observer and critic, as complete a record of a great man's inner life as is anywhere available. Thoreau's Journals served him as raw material for his formal pieces, as a place where he could develop his ideas, as an outlet for his interests in wild life and plants, in writing as an art, in classics of literature, Walt Whitman and other contemporaries, in politics, slavery, individual's relation to the State, etc. The Journals present a portrait of a remarkable man, and are an observant social history. Unabridged republication of 1906 edition, Bradford Torrey and Francis H. Allen, editors. Illustrations. Total of 1888pp. 8⅜ x 12¼. 20312-3, 20313-1 Two volume set. clothbound $30.00

A SHAKESPEARIAN GRAMMAR, *E. A. Abbott*
Basic reference to Shakespeare and his contemporaries, explaining through thousands of quotations from Shakespeare, Jonson, Beaumont and Fletcher, North's *Plutarch* and other sources the grammatical usage differing from the modern. First published in 1870 and written by a scholar who spent much of his life isolating principles of Elizabethan language, the book is unlikely ever to be superseded. Indexes. xxiv + 511pp. 5⅜ x 8½. 21582-2 Paperbound $3.00

FOLK-LORE OF SHAKESPEARE, *T. F. Thistelton Dyer*
Classic study, drawing from Shakespeare a large body of references to supernatural beliefs, terminology of falconry and hunting, games and sports, good luck charms, marriage customs, folk medicines, superstitions about plants, animals, birds, argot of the underworld, sexual slang of London, proverbs, drinking customs, weather lore, and much else. From full compilation comes a mirror of the 17th-century popular mind. Index. ix + 526pp. 5⅜ x 8½. 21614-4 Paperbound $2.75

THE NEW VARIORUM SHAKESPEARE, *edited by H. H. Furness*
By far the richest editions of the plays ever produced in any country or language. Each volume contains complete text (usually First Folio) of the play, all variants in Quarto and other Folio texts, editorial changes by every major editor to Furness's own time (1900), footnotes to obscure references or language, extensive quotes from literature of Shakespearian criticism, essays on plot sources (often reprinting sources in full), and much more.

HAMLET, *edited by H. H. Furness*
Total of xxvi + 905pp. 5⅜ x 8½.
21004-9, 21005-7 Two volume set, paperbound $5.25
TWELFTH NIGHT, *edited by H. H. Furness*
Index. xxii + 434pp. 5⅜ x 8½. 21189-4 Paperbound $2.75

THE WONDERFUL WIZARD OF OZ, *L. F. Baum*
All the original W. W. Denslow illustrations in full color—as much a part of
"The Wizard" as Tenniel's drawings are of "Alice in Wonderland." "The
Wizard" is still America's best-loved fairy tale, in which, as the author expresses
it, "The wonderment and joy are retained and the heartaches and nightmares
left out." Now today's young readers can enjoy every word and wonderful picture of the original book. New introduction by Martin Gardner. A Baum
bibliography. 23 full-page color plates. viii + 268pp. 5⅜ x 8.
20691-2 Paperbound $1.95

THE MARVELOUS LAND OF OZ, *L. F. Baum*
This is the equally enchanting sequel to the "Wizard," continuing the adventures of the Scarecrow and the Tin Woodman. The hero this time is a little
boy named Tip, and all the delightful Oz magic is still present. This is the
Oz book with the Animated Saw-Horse, the Woggle-Bug, and Jack Pumpkin-
head. All the original John R. Neill illustrations, 10 in full color. 287pp.
5⅜ x 8. 20692-0 Paperbound $1.75

ALICE'S ADVENTURES UNDER GROUND, *Lewis Carroll*
The original *Alice in Wonderland*, hand-lettered and illustrated by Carroll
himself, and originally presented as a Christmas gift to a child-friend. Adults
as well as children will enjoy this charming volume, reproduced faithfully
in this Dover edition. While the story is essentially the same, there are slight
changes, and Carroll's spritely drawings present an intriguing alternative to
the famous Tenniel illustrations. One of the most popular books in Dover's
catalogue. Introduction by Martin Gardner. 38 illustrations. 128pp. 5⅜ x 8½.
21482-6 Paperbound $1.00

THE NURSERY "ALICE," *Lewis Carroll*
While most of us consider *Alice in Wonderland* a story for children of all
ages, Carroll himself felt it was beyond younger children. He therefore provided this simplified version, illustrated with the famous Tenniel drawings
enlarged and colored in delicate tints, for children aged "from Nought to
Five." Dover's edition of this now rare classic is a faithful copy of the 1889
printing, including 20 illustrations by Tenniel, and front and back covers
reproduced in full color. Introduction by Martin Gardner. xxiii + 67pp.
6⅛ x 9¼. 21610-1 Paperbound $1.75

THE STORY OF KING ARTHUR AND HIS KNIGHTS, *Howard Pyle*
A fast-paced, exciting retelling of the best known Arthurian legends for young
readers by one of America's best story tellers and illustrators. The sword
Excalibur, wooing of Guinevere, Merlin and his downfall, adventures of Sir
Pellias and Gawaine, and others. The pen and ink illustrations are vividly
imagined and wonderfully drawn. 41 illustrations. xviii + 313pp. 6⅛ x 9¼.
21445-1 Paperbound $2.00